MORE ADVANCE PRAISE FOR
Order of the Sacred Earth

"The Order of the Sacred Earth is a vision as vital and inspired as any on our planet in this time of cultural collapse and regeneration—a gathering together of mystic warriors and visionary artisans of cultural evolution. There are now millions of us—imaginal cells of emerging ecocentric cultures—but what is needed is a consciously convened community that brings us together to synergistically deepen and amplify our artistry and to train and initiate others. Fox and Wilson's co-dreamed vision draws from the very heart of the dream of the Earth."—BILL PLOTKIN, AUTHOR OF *Soulcraft* AND *Wild Mind: A Field Guide to the Human Psyche*

"The creation of the Order of the Sacred Earth is a magnificent step forward for humanity. What we need now are sacred activists willing to come together and live conscious and sacred lives while pooling their resources and passions to preserve the earth and humanity. I am honored to celebrate and join this great adventure!"—ANDREW HARVEY, AUTHOR OF OVER 30 BOOKS, INCLUDING *Way of Passion* AND *The Hope*

"I feel grateful for this inspiring book and the inspiring initiative it launches. The Order of the Sacred Earth gives me new hope; its founders are visionaries who set out a plausible program to engage all aspects of our life, and motivate much-needed change. I hope and pray that their message and their Order will spread and transform our relationships with the Earth and with each other."—RUPERT SHELDRAKE, PH.D., AUTHOR OF *Science Set Free*

"The Order of the Sacred Earth has the potential to be a shapeshifter of our culture, transforming humankind on the individual and community levels to nurture our relationships with all of life. This powerful vision will touch the hearts of sacred activists while helping to heal our Earth."—MICHAEL MURPHY, CO-FOUNDER OF ESALEN INSTITUTE AND AUTHOR OF *The Future of the Body* and *Golf in the Kingdom*

"In this timely book, the authors provide a blueprint for creating a sacred community, one united by compassion, social action, and a commitment to protecting the sacred earth. The historic framework of spiritual renaissance outlined in the book provides a helpful perspective for relating to this call to a new order. May everyone who reads this book be inspired to take the vows of The Order of the Sacred Earth so they may find the clarity in commitment, direction, purpose and vision the authors so generously offer!"—ISA GUCCIARDI, PH.D., AUTHOR OF *Coming to Peace* AND FOUNDING DIRECTOR OF THE FOUNDATION OF THE SACRED STREAM

"The Order of the Sacred Earth enables us to integrate our varied actions worldwide, energizing our quantum connectedness for greater personal and planetary well-being. Accepting our roles as visionaries, co-creators, and Earth lovers, we can be daring collaborators with each other and nature."—J. ZOHARA MEYERHOFF HIERONIMUS, D.H.L., RADIO BROADCASTER, AUTHOR, SOCIAL JUSTICE, ENVIRONMENTAL AND ANIMAL ACTIVIST

ORDER OF THE SACRED EARTH

An Intergenerational Vision
of Love and Action

Matthew Fox
Skylar Wilson
Jennifer Berit Listug

Foreword by David Korten

Monkfish Book Publishing Company
Rhinebeck, New York

Book & cover design by Colin Rolfe

Paperback ISBN: 978-1-939681-86-7
eBook ISBN: 978-1-939681-87-4

Library of Congress Cataloging-in-Publication Data

Names: Fox, Matthew, 1940- editor.
Title: Order of the sacred earth : an intergenerational vision of love and
    action / [edited by] Matthew Fox, Skylar Wilson, Jennifer Listug ;
    foreword by David Korten.
Description: Rhinebeck, New York : Monkfish Book Publishing Company, 2018. |
    Identifiers: LCCN 2017038171 (print) | LCCN 2018013066 (ebook) | ISBN
    9781939681874 (eBook) | ISBN 9781939681867 (pbk. : alk. paper)
Subjects: LCSH: Ecology--Religious aspects. | Environmentalism--Religious
    aspects. | Human ecology--Religious aspects. | Ecotheology. | Vows. |
    Communities.
Classification: LCC BL65.E36 (ebook) | LCC BL65.E36 O73 2018 (print) | DDC
    201/.77--dc23
LC record available at https://lccn.loc.gov/2017038171

Monkfish Book Publishing Company
22 East Market Street, Suite 304
Rhinebeck, New York 12572
USA (845) 876-4861
www.monkfishpublishing.com

To River Matthew Wilson and the next generation of Earth activist healers. May you always live in the truth that humans and the Earth are one.

TABLE OF CONTENTS

FOREWORD
Dr. David Korten

"I promise to be the best lover and defender of Mother Earth that I can be."
Might this sacred pledge required of those who join the Order of the Sacred
Earth save humanity and our Earth Mother? It is surely worth a try.

Individually, we are powerless against the forces of death wrought by
human greed and violence in humanity's ultimately self-destructive war
against life. Only by acting together as lovers and defenders of our Earth
mother will life prevail.

If you are drawn to this book, you likely know that our human relationship to Earth is in urgent need of serious healing. Eco-anxiety—a chronic
fear of environmental doom—is surfacing as a reality-based, pervasive
psychological malady.

I now commonly encounter people asking the ultimate question: Has
the relationship between Earth and humans already passed beyond the
point of no return?

Given rapidly growing climate instability, species extinction, and depletion of soils, fresh water, forests, and fisheries, there is good reason to
believe it has. If we accept that conclusion, however, we turn our fear into a

self-fulfilling prophecy. The more responsible choice is to act with urgency, wisdom, courage, and love as mystic warriors for the cause of life and living Earth.

I am thus drawn to the call of Matthew Fox—my longtime friend, colleague, and spiritual teacher.

The essays and reflections that Matthew Fox, Skylar Wilson, and Jennifer Berit Listug bring together in this book hold true to their promise to prospective members of the Order of the Sacred Earth of an open, creative process of inquiry, love, and action. But the diversity of perspectives can be confusing. As I read the book, I found myself asking, "What's the point? Out of these readings, what am I expected to believe or do?"

Yet by the time I reached the end, I had begun to see the wisdom of the open, emergent process that Matt, Skylar, and Jennifer are advancing. They are inviting all seekers of peace, truth, love, and healing—irrespective of past loyalties and affiliations—to join in the common cause of healing Earth guided by an emergent understanding of what Matt calls Creation Spirituality.

I have long felt an affinity with Creation Spirituality. Only as I read this book, however, did I begin to grasp the deep significance of the joining of these two words. Together they evoke a meaning that moves beyond the tragic distortions of dualism's separation of the spiritual and material dimensions of reality. It is a separation that divides those concerned for the future of life between activists who suffer burnout for lack of a spiritual practice and spiritual practitioners who in their search for inner peace through meditation avert their eyes from the violence and injustice of a deeply troubled material world.

The two words, Creation Spirituality, help us to find common ground as spiritual activists.

The noun, Spirituality, draws our attention to the spiritual ground from which matter emerged. The adjective, Creation, draws our attention to an emergent process that is material in its most evident manifestation. Spirit animates our experience of reality with purpose, intelligence, and agency.

Matter enables the accumulation of learning and the emergence of new capabilities. Without matter, there would be only Spirit. There would be no experience of Creation's unfolding. Neither is complete without the other.

And that brings us to the eternal question: Why the unfolding?

Perhaps the reason is the simple observation that while nothingness is peace; eternal nothingness is boring. We may imagine that the Spirit's initiation of Creation ended the peace and replaced boredom with an endless creative material unfolding.

Here is a deeper possibility. We humans come to know ourselves through our contrast to the otherness that surrounds us. In the eternal oneness, there is no other. With Creation, Spirit introduced the inherent otherness of matter. If it was the Spirit's drive to know itself that led it to manifest as matter, then our human need to know and affirm ourselves through our engagement with others affirms our nature as expressions of the Spirit that manifest as matter in a creative drive to know itself and its possibilities.

Our earliest ancestors discerned Creation's purpose by observing what nature does. Our more recent ancestors turned from that understanding to texts recording the words of past prophets. Science now gives us a revealing story of Creation's unfolding since the literal beginning of time. That story, combined with the recent contributions of quantum physics and the life sciences, gives us a rich and complex understanding of Creation's unfolding. In that understanding we may see a clearer picture than we have ever had before of Creation's apparent purpose and our own place within it.

The scientific understanding of the path of Creation has come mostly within the lifetime of my generation. It was only in the 1960s that evidence for the Big Bang theory began to eclipse the Steady State theories of the universe and to substantiate a recognition of Creation as an unfolding process. Even more recently, we have begun to discern that Earth's earliest and simplest organisms joined with Earth's geological structures to create and maintain the surface environmental conditions required for the emergence of more complex organisms.

A bit earlier, in 1923, Edward Hubble published his data that burst the idea that our sun's galaxy, the Milky Way, was the universe's sole galaxy. We began to see that we were part of something even bigger. As new data rolled in, science expanded its estimate of the number of galaxies. As recently as 2014, the estimate was 100 billion. Then, in 2016, with new data from the space-based Hubble telescope, the estimate leaped to between one trillion and two trillion galaxies—a vastness beyond human comprehension. It is no surprise that we have only begun to recognize the profound meaning and implications of these scientific advances.

Linking these new scientific findings to our spiritual understandings is a foundational part of the mission of the Order of the Sacred Earth. Matthew Fox has done this for decades. Many of the contributors to this collection do so as well.

We now can see the unfolding of life as a continuing, cumulative, collective, and fundamentally cooperative process of building and learning in which each quantum particle, each grain of sand, and each organism—including each human—engages. And, except for humans, they do it without the equivalent of the institutions of law and governance, economics, education, and religion that now so badly fail us. We humans are not likely to give up these institutions, but through a deepening understanding of how Creation self-organizes without them, we may learn to transform them so that they become part of the now desperately needed process of healing our sacred Earth.

For me, my love for and commitment to Earth is an expression of the love and commitment I feel for the wonder and beauty of the larger process of Creation. I have come to see Creation as an expression of the Spirit's striving to express and to know itself and its possibilities as it moves toward ever-greater complexity, beauty, awareness, and possibility.

This brings us to another fundamental question. Does Earth exist for us? Or do we exist for Earth?

Clearly, Earth existed and evolved as a living superorganism for billions of years without need for humans. Post the arrival of modern humans, we lived at peace with Earth for many thousands of years. Ultimately, however, a combination of arrogance and advanced technology has led us to become deadly disrupters of living Earth's capacity to create and maintain the conditions essential to its own existence as a living being.

To the best of our knowledge, in all the vastness of a cosmos with a trillion plus galaxies, Earth is the only planet with the conditions essential to life as we know it. Why can we find no other?

One current theory suggests that perhaps life did evolve in similar ways on other planets and eventually gave birth to human-like species that ultimately destroyed themselves and killed the living planet that birthed them. Perhaps through nuclear war. Or maybe through climate change. Both possibilities are chillingly relevant to our present reality.

For nearly a hundred years, our predominant human relationship to living Earth has been that of an invasive species that threatens the life of its host. Healthy living organisms characteristically mobilize to exclude and destroy invasive species.

Earth may be doing exactly that as it unleashes hurricanes, droughts, floods, and wildfires. And now we are learning of how, as the permafrost melts and the oceans warm, Earth is adding its own release of sequestered carbons to further threaten human survival even though this ultimately threatens Earth's own survival as a living being. It is not so different to what sometimes goes amiss within our own bodies in their struggle to defend against invasive organisms.

Earth may now need the positive potentials of human intelligence and agency as much as we need Earth. It needs us, however, as healers and protectors—in stark contrast to our current roles as conquerors and exploiters. Getting it right will be an ultimate test of our human intellectual and psychological competence and agility.

We have assumed that Earth exists for us. But we are now learning that we exist only as part of Earth, and that it may need our help to restore its healthy function as much as we need it.

If we are to hold any hope of a positive outcome to the disaster we have wrought, it surely begins with an expression of our human love for and commitment to the Sacred Earth we now so badly abuse. Our failure to contribute to Earth's healing might well bring an end to Earth's distinctive contribution to Creation's journey. The ill-conceived solutions of geoengineers compound our past arrogance and may only hasten Earth's transformation into a dead rock.

Ultimately, other planets may bring forth carbon-based life that evolves to create conditions essential to more complex and able organisms—perhaps even human-like species. Perhaps one among them will acquire greater wisdom and avoid our failure of arrogance.

Yet, if any possibility remains that we humans might get it right, let us not go quietly. We are an intelligent, self-reflective species with powerful communication networks. This gives us the capacity to learn, to change, to perhaps become a healer to the Earth we have so abused. It begins with our pledge to be healing lovers and protective warriors.

The founders of the Order of the Sacred Earth ask only that we pledge to love and defend. Beyond that, it is up to we who take the pledge. There are implications for every aspect of our daily thought and action as we advance a transformation of the failed institutions that currently make it so difficult to live in responsible relationship with one another and Earth's community of life.

So, what do we do beyond the pledge? Only together can we hope to find the answer.

INTRODUCTION
Matthew Fox, Skylar Wilson &
Jennifer Berit Listug

Humanity finds itself today in a complex situation where most Westernized people have been so heavily dominated and alienated by religion and patriarchal governance and a materialistic, consumer-driven, extractive capitalism that we have lost our active sense of the sacred living landscapes that we inhabit and that inhabit us.

We, Matthew Fox, a 76-year-old elder, activist, and spiritual theologian; along with Skylar Wilson, a 33-year-old wilderness and meditation guide who leads inter-cultural ceremonies, and Jennifer Berit Listug, a 28-year-old writer, spiritual leader, and publicist, are presenting a challenge and an opportunity in the vision we launch in this modest book. That vision is about an Order of the Sacred Earth.

In times like ours, so marked by apocalyptic goings-on, from climate change to climate change denial, to the failures of education, media, politics, economics, and religion, it is important that we not succumb to despair or to non-action or to reptilian brain action-reaction. We need to go deeper within our own souls and within the genius of our species to find anew what Dr. Martin Luther King Jr. called "the beloved community." Yes, we are witnessing the death of institutions and systems, and of the era that is not serving us nor our Earth well any longer. We need to journey into this dying in order to break into new forms of community, religion, spirituality, and education that will give birth to deeper forms of living and interacting with one another and other beings on this small, intertwined planet. Nothing short of what David Korten is calling "A New Enlightenment" will suffice in activating the energies and insights now needed at this important time.

A death and resurrection is at hand. This might be expected in an apocalyptic time like ours, one where the "end time" of our modern era is fast receding and we reach for new visions. Apocalypse, after all, can also be translated as "Revelation."

We feel that this short book provides a new vision, but one that has precedents in our Western, Eastern, and Indigenous histories. What we are proposing came to us in different ways as visions and dreams several years ago. It is about a new spiritual (not religious) Order. We say "not religious" because it will not be beholden to any religious headquarters nor to only one religious tradition. More and more people are open in our times to the many spiritual traditions and practices that sustain life, that teach us to drink in wisdom from the Earth herself.

Many of us are identifying ourselves at this time in history as "spiritual but not religious." At the same time we believe it is possible for some people to be both spiritual and religious, but people must make an effort; all spirituality requires effort through presence, intention, and direct action. We include action because we are in a time when contemplation alone is insufficient in addressing the needs of our times and the more-than-human world. So our vision of a new order extends to those who call themselves spiritual but not religious, to those who identify as spiritual and religious, and also to those who may call themselves either agnostic or atheist and feel the creative potential to build a community vessel such as the Order of the Sacred Earth (OSE). What is at stake is not a particular religious or spiritual tradition but something much larger: the future of Mother Earth, and, therefore, the future of countless species including our own. All are endangered. Humans can and must make a difference.

The essence of the OSE is a common vow we all will take: "I promise to be the best lover and defender of the Earth that I can be." This sacred pledge is a wisdom practice that we can continually refine and develop as we evolve. This vow will underscore the principles through which we operate and the values we strive to fulfill. To understand the power of taking this vow, we look toward another sacred commitment: The marriage vow. When one takes a vow to commit to another person, then one's life begins to orient around this new union in ways one could not have planned for or imagined before. So we believe that by taking the vow to love and defend the Earth, your life will orient around ecological and social justice in ways previously unimaginable to you.

We are all beginners in this sacred work, both inner and outer. We are not here to judge one another but to support each other in our common efforts—efforts that include transforming ourselves beyond the anthropocentric consciousness we have all inherited from the modern era, as well as efforts to transform the institutions that buttress our culture whether we are talking about education, politics, economics, agriculture, religion, or relationships. Networking with other individuals and organizations doing similar work and bringing such activists together to develop a deeper spiritual grounding will be part of our shared work and what the OSE can offer. We can share in person, online, and in regional gatherings and perhaps in an annual gathering.

It is well known that many people in our time—especially the youth—have withdrawn from institutional religion. And yet, our inherent human need to connect with one another in a sacred and ritual container has not diminished. Nor, as Deepak Chopra has pointed out, has evil diminished on the planet because millions have walked out of church (or the synagogue or the mosque). Evil, anything that would intentionally separate us from wholeness, continues to walk among us, and even to take on wings, it seems, with the current goings on in wars, refugees from war, poverty, and from climate change, extinction of species, calls to hatred and bigotry, and denial of scientific facts about the demise of the planet as we know it.

The question we address in this book might be summarized as this: After religion, what? Or, how can we now build a conscious community that gives us a sense of our common sacredness and purpose?

Our response, coming from a young man, a young woman, and an elder, is this: Time for a Spiritual Order. Some people, on hearing our vision, have questioned the term "Order." Let us elaborate on our conscious and deliberate choice of the word "Order." First, religions both Eastern and Western invoke the term—one finds orders not only in Christianity both East and West but also among Sufism in the Islamic tradition, in Buddhist and Hindu traditions of the East, and one can understand both the Essenes of ancient Israel and Hasidic communities of recent times as Orders within Judaism's rich history. Second, we use the word Order because the OSE will bring *order*, an underlying context, to the many wonderful people, communities, organizations, and movements who are already doing the great work.

Why an Order now? As Matthew points out in his essay, Orders arise when society's spiritual/religious and cultural needs are not being met and when religion, which tends to move and evolve very slowly, is not responding adequately or swiftly enough to changes in culture. We feel this is clearly the situation in the times we live in. Each Order has a certain charisma and a particular mission about it. An Order is more of a verb than a noun. (When it becomes a noun it easily becomes complacent.) Ours is captured in its name, a return of the sense of the Sacred and a movement, called to bring spiritual depth and energy to the defense of the Earth.

Orders respond much more swiftly to the new challenges of history than do religions themselves. The OSE holds the Earth itself as the focus and the sacred container where the current spiritual adventure is to be played out rather than any particular religious institution. But this Order will draw on wisdom and practices from the many spiritual/religious traditions our species has birthed over the millennia. We are not throwing the baby out with the bathwater but taking wisdom from a burning building and re-grounding it in what truly matters—the sacredness of our lives and all lives in the sacred embrace and web of this numinous planet. Here is reborn Wisdom. And with wisdom, play, celebration, and creativity. And the passion to heal; therefore, the ability to be instruments of compassion and justice-making. Therefore love.

We criticize the right-wing consciousness for its far too narrow and ultimately hypocritical and anthropocentric (narcissistic) view of religion, culture, and politics. But we criticize the left-wing consciousness for what is often an attitude of superiority in its disdain for and looking down on the religious beliefs and myths that humans often need to establish norms to live by. Without a context bigger than ourselves, we all—whether we identify as right, left, or none of the above—suffer from an "I am right, you are wrong" attitude that creates strife and reduces all our differences to reptilian-brain consciousness of "I win and you lose." We can move beyond a win/lose way of seeing the world, but to do so we must rediscover the gift that existence is, the gift of the amazing and still unfolding universe, which is two trillion galaxies big and 13.8 billion years in the making—and the gift of this sacred Earth, special and beautiful, but ailing and in peril because humans have been too anthropocentric, too narcissistic. Therefore, the OSE exists as much to bring a spirit of activism into our spiritual practice, as it does to bring a sense of spirituality and the sacred into our socio-political actions.

And even more, an Order of the Sacred Earth can move us beyond our anthropocentrism to places where we all can encounter again the well-springs of joy and beauty, gratitude and creativity from which we derive and which will alone arouse the needed energy to carry on new expressions of living as humans in a special home, our beautiful planet Earth.

A wise elder, John Congar, now 82 years old, recently offered this response to the vision of the OSE: "The OSE is radical in a non-radical way. It empowers people at the grassroots level to use their spirituality and lives and commit to something. Committing themselves to guidance and training—like St. Francis called forth in his day. It offers a spirituality for ordinary people; it will frame itself. The OSE holds a huge potential for mobilizing people—especially those in their young 30s. It is wonderful that you have a couple of that generation running it as you get started. The OSE is *not* a long seminary experience thing that priests go through.... The key to OSE is its common values and spirituality. The revolution should come from 30-somethings."

This response was from an esteemed elder. Another response came from a 26-year-old woman who said: "My generation needs this Order so badly. Why? Because we are so distracted and dispersed due to social media, etc. We need focus. OSE would give us this. With that focus we can do great things."

The recent happenings on our planet, the arguments over climate change and immigration and religious strife, the economic and political insecurity, especially since the November 2016 election, and, more recently, the Trump administration pulling out of the Paris Climate Agreement, seem to us to have humbled us. We are questioning our assumptions (and projections) as we look for answers and directions to take as we struggle to understand those who think differently from us. We are, hopefully, ready to receive again a sense of the sacred. The late eco-theologian Thomas Berry felt that recovering a sense of the sacred was at the heart of the renewal of our species. He wrote:

"An absence of the sense of the sacred is the basic flaw in many of our efforts at ecologically or environmentally adjusting our human presence to the natural world. It has been said, 'We will not save what we do not love.' It is also true that we will neither love nor save what we do not experience as sacred."

If we take a look at past historical moments we see in the West movements of various stripes that rose to the occasion when the times demanded it. Whether the "desert fathers" of the fifth century responding "No" to the marriage of Christianity and the Empire; or the birth of the monastic tradition by

St. Benedict in the sixth century; or the new orders of Francis and Dominic in the thirteenth century; or the Protestant Reformation in the sixteenth century; or the Jesuit Order established in the same century—it is easy to recognize that Spirit is not silent when crises hit. Spirit inspires and Spirit acts. In the third century in China the dissolution of the Han dynasty occurred, but the result was the birth of a period when Buddhist monks and Confucian scholars and artists gave expression to new visions and new thoughts at the deepest levels of human consciousness. These new forms allowed the Chinese to survive as a people and as a culture. Wisdom traditions were reborn and carried people far beyond the daily reports of journalists recording daily affairs; they were expressions of the principles guiding human life within the very structure and function of the universe itself. This is what the Water Protectors at Standing Rock have done. The Order of the Sacred Earth can be a similar emerging new form that carries this energy forward now.

We feel that it is more than coincidence that the formation of the Order of the Sacred Earth came to fruition in 2016, the 800th year anniversary of the founding of the Dominican Order and the 807th anniversary of the founding of the Franciscan Order, and that the OSE is went in 2017, the 500th anniversary of the Protestant Reformation. There is something finished—but not forgotten—about these past movements.

The eras that spawned them are behind us. But we sense that a parallel energy is alive and afoot in our time, a movement toward social and ecological justice. Like glowing embers ready to flare up into a fire, or subterranean plates shifting, ready to become an earthquake that will reshape the entire landscape as we know it, this movement is a rich potentiality, ready to blossom into a full revolution. Our context has grown. Our knowledge of our one planet and its unique place in an ever expanding cosmos illuminates humanity within a new earthly and cosmic perspective. It is now time for our wisdom to expand accordingly.

Included in wisdom is our capacity for gratitude, love, and respect. We feel the Order of the Sacred Earth can play a dynamic role in this expansion. Read what follows and see if you agree. Become part of something larger than yourself and our combative histories—part of something that is alive, vital, and nourishing, in which we can learn to set ourselves free in the fullest sense of that term. Free to serve. Free to give back. Free to celebrate. Free to contribute to the return of community and a thriving planet.

February 25, 2017
Oakland, California

PART I

THE ORDER OF THE SACRED EARTH
Matthew Fox

Today many people, especially young adults, are surmising that the times are too dire and the demands too great to be journeying with all the paraphernalia of religions that has accumulated during the past eras. We need to travel with "backpacks, not basilicas" on our backs. We also need to "take the treasures from the burning buildings" that were our religious institutions of the past.

We have all heard the story of how Nero fiddled while Rome burned, but today the Earth itself is burning and many are still fiddling—not just climate change deniers but even those supposedly in the know and paying attention to what scientists are telling us about the waters rising, the snows melting, the disappearance of countless species of animals, birds, fishes, trees, and forests. We can easily be so swept up in our anthropocentric work, media, social media, and daily obligations that we lose sight of the burning going on around us. We fiddle while the Earth burns. Academia fiddles, economists fiddle, politicians fiddle, media fiddles (and titillates), religion fiddles as it argues over doctrines, dogmas, buildings, rules, legalities, accounting, power games, ordinations, men, women, gays, straights, other religions, and more.

Why OSE?

At this critical time in human and planetary history, what Buddhist scholar and activist Joanna Macy calls "The Great Turning," the world does not need a new religion or even a reshuffling of our old religions. It does not need a new church either. *What it needs is a new Order,* that is to say, a community and movement of people from varied backgrounds of belief systems (or non-belief systems) who share a sacred vow to preserve Mother Earth and to become the best lovers (mystics) and defenders (warriors) they can be on behalf of Mother Earth. A post-denominational Order and a post-religious Order. Therefore, a *Spiritual Order.*

On September 17, 2014, I was awakened at four o'clock in the morning with a simple and clear mandate: "Do this!!!!" Later in the day I wrote the following note to myself on a scrap of paper spelling out what the dream had told me to do: "To launch a new 'religious' order which is in fact a *spiritual* order that is deeply ecumenical and creation centered, allowing for people to more easily and joyfully carry on their varied vocations to save Mother Earth within a loose but real sense of community. It would take us beyond Institutional Religion and Institutional Education as we know them."

History is calling not for another religious order subject to a religious headquarters or bureaucracy but for *a spiritual order,* an order dedicated to implementing authentic spiritual values in our souls and our institutions and birthing new ones along with societal networks. Like the desert fathers who rebelled against the church's alliance with the Empire in the fourth century; like St. Benedict (480–550) and Saint Scholastica (480–543), who saw a profound need and launched an Order to reach that need after the darkness of the post-Roman Empire times collapsed all around them in the sixth century; like St. Francis (1181–1226) and St. Dominic (1170–1221), who responded to the critical religious crisis of their day when the monastic orders were too fat, lazy, and comfortable to break with the privileges accorded them from the feudal system in which they were entangled; or like the Beguines who rose up in the 13th and 14th centuries to establish an alternative lifestyle and commitment for women outside the institutions of both marriage and monasticism and did so precisely as a persecuted minority, namely women—our times too call for a revision and renewal of the spiritual inheritance of our ancestors. Today's crises are clear. But ways out that offer hope are few and far between.

Our times call for not just a renewal in the Christian tradition; all the world spiritual traditions need to wake up and rise up. The young, who are the recipients of a planet dwindling in health and diversity and who now constitute over 50 percent of the world's population, deserve nothing less. Indeed, many among them feel called to lead and to live generous lives in birthing a new spiritual vision. Many young people are being *called* today—they are not just seeking a job or profession but responding to a call. This call may be coming from future generations, from ancestors, from Gaia herself, or from all of these sources. It is deep and it will not be compromised.

The new spiritual order will cut through the Gordian knot of entanglements and burdens and thousands of years of religious accretions to get at the heart of spiritual practice in a time when all hands are needed on deck to stem the tide of onslaught that anthropocentrism has wreaked on all elements of society—religion, education, politics, economics, and media. Pope Francis has rightly called this anthropocentrism by another name: Narcissism. There is such a thing as species narcissism, and modern history, which so abused and exploited the rest of nature, has laid on the current generation that onerous burden.

How does OSE cut through the knots? How does OSE take treasures from the burning building? It does so by borrowing the ancient practice, found in the East as well as in the West, of *taking a vow and creating a community based on this shared vow.* A vow is a sacred promise that allows one to focus one's work and lifestyle around a *value* and commitment to that value that one holds dear. The value that OSE is holding up as dear and that many today can identify with is simply this: *To defend Mother Earth, to work and live as generously and wisely as we can on behalf of Mother Earth and her creatures so that future generations might live and thrive and take in her beauty and her health.* To be the best mystics (lovers) and prophets (warriors) we can be on behalf of Mother Earth. Such a pledge is not in conflict with the prospering of our own species but a requisite for it.

Such a vow is what will form the basis of the order or community of the Sacred Earth here called the OSE. A particular lifestyle is not required—members of the Order may be married (gay or straight); single; celibate; parents or not; it may engage community literally speaking or more virtually speaking. The key is that whatever one's lifestyle, eco values permeate one's decision-making. "How is what we are doing going to serve generations from today?"

A particular profession is not required—rather the beauty and glory of OSE will be a variety of workers and professionals who share a common value and a common vow. We may be artists of all kinds: musicians, potters, craftspeople, dancers, writers, filmmakers, painters, and more. We may be farmers or mechanics, carpenters or electricians, teachers or professors, nurses or doctors, clergy or businesspeople, engineers or scientists, managers or bankers, politicians or journalists, accountants or salespeople, monks or nuns, etc. etc. We are parents and grandparents, young and old. What binds all together in community is a common vow to bring values of eco-justice into their work world and their citizenship and communities whether that be in the greater world of politics, economics, religion, media, education, business, etc.

About Vows

Most Westerners know about vows through the marriage vow and some have heard of vows that monks or nuns take as well. The marriage vow is considered sacrosanct and important (although it is often cut short by differences between the two parties that surface after the glow and optimism of a wedding moment burns less brightly). The vow we are speaking of is like a wedding vow insofar as it too is sacrosanct, but divorce is hardly on the agenda.

Why do people take vows? Why did Mahatma Gandhi take numerous vows in his lifetime?

A vow allows one to focus.

A vow allows one to look ahead and define the future choices we make in light of the value one has committed to at the time of pronouncing a vow.

A vow clarifies when the confusions and problems of life can easily distract or set one on a detour from one's life goal and purpose.

A vow allows one to gather all one's energy for a particular and noble purpose. It allows for, indeed calls for, some heavy lifting.

A vow supports one's vocation in good times and bad. In the time of a "Great Turning" vocation is everything. The calling of the human species but also the calling of the individual and the calling of our communities speaks more loudly. A vow assists us to define and clarify vocation and to keep it on track even though it may evolve dramatically as circumstances and culture evolve.

Who is Welcome in this Order?

- Everyone who cares deeply about the fate of the Earth and wants to contribute to her healing and survival.
- Everyone therefore who cares about the next generations of humans *and* other creatures whether four-legged or winged ones, finned ones or

slithering ones, whether tree people or water people or forests and soil and air and therefore healthy food and bodies and minds and spirits.

- Those who respect the ancestors.
- Everyone—whether Christian (Protestant, Catholic, or Orthodox varieties), Jewish, Muslim, Buddhist, Hindu, Indigenous, Sufi, goddess, agnostic, atheist, seeker—you are welcome.
- Whether gay or straight, married or unmarried, single or divorced, you are welcome. All lovers are welcome.
- Whether formally educated or a seeker who is learning from the University of Life itself, you are welcome.
- Whether carpenter or farmer, mechanic or businessperson, artist or teacher, healer, or preacher, secretary or inventor, rich, poor, or in the middle, you are welcome.
- Whether you and your ancestors are black or white, Asian or indigenous, European or African, North, South, East, or West, or combinations thereof, you are welcome.
- Whether you are 88 or 18, 45 or 25, 65 or 35—all ages of adults are welcome! Intergenerational wisdom is key.

But welcome to what? To contribute—to bring your gifts—to the common table for the common good in the name of our best intentions and our common ancestors for the sake of a common goal: Eco-justice and sustainability of this one earth with its potential for teaching us how to live harmoniously with liberty and justice for all.

In a time of chaos, a little bit of order can be good. Not law and order but Spirit and order, creativity and order. A spiritual order that wells up from that deep place in most all of us where vision and generosity, life and eagerness, spring from. A spiritual Order to bind, support, energize, create and learn together. Because our times are new, the dangers are real, and evil happens, we need to resist and offer other avenues to engage and live joyfully and justly.

Nourishing Mystic-Warriors

Another dimension to taking treasure from the burning building of organized religion is the work of creating *mystics* and *prophets* or *warriors*. All healthy religion creates mystic-prophets or mystic-warriors. What is a mystic-warrior? A mystic warrior is a lover (a mystic is a lover—of Life, of Existence, of God or Spirit). A mystic says "Yes" to life even when life is hard and demanding. A warrior or prophet is one who stands up to defend what one cherishes and loves, a prophet "interferes," as Rabbi Heschel teaches. Thus the warrior/prophet says "No" to life's enemies, to injustice and all that which interferes with Life.

There is a connection between the mystic in us and the warrior in us. As William Hocking put it over 100 years ago, "the prophet is the mystic in action." The mystic is the contemplative in each of us. It represents that side of us that is happy being alone to contemplate and be with the miracle of existence. The mystic is at home with stillness and silence (says Meister Eckhart, "nothing in all creation is so like God as silence"). The mystic cleans out his or her psychic basement and attic full of bitterness, anger, revenge, or lack of forgiveness in order to see life head-on again like we did as children. The mystic is the child (*puer* or *puella*) in us that wants to "play with God before the creation of the world" (Prv 8).

Jesus advised that until adults become like children they will never receive the kingdom/queendom of God. Mystics are not afraid to make room for the child in their own souls and for the kingdom/queendom of God in their soul and in their lives. The mystic is not afraid of joy but open to it in all its manifestations.

A warrior who is not a mystic is dangerous, most probably a zealot who works out of unexamined psychological needs (quest for power? for fame? for revenge?) and most likely out of the reptilian brain (eye for an eye and tooth for a tooth), action/reaction, unexamined action. The warrior's mysticism allows him or her to work from a place of quiet and stillness and *non-action* therefore. In this way love is returned for hatred and in this way things can change and transform in a deep and lasting way. The sins of the past are not passed on to the next generation. Non-violence supplants violence and cycles of hatred are broken.

How do we develop our mysticism, which in turn becomes the garden that nurtures the warrior? Meditation and mindfulness are such ways, and important ways. Learning to let go of thoughts and projects temporarily so that we can be emptied is very important. Another way to develop our mysticism is to find models of people who have done this in their lives, contemporary people but also ancient peoples, and to learn how they grew their souls so large. In my recent book, *Meister Eckhart: Mystic-Warrior for Our Times,* I tell the story of just one person who rightly deserves attention for having accomplished a fine marriage of Yes and No in his life and work. Like many mystics of many of the world traditions, Eckhart was not always the most popular person in town for he spoke truth to power and truths to everyday citizens that were considered a threat to the status quo. This is how mystic-prophets are; they often get in trouble by speaking the truth.

Many and varied spiritual practices can be employed to nurture the mystic-warrior in us all, and this is especially true today when so many of the world's spiritual traditions are unveiling their riches and are offering their inner technologies to the whole world. Yoga, Zen, Tai Chi, haikus, Sundances, vision quests, sweat lodges, pilgrimages, times of fasting (Ramadan), chanting, dances of universal peace, cosmic masses, labyrinth-walking, Burning Man, psychological introspection, reiki, as well as art as meditation, practices of painting, clay, poetry, dance, filmmaking, photography, music—many are the practices ancient and new that gift us with ways to calm the reptilian brain, i.e. to meditate.

The lives and teachings of our great mystic-prophets are gifts to support us. Countless are the persons today who have profited from the stories and writings of people like Rumi, Hafiz, Jesus, Mohammad, Lao Tzu, Buddha,

Rabbi Heschel, Howard Thurman, Thomas Merton, Hildegard of Bingen, Moses Maimonedes, Thomas Aquinas, Meister Eckhart, Julian of Norwich, Nicolas of Cusa, George Fox, Dorothy Day, and many, many more.

There are also the Sacred Scriptures of so many traditions—the Bible, the Upanishads, the Vedas, the Tao te Ching, the Quran, and many more.

There are rituals from many world traditions including the Mass, the Liturgy, Zikr, Shabbat, sweat lodges, sun dances, vision quests, and more.

There are feast days from the world traditions, including Hanukah, Christmas, Easter, New Years, Passover, Yom Kippur, and ways of fasting such as Ramadan and Lenten fasts.

A Learning Community: Learning as a Spiritual Practice

Practices of study and learning for many people today have taken on what seems like a strictly secular purpose—to get a job or be licensed in a profession. But if study is approached through the lens of a sense of the sacred and of a call to serve, learning becomes a spiritual practice that very much nourishes one's vocation. A vocation is a calling to serve a noble purpose beyond just putting food on the table for one's own family (which is itself a noble purpose, but if isolated can be short of the nobility we are all called to). The greater purpose of work is to spread joy, healing, and prosperity to others and the vow we undergo in OSE allows one to steer our work and professions deeper into directions that carry out our deepest values and best intentions.

Learning and the discipline it takes is an integral part of a spiritual community, especially today when science has so much to teach us about our world, about human nature and where we come from, about the Earth and her marvels as well as the perils she and her many endangered creatures face.

So integral is *learning as a spiritual practice* to a spiritual community today that we must shed light on its advantages for all to see and all to undergo. Learning is as important for our humanity as food, water, shelter, or clothes. Learning is one sure way to grow the soul. It must never cease, for, as Rabbi Heschel put it, "learning is not for life, learning is life." The day we cease learning is the day we die (even if we are still standing up).

Learning then must be available to all. Learning—alas!—is not the same as education. Education is meant to be about learning but it often falls short and can be reduced to a kind of ego trip wherein it becomes about... itself. Education can commit a kind of reductionism on the joy of learning wherein its own rules, institutions, dogmas, certainties, power trips, accrediting, and bureaucratic games prevail over the mystery, joy, and creativity of real learning.

Often education is merely about fitting oneself for a job but not for one's work or one's vocation, the reason one is here on this endangered planet at this unique time in its history. Unfortunately, very often education is to learning what religion is to spirituality. It forsakes its deeper self to become an entity in itself, an ego in itself, and therein lies its downfall. When education becomes an entity by itself and for itself it becomes very expensive and very elitist and serves the goals and values of the elite. Much of education has become that way at this time in history.

Thus we must move beyond education to learning. How do we do that? What are the steps to bring authenticity back to education? This effort is so needed and the cost of education is so bloated today that surely revitalizing learning is an essential part of a community of persons vowed to heal the Earth. For the most dangerous species on the Earth is not the great white shark—it is us; humans are far and away the most dangerous species on the Earth precisely because we can use our large intellects and powers of creativity to destroy more efficiently and to take down whole eco-systems, whole oceans, whole forests, whole species to play out our vengeance and hatred of self, of others, of nature, of life itself. No other species does that.

It is our species that needs taming and learning about ourselves and other beings and how we need one another. Learning is one way to counterbalance our potential for evil.

Fortunately at this time in history we are not married to just the educational institutions and models of the immediate past—just as our ancestors in the late Middle Ages were not stuck in the monastic educational system that had ruled for centuries. The birth of the University that occurred at the rise of the new religious orders in the early 13th century turned their back on the monastic establishment and its educational pedagogy. The new orders of the Dominicans and Franciscans came alive under the excitement of a whole new concept: That of the "University," a learning experience that was no longer beholden to a particular feudal or monastic system. Indeed, the idea derived from Islam at that time. The radical new way of learning that was known as "scholasticism" replaced the monastic style of citing authorities with a radical new idea: Asking questions and answering them not primarily from dead authorities but from observation. It is not for nothing that scholars have recognized that the new learning methodology of scholasticism, taken from Islam, formed the basis of modern science by replacing arguments from authorities with arguments from observation and logic.

Today is of course not a time to invoke scholasticism as the basis of a new and renewed pedagogy. Thanks to the internet and social media available around the world today, we can all be exposed to great thinkers of today and yesterday even as we forge new directions for tomorrow. The OSE community must be a *learning community*, a community ever-learning and bringing together the wisdom of our various professions but also our varied and various spiritual traditions, value systems, and psychological schools. We need to train all our chakras and both our right-brains and our left-brains. We must opt for wisdom more than mere knowledge which—alas!—is what most of education as defined today is committed to. We need fewer knowledge factories and more wisdom schools.

OSE and the Movement from Failing Education to Learning

This is a great contribution that OSE can make, and which Creation spirituality has already made to the human race. It concerns a change in pedagogy and a conscious movement from patriarchal to feminist education (consider that wisdom around the world, including in the Bible, is feminine). The banishment of wisdom in favor of mere knowledge has for obvious reasons paralleled the unbridled assault on Mother Nature or, as modern philosopher Francis Bacon warned us, "We will torture Mother Earth for her secrets." Or Descartes, another modern philosopher, who said, "I think therefore I am," as if the thinking ego is at the heart of human learning. It may be at the heart of knowledge but it is not at the heart of wisdom. Modern education, following in Bacon's and Descartes's footsteps, has also paralleled the rise of an exaggerated patriarchy.

Reinventing education is one of the great spiritual works of our time, for education is the funnel through which we pass so many of our workers of all kinds, decision-makers from scientists to businesspeople, from bankers to politicians, from economists to military leaders, from clergy to educators and farmers and those who make decisions on behalf of us and our planet. Education is far too important to leave to outmoded forms that have proven they are destroying the Earth even while claiming to love it. "Most of the destruction of the planet is happening at the hands of people with Ph.D.s," warns "geologian" Thomas Berry. Berry also dares to say that there is such a thing as "academic barbarism." Is academia—including the vaulted accrediting bodies made up of academics and very often anal-retentive bean counters—part of the problem today? Where is there room in our accrediting bodies for an educational model that awakens all the chakras? And both hemispheres of our brains? And puts creativity first? And service to others through our creativity? In short, where is the room for values?

How can we make learning more available? Cheaper? More dispersed? More fun? More inclusive of people of many classes, races, and traditions? More inclusive of the Earth and her more-than-human creatures? We need an exchange of learners for sharing ideas and values and talents, a much cheaper and simpler and more fun way to learn. And one of the things we need to learn anew is *spirituality.*

How does the Order affect education and education affect the Order? Clearly, the OSE is about moving beyond *both institutional religion and institutional education*. It wants to put spirituality first and ahead of religion and learning first and ahead of education. This seems fitting for a postmodern time when forms are seen for what they are—relative and subject to alteration (as in "evolution"). It is the forms of organized religion and of education that have become frozen and dinosaur-like, unable to adapt, too large and weighed down with canons and prescriptions of far too many bureaucracies. The result is that the joy of worship and the joy of living out one's conscience get lost in the maze of rules called religion. Similarly, the joy of learning and the ecstasy that accompanies truth can get equally muffled by the institutionalization we call "education." Both dimensions of life require simplification, simplification, simplification. Where has all the joy gone?

Part of the training for OSE membership can be learning the Creation Spirituality (CS) lineage through online courses and also through certificates or degree programs. The newly launched Fox Institute for Creation Spirituality, headquartered in Boulder, Colorado, can offer this kind of learning opportunity. Workshops and retreats and study groups organized locally are also places for learning. Public rituals and ceremonies can also be understood as sources of learning—that was a deep part of their role in ancient times when the youth were trained in stories that related them to the cosmos itself through ceremony and not through sitting at desks for hours on end. The Cosmic Mass is one model for such experiences today. We need to know the wisdom of the past and a lineage even as we forge a fuller version of the future and marry it with science and with the wisdom of other spiritual traditions old and new.

Lessons Positive and Negative from Past Religious Orders for a Spiritual Order to Heed

One of the treasures we are taking from the burning building is that of a community that takes common vows, i.e. the treasure of a religious order. Consider for example what the spiritual genius of Francis of Assisi brought the world when he attempted to reform the Catholic Church of the 13th century with his new order called the "friars minor" ("little brothers") and which we know as the Franciscan Order. He attempted a re-start of Christianity by emphasizing a return to the poverty of Jesus and an alliance with the poor and outcasts such as the lepers of his day but also with the poor who were the more-than-human creatures who have so little voice when humans gather to make their grand decisions and pronouncements, advancing their agendas often without regard for how they affect other creatures.

The irony of Francis's attempt at religious reformation was that he wanted a simple gathering of brothers who would live a life of vowed poverty; but to get approval for his Order by the religious authorities in Rome he had to draw up a rule and all the laws that would please the bureaucrats in Rome. Francis had said early in sharing his vision that the only rule he wanted was that of the Gospels, but that was not enough for his religious "superiors." The result was that, two years before he died, he let go of the Order and others drew up rules and laws that he so much did not want. His vision and religious Order were compromised. I believe there is a direct link between their taking his Order away from him and his death. Within a generation his Order was enlisted to play the role of Inquisitors in the papal inquisitions that followed. Did he foresee such a future? I suspect he did. (His peer, St. Dominic, had a parallel experience insofar as his brothers too were enlisted as Inquisitors a generation after he died.)

This is a noteworthy element to the OSE. We can and must learn from such histories and the painful lessons they teach us. The OSE is not a religious Order—it accepts no accreditation from any religious hierarchy on Earth. It is born of spirituality, not religion. It is not meant to be a bureaucracy in any shape, manner, or form or to be beholden to any headquarters anywhere. It is a community and a movement, not an institution; a verb, not a noun; a gathering of people very diverse but drawn together by a common value: the survival and thriving of Mother Earth.

The OSE is not a religion because portions of humanity may well have outgrown religion. It is a movement to gather humanity to pay attention and to focus on the great issue of our time (Thomas Berry called it "the great work"), which is the survival of our planet in all its diversity, beauty, and magnificence. It is a community of sisters and brothers dedicated to saving the Earth in whatever ways they can as citizens, as workers, as parents, as elders, as young adults, as humans who care.

The OSE is in no way anti-religious however. Persons who are religious are welcome into this community along with those who do not identify as religious. Spirituality, however, is required, and that means only a willingness to attempt to live life fully and deeply and not skate along on the surface of superficiality, tribalism, or materialism/consumerism. Spirituality is best tested by our generosity and courage and our willingness to stand up for generations still unborn by living lives of gratitude and awe, creativity and healing, compassion, and justice.

Though teachers live and die, many *teachings* are available to us, and it is expected that members of this Order will never cease to study and to learn. Many are the spiritual traditions that celebrate how study and learning, when the intention is more than ego and power, and the heart is included along with the head, is indeed spiritual practice—a prayer if you will. The internet today offers a *way* to continue one's learning and from the comfort

17

of one's own home for many people. There is far less need for institutions of higher learning as in the past, and new teachers need not be pursued as if they were movie stars chased by paparazzi or the new 'fast food' of the day. One does not get tired or bored when one is exposed to wisdom.

Elders and Young Together

Another dimension we can expect in this new spiritual order is a lively marriage of generations and with it a birth of *intergenerational wisdom.* As baby boomers more and more reach the age traditionally called "retirement," there is a crying need to toss out that nomenclature. To step away from one's job does not require retirement. Older people carry too much wisdom and experience to be put out to pasture or to be told to play the golf course or the stock market or watch television for the rest of their years. The older people seek *refirement and rewirement.* Let these replace the dangerous nomenclature of *retirement.*

The OSE can help considerably with both refirement and rewirement. What is the fire in your belly after putting bread on the table for the younger generation is finished? Seek out that fire; follow it. Very often the message that arises is that older people feel called to work with the youngest generation. Grandparents and grandchildren—therein lies an organic and natural relationship. The firing up of values for the grandchildren and great grandchildren—that is key, and that has been the role of elders for tens of thousands of years. This is why elders are honored in all of the indigenous and ancient societies we know of. A rebirth of eldership and the role it can play in leadership is in order especially today.

But to be refired, elders also have some *rewiring* to do. Too many older people lack a full development of their right or mystical and intuitive brains because not only education but religion itself during the past several hundred years in the West has been severely out of touch with the mystical brain. A kind of mystical illiteracy reigns. Albert Einstein himself observed this when he commented that we have been given two gifts: that of rationality and that of intuition. Rationality is meant to serve intuition because that is where values are to be found—not in the intellect as such.[1] To engage the mystical (or intuitive) and contemplative brain again is to rewire ourselves. That is possible, and with it will flow more joy and creativity, freedom, and playfulness. Also, a more critical look at values for without training our intuitions we are merely immoral robots playing out the so-called values of our culture. With this refirement and rewirement young people will find allies among the elders that they did not know they had and the old will learn from the young. Out of this mutual learning an era of *intergenerational wisdom* can emerge. The OSE can assist considerably in helping fan the flame in the belly of older people (including but not limited to the fire of moral outrage at the way the Earth and her marvelous creatures are being treated) and in helping to rewire people both old and young. This rewirement occurs by emphasizing the right brain, which has been overwhelmed ever since the Enlightenment period by the verbal left brain. To study the mystics and to undergo spiritual practices, including mindfulness and meditation, art as meditation, and other ways to awaken the mystical part of our souls, the OSE is committed to such inner work. To encourage all members of the OSE community to find what practices make them alive, on fire, and creative is to support a community of wisdom-makers.

The young too have a fire in their bellies, and the OSE can help steer this fire not into the selfish arena of "How can I make the most money?" and not just into venting one's anger out of frustration but into the vast arena of one's true vocation: "Why am I here on Earth at this critical time in Earth and human history? and how can I make my unique contribution to the future?" Good elders make good listeners and elders today must first of all listen to the stories and the vocation struggles of the young, for many hear themselves called to serve in special ways at this unique moment in human and planetary history.

---

1   William Hermanns, *Einstein and the Poet: In Search of the Cosmic Man* (Brookline Village, MA: Branden Press Inc, 1983), pp. 135, 103.

The community that the OSE will become will be a community that honors the wisdom of old and young alike, for wisdom comes from the young and especially the new questions they ask. Wisdom can also derive from the old and their years of experience and stories they have to share, especially stories about courage. A new flow of communication from elder to young and young to elder is in order. Generational diversity is needed. A shared interest and practice in spirituality (as distinct from mere religious piety or identity) is required. The OSE can provide such a formless and opaque form through which Spirit can move and breathe and speak its will—provided it remains light and transparent in its own forms.

Recent scientific studies have demonstrated that the reason our neanderthal ancestors died out while our homo sapien ancestors survived was not—as was previously thought—because we beat them up in wars. Rather it is because neanderthals tended to die by the age of thirty; in other words, they had no elders and operated as two generations only. Our human ancestors on the other hand lived long enough to have grandparents, to have two generations involved in raising the young and a lifespan that stretched to three generations. This helps to explain why so many indigenous peoples celebrate eldership; it is a thank you and also a recognition to the elders that our very survival depends on them.

Today there is a new impulse to awaken the wisdom of young and old alike and to welcome intergenerational wisdom across the board. This requires certain humility from the elders who need to learn to be good listeners and learners, seeing the young as their teachers and not only as their students. But humility is required from the young too who do not have all the answers and do not live in a homogenous world where only their peers have truths to share.

Training

Past students of mine are currently in the process of launching a school in Creation Spirituality called the Fox Institute for Creation Spirituality. As envisioned it will offer master and doctoral degrees in creation spirituality as well as certificate programs. But much of its contribution could be to offer training to members of the Order of the Sacred Earth. Whether members choose to register as degree candidates or simply take courses of a certificate kind, it could be a very useful training program for OSE members since it would be covering areas that are important for all OSE members to deepen in awareness, whether courses on the mystics or on art as meditation (to develop one's own mysticism) or on contemporary science or psychology or reinventing one's profession using spiritual values, the classes should prove ideal and in fact necessary for one committed to both a vow to love and sustain the earth but also to deepen one's journey and commitment along the way.

Training will be an integral part of the OSE as it is of any religious order. Psychologist John Conger, a wise elder whom I spoke with about the OSE, had several very enthusiastic responses. One was this: "It will lead to training, and the search for Truth. Truth is synonymous with God, the order that is beyond us. I don't care and the OSE doesn't care what you believe but who you are. God is the underlying sense of truth that all humans ultimately know exists. An underlying meaning. Truth is what matters. It is about being in harmony with what people mean by 'God' and with the basic rhythms of this world. A warrior is one who is grounded and present. A vow is so powerful a means of focus; it helps to gather a person, especially the young as we face the future."

He went on:

"The sooner you launch the OSE the better—including its school and training, which is about prayer and action. The alphabet has only been with us 3,800 years—we need to evolve. Taking a vow is an evolutionary step and could hasten our evolution. This is especially true of men who developed as warriors. While women planted things and weaved baskets and clothes and made pots, the men were jumping on the back of wildebeests, etc. Maleness is still young. It needs to develop, and the sooner the better. A community bound together by a vow takes the best from religion while flying in the face of institutional religion, which has so often sold out to governments and been used as a means by which governments control people more effectively. the OSE would *not* be an institution that can be co-opted but a *community.*"

He also commented on the training aspect of the OSE this way: "People can't afford school anymore—education needs alternatives. Professors and teachers are badly treated so a learning project that accompanies the program makes lots of sense." He saw it as an alternative to today's version of education when he said: "Your books, Matthew, should be read by 30-somethings. The link to the new school, Fox Institute for Creation Spirituality (FICS), gives the OSE more bite—'I can have a degree in this' people will realize. Loyalty to certain principles is key. BE VERY clear—about Creation Spirituality and protecting the Earth with mysticism and creativity; they will get into it. A school too—FICS—yes! Compare the work of St. Francis and the current Pope by the same name. Pope Francis is striving for the same spirit as Francis. So might OSE."

Adam Bucko, an accomplished man in his mid-30s, and head of The Reciprocity Foundation said the following: "OSE is where things need to go—replacing a degree with training that leads to vows is key. A vow is the beginning and you live them and don't stop learning." Indeed, my vision is that integral to the vow and the community is continual learning, which is not unlike continual creation, continual creativity, or continual resurrection. Adam continues: "There is little good training for spirituality any place. A school like this would really work! Vows, not degrees! Building courses around mystic-warriorhood, 'Eckhart and Gandhi' courses. So few mystics are being taught in other schools. Julian of Norwich and Dorothy Day. The project is real exciting and would be embraced by different communities.

Part of its work would be to develop a language that speaks to all. Mentorship would be important! Being available. Using D Min grads as mentors. Service—not just a classroom. Native American elders—Pancho and others—offering a team to create. A call to commitment to help the world along with personal spirituality—the emphasis is about commitment, not a degree!

"What kind of training really works? Training must be transpersonal and contemplative but also lead to action. This vision could speak to different groups and truly be amazing. Eckhart and Hildegard, Father Bede, and liberation theology are not being offered anywhere. Very little mysticism is offered anywhere. We can give training to many other groups."

A 26-six-year-old woman had this response to the idea of the OSE: "My generation needs it so badly. We can be so easily distracted with all the social media and such and our lives lack depth and meaning; they become very hollow and shallow and we are often afraid of commitment. A vow would be a great way to commit! The idea of a vow that truly focuses on the meaning of our lives makes all the sense in the world. I want to be a part of this and I know many others who would be joyful about such an invitation."

Why Join the OSE?

Many people today are feeling a calling, a vocation, to do something about the demise of Mother Earth as we know her. This calling is coming from Gaia herself and therefore from the Creator. The rainforests and soil, oceans and rivers, climate change and disappearance of species of animals and plants is arousing many to action and to reconsider their lifestyles and the footprints we leave on the Earth. What will future generations say if we remain indifferent or forgetful or living "life and business as usual" in so critical a time? The consciences of many are being awakened.

In such a context an Order that brings together the best wisdom of science as well as that from our varied spiritual traditions could play a powerful role in creating a world-wide community and movement of common sense and deepening of heart, purification of intentions and support of individuals and groups that commit to healing the Earth. It would seem that such an Order could contribute to the following *advancement in human evolution* and its very existence would further that advancement more quickly.

1. Community support and nourishment for one's deep vocation. The OSE gives you allies, spiritual brothers and sisters who share common values and common goals as a person and as a citizen on a dying planet. This alleviates feelings of isolation or being alone.

2. The more rapid maturity of the human species might occur in its evolution from reptilian-brain dominance to compassion (mammal brain emphasis) as primary for our survival and sustainability and that of the Earth and her marvelous panoply of creatures.

3. The healing of Mother Earth could be assisted.

4. Learning more and journeying deeper into one's mystical life and one's prophetic or warrior vocation. Access to ancestral wisdom by way of common study and living out of the lineage of mystic-warriors of the past, including but not limited to such persons as Hildegard of Bingen, Meister Eckhart, Thomas Aquinas, Jesus, Paul, Gandhi, Martin Luther King, Jr., Howard Thurman, Rabbi Heschel, Thomas Merton, Rabbi Zalman Schactner, Dorothy Day, Father Bede Griffiths, and many others.

5. Assisting the renewal of religion as it strives to move from authoritarianism and from the literalism and preoccupation with sacred book texts to becoming an instrument of courage and compassion on behalf of the sacred text and context of nature itself.

6. Assisting the renewal of religion as it strives for an ever deeper deep ecumenism or interfaith, interspirituality experience and learns to share its wisdom of inner technologies that calm the soul and its values of compassion and justice to heal society and human interaction with the more-than-human world.

7. Assisting the renewed marriage of science and spirituality. For too long throughout the modern era religion and science have been split in the

West. In our times, a deep and healthy spirituality welcomes the wisdom emerging from postmodern science.

8. Assisting the renewal of education so that it includes all human potential, including the intuition or right brain and creativity as well as all the chakras.

9. Assisting individuals to focus their goals and values in their living and citizenship and work.

10. Assisting to support and energize the younger generation.

11. Assisting to support and focus the older generation so that they do not live selfishly but in community with the younger generation thus birthing a period of intergenerational wisdom.

12. Assisting the important vocations of parenting and of grandparenting.

13. Nurturing what is known as the "Great Work."

14. Assisting in both the "inner work" of preparing one's soul and psyche and the "outer work" of activism in the culture.

15. In a time when many religious institutions have rendered themselves banal and irrelevant and without adventure or courage, the OSE offers a form that is flexible and not rigid, open but still holding parameters, by which to guide one on a deep, useful, and adventurous spiritual journey.

16. A great way to serve whether one be of Christian, Jewish, Hindu, Buddhist, Sufi, indigenous, or atheist tradition.

17. Fun. Healthy ritual and healthy service to the planet on behalf of future generations will make one joyful. But the *way* must be as mystical and joyful and full of fun as the goal. Thus one works, as all real mystics do, "without a why or wherefore" but for the sake of good work.

18. Drawing on traditions but not idolizing them. A simplifying of our varied, rich, and diverse religious teachings without the burden of great institutional upkeep or investment is possible.

19. Creativity gets awakened and creativity is a major value in humanity's evolution and in the creation spirituality tradition. In that tradition the first paths (the via positiva and via negativa) lead up to creativity and

the last one (*Via Transformativa*) leads away from it (the *Via Creativa* being the third path). Creativity, after all, is the heart of what most distinguishes us as a species, and it rarely receives the attention it deserves in either education or traditional religious teaching.

20. A vow offers a *clarity of commitment.*

Practices Important to an OSE Community Commitment

Practices are made available and are encouraged for OSE members to participate in. Following are a few:

1. Lectio divina. The monastic practice of reading and studying with one's *heart* as well as one's head is valuable still today. One may choose to study scriptures (of one's own or of other traditions or both) as well as the mystics as well as science (since, as Thomas Aquinas warned us, "a mistake about creation results in a mistake about God"). When one reads the mystics one ought to stop when one is struck with awe or insight and turn that teaching over in one's heart before moving on. One dwells with a mystical insight, one does not race on beyond it.

2. Praying the news. Information of what is going on in the world is very important. But one can be overwhelmed by bad news that makes headlines every day as well as be distracted by an onslaught of trivial news and entertainment. Therefore it is useful to *pray the news.* How does one do this? One way is by employing the four paths: Look for the *Via Positiva* news and dwell with that; the *Via Negativa* news that calls for grieving and other actions and dwell with that; the *Via Creativa* news—what are people giving birth to that is useful? And the *Via Transformativa* news—where is justice and therefore peace really happening? And how can I contribute to that? Turn the news over in one's heart therefore.

3. Study Groups. Getting together regularly to discuss an important book or topic that raises spiritual issues (for example, the new science or

critical thinking about religious Scriptures and sources) or shared reading of the mystic/prophets can be a powerful experience of sharing ideas and passions and values.

4. Study. This is spoken of in the previous section on "Training." Study is a spiritual practice if one brings one's heart to the task. Study of anything—for all of creation is holy.

5. Chanting. Create mantras from your favorite scriptures or mystic teachers and chant them on a regular basis. These mantras are brief sayings that one repeats over and over.

6. Yoga practices.

7. Tai chi practices.

8. Silence practices. Emptying the mind.

9. Art as meditation—dance, music, poetry, clay, painting, mask-making, film, photography, video-making, etc. When the emphasis is on the process and not just the product art is a spiritual practice.

10. Exercise as meditation—running, swimming, hiking, walking, climbing, sports, and more. Be open to the alternative state that exercise often brings you to.

11. Work. Pay attention to your own profession as an avenue to spiritual healing of self, others, and the planet. Ask how you can improve the way it is gifting—or failing to gift—others and culture itself. Think critically about your profession: What is positive? What needs improvement? How much joy is it bringing to others (and to yourself)? How can it serve more fully?

12. Any practice that deepens your Yes to life or your No to injustice that interferes with life is a prayer practice given our understanding of prayer as "a radical response to life."

13. Grieving rituals. It is so important to grieve today and to cleanse the heart of the anger and sorrow that can burden us and block our creativity. A number of grieving practices have been developed by the CS tradition in our time such as the via negativa practice of the Cosmic

Mass and also beating and wailing with a hand drum for fifteen minutes per day. Be on the lookout for other grieving practices from various cultures and spiritual traditions.

14. Rites of passage. Whether welcoming a new born child into the universe or celebrating the coming of adulthood in puberty or marriage or graduation or becoming an elder or dying—all these rites of passage and more deserve our attention and our creativity to render them powerful and meaningful in our time.

15. Walking (with cards or in person) the Stations of the Cosmic Christ can awaken an eco-consciousness and a return of the sacred awareness deeply and swiftly.

16. Group sharing of any of these practices named above can often deepen their experience.

What is Needed Today?

The next level of human evolution requires an explosion of mystic-warriors feeling a common call to defend Mother Earth. It is not important from what tradition one derives but rather how fully, courageously and generously one is living out one's life as a mystic-warrior on behalf of Mother Earth. It needs to steer contemplatives into action and activists into contemplation so that a deeper activism emerges.

The Awe that the sacred arouses is the basis of this mysticism or love affair with Mother Earth. The world needs contemplative activists and active contemplatives—mystic-warriors therefore—people committed *to interfere* (the primary work of the prophet) with the ongoing destruction of Mother Earth.

The world needs communities of people loosely bound in confederation and support of one another who commit to this task, which Thomas Berry called "the Great Work." A common and sacred vow would bind them together and define their common commitment and even identity.

In whatever one's work or profession, family or lifestyle choice, or one's citizenship decision-making, this vow would be a sacred pledge all make on behalf of saving Mother Earth.

The world needs real engineers and scientists, healthcare providers and clergy, artists and educators, businesspeople and computer specialists, journalism and media experts, farmers and politicians, inventors and homemakers, parents and grandparents, children and teenagers, young and old—all committed to the task and to supporting one another.

Time is running out for our species as we know it and for the Earth as we know it with its immense diversity and beauty. Deep ecumenism or interfaith and interspirituality is required, namely the gathering of all the wisdom teachings of the world's spiritual and religious traditions along with science so that people, and especially the young, can be not only motivated but empowered through spiritual practices to live full lives of both contemplation and action.

The world needs a profound change of consciousness and expansion of human consciousness that moves us beyond Tribalism (though "tribes" are very useful and even fun to dwell in) to a consciousness of the whole, a postmodern consciousness therefore. The vow we share in common is a vow of *service* that supports those in service to Earth and one another.

Much community-building can happen online but some of it can and ought to be in person as well with small community gatherings and even larger regional gatherings once or twice annually. The community we are envisioning is a *light one*—it is not a legal or institutional bond (no legal commitments by any one central headquarters for example) but *a bond of shared values* and shared efforts to live those values. No one should underestimate what we can teach one another by our efforts including both "successes" and "mistakes." Peer group education will prevail.

These gatherings may and will take varied expressions from common meals to common rituals to group discussions and group book readings and group dances. Doing service together is the key. Belonging to the

Order will give energy for one's work and vocation. Leadership would be more about facilitating than giving orders and men and women ought to lead together or alternatively to ensure gender balance.

What is Creation Spirituality?

Creation Spirituality is both a tradition and a movement, celebrated by mystics and agents of social change from every age and culture. It is the oldest tradition in the Bible (the "J" source) and is also the tradition of the historical Jesus himself since the wisdom tradition of Israel from which he derives (all scholars agree on that) is thoroughly creation centered. I maintain that there is a Creation Spirituality tradition throughout most of humanity's religions and philosophies. After all, we all have creation in common.[2]

Therefore Creation Spirituality (CS) forms a foundational dimension to an Order of the Sacred Earth. Honoring all of creation as Original Blessing, Creation Spirituality integrates the wisdom of Eastern and Western spirituality and global indigenous cultures with the emerging scientific understanding of the universe and the passion of creativity.

CS acknowledges the following principles:

- The universe is fundamentally a blessing. In Creation, God is both immanent and transcendent. This is panentheism, which is not theism (God out there) and not atheism (no God anywhere).

- God is as much Mother as Father, as much Child as Parent, as much God in mystery as the God in history, as much beyond all words and images as in all forms and beings.

- In our lives, it is through the work of spiritual practice that we find our deep and true selves. Our inner work can be understood as a four-fold journey involving: awe, delight, amazement (known as the *Via Positiva*); silence, darkness, suffering, letting go (*Via Negativa*) —birthing,

---

2   See Matthew Fox, *Creation Spirituality: Liberating Gifts for the Peoples of the Earth* (San Francisco, CA: HarperSanFrancisco, 1991).

creativity, passion (*Via Creativa*); and justice, compassion, healing, celebration, service (*Via Transformativa*).

- Every one of us is a mystic.
- Every one of us is an artist.
- Every one of us is a prophet.
- Diversity is the nature of the Universe. The basic work of God is compassion and we, who are all original blessings and sons and daughters of the Divine, are called to compassion.
- There are many wells of faith and knowledge drawing from one underground river of Divine wisdom. The practice of honoring, learning, and celebrating the wisdom gathered from these wells is deep ecumenism.
- Ecological justice is essential for the sustainability of life on Earth.

CS begins with Original Blessing, not Original Sin. An Original Blessing theology begins with the notion that life and existence are good ("blessing" is the theological word for "goodness") and indeed "very good" as the first page of the Bible (Genesis 1) declares. Buddhists talk of an "original purity" and Hildegard of Bingen talks of an "original wisdom." It makes a big difference psychologically and sociologically whether one looks on life primarily as an original blessing rather than foremost as an original sin. The latter feeds pessimism, self-doubt, despair, dependence and co-dependence. It can easily lead to what feminist poet Adrienne Rich calls man's "fatalistic self-hatred." It is also the philosophical basis of consumer capitalism, which begins with the notion that we do not have within what is needed, we must buy some external object to be whole again. Original Blessing on the other hand empowers—we are all here as a blessing to one another and to the Earth and it is our responsibility to live out our capacity to return blessing for blessing.

Original Blessing also takes us beyond anthropocentrism or human narcissism, which has so dominated the modern era because the message is not just that we are blessings but that the 13.8 billion years of the universe that birthed our amazing planet and ourselves and all the other beings on this planet were also *years and eons of blessing.*

To begin human consciousness with teaching about "original sin" is to begin with anthropocentrism. The universe did not sin in bringing about this amazing planet Earth, nor in bringing about our species (though it did take a big leap and tempt fate by imbuing our species with so much strength of intellect and creativity and apparently so little wisdom by which to guide us along the way).

To speak of blessing is to be on the lookout for goodness (not fault-finding). Meister Eckhart asks, "Who is a good person?" And he answers his own question this way: "A good person praises good people." A good person is on the hunt for goodness all around him or her and is emptied of envy and eager for shared communion and work with good people.

- CS welcomes science because CS seeks to know all we can know about nature and creation. As Thomas Aquinas warned us in the 13th century, "A mistake about creation results in a mistake about God." So too, insight about creation results in insight about God. Why would spirituality be anti-intellectual or anti-science—unless of course science itself becomes arrogant and unwilling to explore the full spectrum of human experience and potential including our capacity for moral decision-making and for transcendent experiences?

- CS is creative and encourages creativity, which is, after all, the one gift our species has going for it. To be creative is to be not complacent or compliant, not passive or subject to couch-potato-itis. It is our creativity that has to explode at this time in history to fashion alternative ways of living on the Earth, ways that do not exploit the Earth or abuse it. Alternative energy and technologies and agriculture that pass on a healthy and clean planet all can come about when our creativity is invoked.

- CS is about deep ecumenism, or interfaith and interspirituality, drawing wisdom from all our spiritual traditions plus the wisdom that science is capable of as well (including the psychological sciences). CS resists sectarianism and division, which is a religious version of tribalism, and it celebrates diversity of all kinds such as nature itself does. "*Vive la difference!*"

- CS is not homophobic because nature has seen fit to foster over 464 species with homosexual populations, of which the human species is one. Science has spoken on the reality of homosexuality, which is found in about eight percent of the population among all human tribes, and science ought to be listened to.

- CS is earthy, not earth-denying. The lower chakras, which include our sexuality and our anger or moral outrage as well as our connecting to Mother Earth, are to be respected, honored, and educated for the greater good of the individual and society. Indeed, our sexuality is a perfectly valid expression of mysticism and should not be seen as merely a "moral problem." The ecstasy of lovemaking leads us to the Divine who is present as a Buddha Nature, Cosmic Christ, or Image of God in our love relationships just as the "Song of Songs" teaches in the Bible.

- CS honors the Cosmic Christ, Buddha Nature, or Image of God that is within all beings including ourselves. This becomes the basis of respectful and even reverential relationships with the Earth and all her creatures and with ourselves and other humans as well.

- CS is open to other forms of spirit besides humans. Angels and spirits are often a part of our everyday lives if we ask them to be.

- CS is eager to birth new (and often old) forms of ceremony, ritual, and liturgy, for community prayer is often a deep and fun way for different generations to interact and for wisdom to be passed on from young to old and old to young. Employing recent art forms as well as ancient ones seems appropriate and necessary.

- Creation Spirituality is the opposite of fundamentalism, fascism, control-oriented religion, and the idolatry of surrendering one's conscience in the name of "holy obedience." It resists worshipping a punitive Father God.

- CS is feminist in the sense that it honors the wisdom of women and calls for a needed balance of feminine and masculine energies including in the Godhead itself, God being "both Mother and Father." CS opposes patriarchy because it seeks gender balance both as a personal commitment and as a societal commitment. (One example of the latter would be an educational system that honors not only knowledge and the verbal left-brain, but also wisdom and the more intuitive and mystical right-brain.) Wisdom, after all, is feminine both in the Bible and around the world.

  CS recognizes Erica Jong's definition of feminism when she writes: "By the feminine I mean the nurturing qualities in all people—whatever their sex."[3] Feminism stands up for women's rights and speaks out on women's abuse. It seeks a gender balance in self and in society and its institutions (including but not limited to education). Part of feminism is to recognize the toxic masculinity embedded within Patriarchy that can distort society and individuals, boys and men, but also girls and women, all of whom have an investment in offering healthy masculine modeling and metaphors for the young. The goal of healthy feminism is a "sacred marriage" of deep and healthy feminine along with deep and healthy masculine archetypes.

- CS names the spiritual tradition not in the tired and introspective and unprophetic way of Purgation, Union, and Illumination but in the Biblical naming of the *Via Positiva* (joy, awe, wonder, gratitude), the *Via Negativa* (silence, darkness, grief, suffering, letting go), the *Via Creativa* (creativity), and the *Via Transformativa* (compassion, celebration, healing, justice).

What is Creation Spirituality and an Order that lives out its values? The word "creation" includes the entire cosmos, and CS is mysticism (being a lover of Mother Earth, one who tastes the *Via Positiva*) but also one who is at home with silence as well as with grief and darkness and suffering (the

---

3   Erica Jong, "Visionary Anger," in Barbara Charlesworth Gelpi and Albert Gelpi, eds., Gelpi, *Adrienne Rich's Poetry* (New York: W.W. Norton, 1993), 172.

Via Negativa). Such a person has learned to calm the reptilian brain and this calming is done via meditation, being at home with silence and solitude. CS recognizes that all humans are creative and we are part of a richly creative universe (a star is being born every fifteen seconds). The question is: "What are you creative at?" (the *Via Creativa*) *and* "How can you steer your creativity toward healing and reviving Mother Earth?" (the *Via Transformativa*). The late Dag Hammorskjold used to ask: "Do you create or do you destroy?"

Thus CS is also about prophecy or warriorhood, for it stands up to injustice in any of its expressions and it does so with both creativity and courage. CS is in touch with moral outrage and therefore does not indulge in passive-aggressive games (which often derive from the repression of anger) or violence on the other hand. Again, one has learned to do inner work on one's own tendencies to violence and to find creative expressions that are non-violent and that re-cycle violence.

CS is earthy; it is of the earth and on behalf of the earth and honors the earth as an "original blessing." It also honors our bodies along with other bodies—that of animals, birds, and fishes and trees, plants, flowers, forests, water—as the sacred and precious entities that they are. Our bodies are of the Earth and are sacred and deserve healthy food and water and exercise and caring. CS loves the body and is not stuck in abstractions but in love of one's own and others' bodies. After all, Mother Earth has birthed our bodies and rendered them holy over 4.5 billion years of trial and error.

CS is joyful; it is not afraid of fun or laughter but sees them as exercises in letting go. The Upanishads say that all creativity brings joy—"Know the nature of creating/ Where there is joy, there is creating. Know the nature of joy."[4] Thus CS, whose central practice is about creativity, is inexorably about joy as well. Justice is the form that allows joy to happen; injustice interferes with joy. Joy is not diminished by suffering. Joy wraps suffering in its arms. Joy endures through suffering.

CS is contemplative as well as active. That means that it teaches and respects the practice of stillness and emptying and mindfulness. Stillness is

---

4   Juan Mascaro, trans., *The Upanishads* (New York: Penguin, 1965), 119.

the door to encountering the Divine Silence and the Presence that is greater than ourselves.

CS is about being in love with Love and Life and Isness or Existence and the Cosmos and God. For if "God is love," then our being in love is our being in God. CS therefore is not anthropocentric by any means; it is not concerned with what Howard Thurman calls our "little God" whom we worship at "our little altars." There is nothing little or puny or sectarian about Life or Isness or Existence or the Cosmos. As Meister Eckhart put it, "God is delighted to watch our souls enlarge." We are here not to settle for tidiness, comfort, security, or smallness—but to engage in the cosmic adventure that the Universe itself represents and that we are fully capable of and desirous of. We long for a place in the grand world of existence, to celebrate the grandeur of existence and no one should be deprived of that greatness.

CS is a tradition of many mystic-warriors; the communion of saints, our ancestors, provide many examples of these mystic warriors in love with Love, Life, Isness, Existence, Cosmos, and God. CS studies the teachings of these lovers or mystic-warriors.

CS is ecologically minded and ecologically committed. It works in many fields and with considerable and ever-expanding imagination to make a difference to slow down global warming and climate change and other expressions of injustice as it works hard to interfere with the suffering of Mother Earth and her creatures.

CS is future-oriented but respectful of the past and our ancestors. We cannot, however, be stuck in the past. CS spells "tradition" with a small "t," not a large one. Tradition is not an idol; it serves as a source of renewed energy and purpose and inspiration for us to match the courage and creativity of our ancestors. Evolution is a process that embraces all cosmic history as we know it, it is a process wherein all forms come and go, die and are reborn, and absolutism does not occur in nature. Evolution mirrors the "Paschal mystery" of Life, Death, and Resurrection.

CS embraces a "preferential option for the young." With more and more of the human population being young people, it is important to encourage creative imagination and look to the future with hope and visions of what is possible. We must be careful of seeing the future as only problem-oriented, devoid of promise and possibility, mired in impossibility and the despair it breeds. As the eco-philosopher David Orr puts it, "Hope is a verb with the sleeves rolled up." Work for justice and healing brings hope and hope invites us to new possibilities that will excite the young and encourage them to give birth and grow their bodies, minds, and souls to be generous in creating new forms of living on this Earth in an ever-more respectful way.

CS is young, ever new and ever beginning anew for that is where the Divine is to be found, "in the beginning." According to Meister Eckhart, God is "the newest thing in the universe" ("Novissimus").[5] In God there is no room for *adultism* or *ageism*. If anything, a "preferential option for the young" is required today, for it is the young who are inheriting a deeply sick and rapidly diminishing planet. The young are the poorest of the poor at this time in history; they deserve to be listened to and worked with— WITH, not over. As the older ones begin to take their calling to eldership more seriously and move from a consciousness of retirement to one of *refirement* and *rewirement* they will happily find allies with the young and a new era of intergenerational wisdom will rise. The old will not resent the young (adultism) but will link up to work with the young and support their efforts at creative and courageous action as well as fun times.

CS is about a simplifying of one's lifestyle, for how else can we guarantee that the Earth will survive the human experiment?

CS is about spirituality and not religion as such. It can find common ground with religion and faith believers but it does not put faith understood as concepts, dogmas, or doctrines ahead of experience. Indeed, "praise precedes faith," as Rabbi Heschel teaches, and so praise, the *Via Positiva*, pre-

---

5   Matthew Fox, *Passion For Creation: The Earth-Honoring Spirituality of Meister Eckhart* (Rochester, Vt: Inner Traditions, 2000), 112.

cedes faith and indeed all the four paths do. It is spirituality that renews religion and not the other way around.

CS resists the preaching of *cheap guilt* that disempowers people and reinforces shame and pessimism and fails to honor or to unleash the power of creativity. Whether this teaching of guilt comes through ideologies of original sin in religion or of original sin in consumer capitalism, it is equally pernicious. CS resists guilt by putting forward a consciousness of original blessing wherein all of nature, all 13.8 billion years that have brought us here, the vast universe with two trillion galaxies, each with billions of stars, all this is an original blessing. As are we. Our time is a blessing; our bodies are a blessing; our minds and imaginations are a blessing; our hands and our feet are blessings; our capacity for work. play, love, lovemaking, birthing, parenting, interacting, serving—it is all a blessing. Even our suffering and our grief can be a blessing. Patriarchy has an investment in guilt, shame, and pessimism. The joy of life is lacking there. Wisdom, on the other hand, celebrates eros, pleasure, and the joy of living. Creativity banishes pessimism.

Lessons from Traditional Vows and Religious Orders

Traditional vows of orders in the West have usually included the following: Poverty, Obedience, and Celibacy. Monks have often added a vow of Stability. Of course married couples undergo a vow of marriage—vows to be faithful "until death do us part." What light do these vows shed on the Order of the Sacred Earth? What lessons are there within this tradition to take from the burning building?

First, we recognize in the traditional three monastic vows that something is being said about three profound dimensions of human reality: economics and money; government, decision-making, and community organization; and sexuality. All three of these dimensions to human living are significant to individuals at a psycho-spiritual level as well as to the culture at large. Thus they remind members of the OSE community that these issues will not go away but are always present and indeed at the forefront of the human condition and our interaction with others. Let us consider each.

1. Regarding Poverty, the OSE recognizes this as an awareness of the value of simple living and of resisting the dominant cultural myth about consumerism, the idolatry of money, the idolatry of always having the newest fashion, the addiction to shopping, spending, and working to become a squirrel in a cage called the shopping mall (or internet shopping). Instead of such pitiful reductionism on the great purposes for which we exist on the earth, instead of settling for addictions of power and money and shopping, OSE community members would be ever vigilant to live lives of simplicity and to support those who have less. A "preferential option for the poor" seems very much in order. The Earth cannot sustain a constantly expanding Gross National Product—gross indeed since it borrows from future generations. Excessive materialism can so readily despoil the health and beauty of the Earth as well as the souls of those who make excess their god or idol. Ayn Rand not withstanding, greed is not a virtue, and no authentic spiritual teaching has ever held avarice up as a common good.

OSE members ought to be actively involved, according to each one's gifts and resources, in developing, creating, debating, and encouraging a New Economic System that works for everyone on the planet—not just all two-legged ones but all beings, the oceans and fishes, the forests and trees, the plants and animals, the birds and the weather. An economic system based on community, not on rapacious profit—that is what a vow to support Mother Earth requires. That is a 21st century version of the vow of poverty.

2. Regarding governance, we have come a long way since a vow of obedience that meant a vow to obey the admonitions of "father abbot" or a vow to a "superior general" to obey the pope and the "superior general's" admonitions. There has been such a thing as the American Revolution and the ideal of democracy and parliamentary decision-making or decision-

making by representatives. But these advances in human governance can themselves come to dark times and be co-opted by powerful forces including corporate lobbying and paying for votes and voters and all kinds of skullduggery enhanced by lobbyists and so-called laws of the Supreme Court that tell us corporations are citizens and money is speech and corporations have religious rights and more.

It stands to reason then that members of the OSE will stand up for the rights both of individuals and of the commonwealth, the community of Earth dwellers including those not yet born and including the more-than-human beings who rarely get a voice in economic or political decision-making. Democracy is a fine goal and ideal but it has diverse expressions and has its intrinsic limits and to be real must recognize that not only individual rights are important, but Earth rights and community rights in the fullest sense of that word are also important. Our survival depends on our recognizing the rights of all beings, that is to say all citizens on the planet.

Within its own modest structure the OSE will be grounded most in local communities where interaction and decision-making can happen both online and in person with regular (but not overly frequent) gatherings that are face to face. Special attention will be paid to issues of gender balance in terms of leadership and of leadership being temporary and not for lifetimes. Of course the smaller and local OSE communities will want to interact with other OSE communities as well, and much of this can be done online though, again, annual or regional get-togethers seem appropriate.

Because the OSE is consciously and deliberately simple and light and not burdened with property or legal status even, bureaucracy can be kept to a minimum and democracy to the maximum. Respect for the individual and his/her decision-making is paramount.

For the beginning season of the Order we look forward to a young pair of co-directors who will help steer the Order in its initial phase. Included in their tasks will be a modest but proper disseminating of the news about the

Order and creating web pages, blogs, and other means for intercommunication among members.

3. Sexuality. Our ancestors were not blind or stupid. They knew about the power of the second chakra, our sexuality that we all carry within us and which can be an expression of our deepest spiritual longings (we spoke earlier of the "Song of Songs" in the Bible that celebrates lovemaking as a theophany or mystical experience). Precisely because it is so foundational to our survival, the birth of children and the keeping together of family life and the survival of the "tribe," sexuality can also be an avenue of profound distraction, addiction, and hurt. People who break their marriage vows, for example, often break the heart of one they love or have professed to love. So sexuality, so sacred a reality, can also carry a large shadow.

Taking a vow of celibacy was not just a psychological decision among our ancestors; it also had profound social implications, for it was the most certain expression of birth control when other means of birth control were often rare to find. It was also a potential means of liberation of women and gay people from cultural norms that required marriage (often with someone whom one did not love or could not love). Today of course we have other and numerous forms of birth control and we have a burgeoning movement worldwide of gay rights, including the right to marry and to parent, and a steadily rising movement of equality for women.

Thus it can be said that the insight borrowed from the past around the psychological and spiritual and sociological importance of sexuality has been simplified considerably by modern science and technology. For example, knowing that homosexuality is not a "disease" or a "sin," frees one and a society from its homophobic burdens and releases the energy of gay and lesbian people to be their best selves and contribute their many spiritual gifts to the larger community.

Psychology is a tremendous asset in assisting us to look at our sexuality more honestly and more directly but it is not enough. We also need spirituality to remind us of the sacred dimensions to sexual experience, the return of the wild God of passion amidst mutual exchange and communication and pleasure-giving. The conception and birth and raising of children is no small matter. In this context, then, what is needed regarding sexuality is this: Responsibility. We are all called to be responsible with this great power that our second chakras carry. Among the responsibilities to consider are the following:

- Not bringing children into the world who, to the best of our awareness, will not have the guidance and care that a loving home and family can provide. Thus the need for birth control.
- Not bringing excess numbers of additional children into the world at all since 8 billion people on the planet is stretching things already and causing many other species to suffer and even disappear. Thus the need for birth control, family planning, and to consider adoption of children are very real moral decisions. To pay attention to the children who are here already and need the assistance of home and parental caring must be paramount.
- Not spreading sexual diseases, thus using birth control and common sense and inner discipline.
- Trying not to break others' hearts by betrayal of love or promises made to another lover.
- Recognizing the reality of sexual diversity and rights of sexual minorities including homosexuals and transgender persons. Standing up for those rights whether of ourselves or others.
- When vows are made of marriage fidelity, to know the seriousness of such commitments and make every attempt to keep them.
- Ever increasing awareness of the shadow side of sexuality such as sexual abuse, sexual slavery, forced liaisons, rape, diminishment of women or gay people, and truly standing up for those so abused.
- Educating oneself in the traditions of erotic mysticism, sexual mysticism, sacred sexuality, and tantra, so as to be the best lover one can be

and the fullest, so that not just the ego is involved but the full self, the spiritual self, the spontaneous and passionate self.

- With these practices and responsible sexuality, hopefully the joy of sexuality may return again to displace boredom or power games. In this context, we recover the ancient traditions of sexuality as a source of learning and of spiritual experience including but not limited to the birth and rearing of children.

4. Stability. The monastic vow of stability essentially meant that members agreed to remain in the same monastery for their whole lives. Such a vow guaranteed that a person promised loyalty to a particular community and locality. We might translate that vow to today's situation in this way: A commitment to a bioregion makes sense if only so that one may truly get to know it and to study it and to learn to love it and stand up for it. This does not mean one is not free to move to other locations, but it suggests that going deep into one's own place is important wherever one finds oneself.

A sense of place is important. A knowledge of one's place is important and not only in order to defend its healthy order when required but for another reason as well: Spirituality requires a love of one's place, roots in one's place, being at home within one's locale. This relationship to place is part of the first chakra and it is also the meaning of *humility*, which comes from the Latin word for "earth." Creation Spirituality is not about an abstract love but about a local love as well as a cosmic love. We live locally in a particular time and place and eco region and that deserves to be acknowledged and sacralized. As Howard Thurman put it, "the more I relate to the universe everywhere I must relate to something somewhere." A cosmic consciousness requires a local rootedness.

5. Another vow that is, of course, far more familiar to more persons than are the traditional three or four vows of monks, nuns, and religious order members is that of a marriage vow. More light is shining on the marriage vow these days as gay couples strive mightily to overturn laws and practices in many countries and religions that prevent their participation in mar-

riage. There is a rush among gay couples and an eagerness among many to line up to speak their vows of allegiance and love and monogamy to one another. The marriage vow is receiving attention it has rarely achieved of late in these new circumstances.

The OSE celebrates love and the diversity of love. It celebrates marriage vows and commitments of all kinds. The excitement about a new population becoming eligible to share marriage vows underscores the value of a vow. Such a promise is of deep meaning to the individuals involved but it also means something profound to the community at large who eagerly join in the celebratory occasion. Those in vows are not only celebrating their love in a public way but are also asking the larger community to support them in their daring and deep journey of commitment "in good times and bad, in sickness and in health." A vow is a sign of hope, of a possible future, of the power of commitment. Love is always optimistic, it reaches for a horizon and a common dream.

In the OSE there will be openness to marriage vows whether heterosexual or homosexual but also to other forms of living together, including vows of celibacy. Living singly is a viable lifestyle as well. And of course divorce does happen, often for the better. There is no one way to sanctify human relationships, including one's relationship with oneself. *Vive la différence*! Celebrate diversity!

It follows that a vow to respect Mother Earth and work to defend her as mystics and warriors would indeed incorporate updated versions of vows that our ancestors respected and often undertook. This incorporation of the wisdom of the past is very valuable; it assures a link with the ancestors without being lock-step living and stuck in the past. This is a postmodern approach to vows: To respect the past and adapt it while living for the future. It does not mean throwing out all efforts at wisdom from the past. But it does mean orienting ourselves to the future and those not yet born.

It is telling, we think, that the beginning of this new order's formation for our new times was in the year 2016, which is the 800th year since the launching of the Order of Preachers by St. Dominic, who was a contemporary of St. Francis of Assisi. Dominic came from Spain, which held the most advanced part of Christianity at the time because of its centuries of peaceful interaction of Muslims, Jews, and Christians, and because Islam was the intellectual dynamo of the Western world. In Baghdad, Aristotle's works were being translated into Latin and sent into Europe via Spain. Science, mathematics, architecture, and education were all being reinvented by Islam at that time (thus the term "Arabic numerals"). From Islam via Spain arrived the concept of the university and of scholasticism, which was in many ways a scientific basis for learning since it emphasized evidence and logic over citing of authority.

While Dominic and Francis shared much in common, including a fierce critique of the laziness of the monks of the day, Dominic was different from Francis insofar as he very much supported the new university movement, and within two years of the Order's birth he sent several of his men into the universities, including those of Paris, Cologne, and Oxford. These universities were, among other things, taking the power of education away from the monastic establishment located in the country-side and supporting the declining feudal system. They arose in the newly flourishing and expanding cities where youth were escaping the monastic hold on the feudal society and streaming into cities such as Paris, Bologna, Naples, Cologne, and more. Many students and faculty members from the first generations of the new universities were drawn to join the Dominican Order at that time.

In this section I have urged that we learn from the Orders of the past—both their successes and their failures. The second-generation Dominicans, like the second-generation Franciscans, soon were hired by the Vatican to wage the first Inquisition, that against Albigensians in southern France. A few centuries later they would be at the helm of the Spanish and the Roman Inquisitions, both in Europe and in the New World, along with the Franciscans. Those were not the most memorable accomplishments of the Franciscan and Dominican movements. Some members of those Orders, such as Bartolome de las Casas in Latin America, resisted the right-wing political misadventures of the religion of their times, however. De las Casas fiercely supported the indigenous peoples of the Americas and traveled to Spain to argue his case before the monarchy.

Conclusion: Responses to the Idea of OSE

One person in his 30s remarked about the new Order of the Sacred Earth: "This *is* the new reformation! It articulates a new expression of religion in an accessible form." The 81-year-old psychologist John Congar had this response to the idea of the Order: "The Order gives identity; it can be a powerful empowering moment for young adults. I see it as a group of knights—warriors of the Spirit—who get their feet into the same earth as me. Sew the young people into the plan; let them identify with it and write about it and spread the word about it. Give them honor. They will make it grow and continue. Invite them to be leaders. Empower them."

This I have tried to do by reaching out to Skylar Wilson and his partner, Jennifer Berit Listug, to encourage their leadership in the OSE at its start. When one reads their vision in tandem with that which I have laid out here, and when one considers the responses from John Conger, a wise elder, along with Adam Bucko, who in his mid-30s, works with young adults living on the streets of New York City, and the 26-year-old woman whom I have cited perviously who declared, "This is exactly what my generation needs," *one might get the idea that a Spiritual Order such as I have talked about here is an idea whose time has come.* It cuts across generations and it cuts across spiritual traditions and through cultural and religious divides. It offers a form but of a minimalist and flexible kind, one that trusts human individuality and creativity and leaves lots of room for Spirit to act. The OSE is a vessel that awaits energized persons to employ it for energizing others. It is "in the air," and we need to act on it, for time is running out for our species and a new Spiritual Order can profoundly assist our wake-up and renewal.

It is in this spirit that Skylar, who is the current director of our Cosmic Mass ritual and is 33 years old, has composed his vision on the new spiritual Order, which follows, as has Jennifer. In addition, we have invited a number of other persons to respond with brief versions of their own visions and have paid special attention to age diversity so that young people and elders are fully represented. So great has been the interest in responding that we cannot put all the essays into this volume, which we wish to keep small. Thus we will have a blog online where we will reproduce some of these other visions and invite others not invited directly to contribute. In this way, too, a living and vital vision-sharing is set into motion.

An Historical Reflection from Pere Chenu and a Contemporary Challenge from Naomi Klein

Renowned medieval historian M. D. Chenu underscores the contribution the new movements and orders made to the Evangelical Awakening of the late 12th and early 13th centuries that provided a spiritual basis for the "only renaissance that succeeded in the West," the 12th-century renaissance that was from the grassroots and not top-down. These movements provided a deep "sociological" and "political" as well as "theological" awakening. They precipitated a break with the "myth of Constantine" that continued to buttress a false theological narrative that put empire before the teachings of Jesus and held the papacy up as heir of the Roman Empire. The new movements/Orders "treated it [the myth of Constantine] with contempt," notes Chenu, and instead a new emphasis was placed on "reading the signs of the times" rather than wallowing in past history, much of which was fiction.[6]

The new Orders took up the energy implied in the text of the prophet Joel recited by St. Peter and saw it as a call to action coming from Spirit.

---

6   M. D. Chenu, o.p., *Nature, Man and Society in the Twelfth Century* (Chicago: University of Chicago Press, 1968), 266-267.

47

"I will pour out my spirit upon all of mankind, and your sons and daughters will be prophets. Your young men shall see visions, and your old men shall dream dreams." (Acts 2:14-21) (Intergenerational wisdom indeed!) In the midst of "contemporary social stagnation," the new Orders woke up a people and launched a new era characterized by "an active presence of the gospel" in its support of the poor, where "the word of God was announced as real and present by action of the Holy Spirit in a vibrant church and a revitalized theology."[7]

Part and parcel of the appeal of the poverty movement was its sense of appeal to the "outlaws," who were "living on the fringes of society." This included the new merchant class represented by people like Peter Waldo, the son of a merchant from Lyon, and Francis, the son of a cloth-maker from Assisi. A "sharp anticlericalism directed against feudal prelates and rich monasteries" was part of the appeal as well; resentments against feudal society were tapped into. Education was part of the battle for, "as always, students were at the center of a most active ferment in which intellectual culture and fresh spirituality collaborated and even produced new institutions." In 1201, four professors and 37 students at the University of Paris founded an Order of the Valley of Students "committed to the total rejection of property and of temporal lordship." Feudal Christendom was being challenged by gospel values organized into a "disruptive force."[8]

The parallels with our times abound where many today are "treating with contempt" the inherited myths of neo-liberalism and religious hypocrisy found among politicians as well as churches and others buttressing an ideology of empire and of exploitive capitalism. An Order today, like yesterday, can provide new energy and new hope for those organizing at the grassroots toward a profound transformation of sociological, political, economic, and theological structures. Religious mythology was "desacralized" by the 12th-century movements not only philosophically but in "the polit-

---

7   Ibid., 269.
8   Ibid., 243f.

ical order itself" as a necessary step to launching a new vision of service by forcing "the papacy out of politics."[9]

The stakes were high—as they are today with the plight of the Earth at the hands of exploitive capitalism and the myths that buttress it. Letting go of "pseudoreligious myth" was an integral part of the battle.[10] How can one commit to an authentic sense of the sacred if consciousness is cluttered with pseudo mythologies of dubious religious and corporate ideologies? Then, as today, spiritual depths of courage and vision and intellectual rigor and organizing was required. Might the Order of the Sacred Earth offer such a vessel? Might it provide a spiritual rootedness to the movements of ecological transformation so needed today?

I believe that the work of Naomi Klein, as in her important book *This Changes Everything: Capitalism vs. the Climate*, offers a veritable Bible for the Order of the Sacred Earth. Klein, who describes herself as "Jewish, atheist, and a feminist," brings together in that book the bad news of our time vis-à-vis the ongoing ecocide as well as the good news of movements like Blockadia, including global grassroots movements, indigenous movements, 350.org, and more for us to emulate, support, and learn from. In addition, she offers a sound critique and analysis of what is truly going on in our world today. She criticizes both right and left responses to the crises of our time. It is in this vein that I see *This Changes Everything* as sounding a clarion call for a movement like the Order of the Sacred Earth. Such an Order might also contribute to changing everything; it is needed. We need to change human consciousness from the inside out.

To cite just a few of her wise and challenging observations:

- We are so much more than we have been told we are.[11]
- Free market ideology has been discredited by decades of deepening inequality and corruption, stripping it of much of its persuasive power (if not yet its political and economic power). And the various forms of

9   Ibid., 265.
10   Ibid., 266.
11   Naomi Klein, *This Changes Everything: Capitalism vs The Climate* (NY: Simon & Schuster Paperbacks), 465.

magical thinking that have diverted precious energy—from blind faith in technological miracles to the worship of benevolent billionaires—are also fast losing their grip. It is slowly dawning on a great many of us that no one is going to step in and fix this crisis; that if change is to take place it will only be because leadership bubbled up from below.[12]

- So how do you change a worldview, an unquestioned ideology? Part of it involves choosing the right early policy battles—game-changing ones that don't merely aim to change laws but change patterns of thought....The very process of arguing for a universal social safety net opens up a space for a full-throated debate about values—about what we owe to one another based on our shared humanity, and what it is that we collectively value more than economic growth and corporate profits.[13]

If we are to have any hope of making the kind of civilizational leap required of this fateful decade, we will need to start believing, once again, that humanity is not hopelessly selfish and greedy—the image ceaselessly sold to us by everything from reality shows to neoclassical economics.[14] To me these observations resonate powerfully with a vision of a new spiritual Order, one that affirms that humanity need not submit to selfishness and greed; that ours is indeed a "fateful decade," things must change and change fast; that a full-throated debate about values is long overdue; that leadership must bubble up from below; that we cannot afford 'magical thinking' about the idols of technology and the market place; *and* that "we are so much more than we have been told we are." In a follow-up book, *No Is Not Enough*, Klein offers additional wisdom.

---

12   Ibid.

13   Ibid., 461.

14   Ibid. To me, this echoes my teachings of "original blessing" and also of the ten archetypes of the Sacred Masculine destined for a "sacred marriage" with the Divine Feminine as I laid both out in my book *The Hidden Spirituality of Men: Ten Metaphors to Awaken the Sacred Masculine* (Novato, Ca: New World Library, 2008). A Native American elder who has worked in prison ministry for 12 years told me: "This is the first book I have found that men in prison will read and cease their projections and instead find the nobility inside." It is that "nobility inside" that must replace the "fatalistic self-hatred" that poet Adrienne Rich thinks occupies many men's self-consciousness.

- That we are inundated with "a great many dangerous stories our culture has been telling for a very long time. That greed is good. That the market rules. That money is what matters in life. That white men are better than the rest. That the natural world is there for us to pillage. That the vulnerable deserve their fate and the one percent deserve their golden towers. That anything public or commonly held is sinister and not worth protecting. That we are surrounded by danger and should only look after our own. That there is no alternative to any of this."[15]

- That these stories feed "a culture that grants indecent levels of impunity to the ultrarich, that is consumed with winner-take-all competition, and that is grounded in dominance-based logic at every level.... The values that have been sold to us through reality TV, get-rich-quick books, billionaire saviors, philanthrocapitalists. The same values that have been playing out in destroyed safety nets, exploding prison numbers, normalized rape culture, democracy-destroying trade deals, rising seas and privatized disaster response, and in a world of Green Zones and Red Zones."[16]

- That we need to overcome our "biases and prejudices, the ones that have kept us divided in the past. This internal work is crucial as we come together in resistance and transformation."[17] To me, this latter point demanding internal work is a call to spirituality; it confirms in my mind an invitation to an Order of the Sacred Earth.

- Klein sees hope coming from "new political formations that, from their inception, will marry the fight for economic fairness with a deep analysis of how racism and misogyny are used as potent tools to enforce a system that further enriches the already obscenely wealthy on the backs of both people and the planet. Formations that could become home to the millions of people who are engaging in activism and orga-

---

15   Naomi Klein, *No Is NOT Enough* (Chicago, Il: Haymarket Books, 2017), 257f.
16   Ibid., 258f.
17   Ibid., 256.

nizing for the first time, knitting together a multiracial and intergenerational coalition bound by a common transformational project."[18]

- Klein endorses the value of "communities and movements…uniting to lay out the core policies that politicians who want their support must endorse. The people's platforms are starting to lead—and the politicians will have to follow."[19] And she beckons us "to choose to come together and make an evolutionary leap."[20]

Might the OSE be extending an invitation to join such a community and movement in an adventurous "evolutionary leap?" It is possible that an Order of the Sacred Earth could be destined to address and hopefully incarnate the sort of wisdom Klein is calling for.

---

18   Ibid.
19   Ibid.
20   Ibid., 266.

THE ORDER OF THE SACRED EARTH
Skylar Wilson

"There is almost a sensual longing for communion with others who have a large vision. The immense fulfillment of the friendship between those engaged in furthering the evolution of consciousness has a quality impossible to describe."
—Pierre Teilhard de Chardin

What Dreams May Come

Two recurring dreams I've had have stuck with me as vital organizing forces in my life. One is soft and contemplative, going inward with a Yin-like quality, while the other has a Yang-like primal feeling with the outward intensity of the warrior archetype. In the first dream, I'm practicing a technique of levitation that I unintentionally come upon in meditation (this felt similar to when I accidentally discovered masturbation for the first time as an adolescent). The technique involved fast and deep circular breathing, similar to the method of playing the wind instrument of indigenous Australia called a yidaki or didjeridu (which I spent six months studying while living near Sydney). After something like an hour of circulating my breath, up and down, below, above, and throughout my body, a blissful feeling of oneness as light as air began to lift my body, and it became possible to levitate above the ground. This technique was somehow part of an ancient conversation with the elements of nature that most humans had lost touch with in the modern era and were rediscovering now. I began connecting with others to practice this enchanted lightness of being on a regular basis for what felt like many years in the dream. The dream ended with the image from afar of five people levitating together in a circle, high above the city of San Francisco at sunrise.

My second dream involved an intimate group of male friends. We were training in secret on a beach by firelight, tending a sacred fire that had existed since the creation of space and time. The training was exciting, wild, close to the ground yet larger than life. It was as if we were breaking new ground to understand and feel many of the powerful secrets of creation through techniques of embodiment and intimacy. A penetrating presence that we cultivated expanded as we carried stones together down Muir Beach, moved with the waves of the ocean, and engaged that which was beyond our understanding. Our training centered on a hyper-focused, raw connection with the Earth and cosmos, accessed through each other's eyes. It was a visceral and interpersonal experience more potent than anything I had experienced in my waking life. My awareness entered into the Earth's presence. Each of us became enlivened by the relational web of presence that danced and moved among us within the firelight. We moved with the elements to activate and pressurize the ritual space that we were creating. Our collective energy compressed into a diamond-like, ecstatic fullness that went through our muscles, hearts, abdomen, and vital organs. More and more people came to the fire as we opened together to the Universe in waves of surrender. It was as if we were being held by the Earth's inner mind and body as we meditated with unwavering focus. We flipped logs down the beach and practiced telepathy by focusing on the reflection of firelight and moonlight dancing upon the ocean. We swam through the waves and into the dark depths of the sea while opening to wildly sensual contact with all of the textures, colors, scents and shapes around us.

The message that I awoke with was this: Communal practices that engage in the sacred, living presence of this land, this planet, and this cosmos can activate our genetic intelligence and expedite our evolution into a new species.

These dreams were about evolving our minds and our bodies. They involved attuning to a subtle order of creativity within each of us and within our wildly intelligent planet. Although this order has been known as the Tao and felt as Qi (or subtle energy) in Eastern traditions over the last 4,000 years (and practiced by indigenous peoples worldwide through countless rituals since long before recorded history), this connection has been overlooked and, in most cases, violently repressed by occidental industrial cultures. Although powerful mystical practices have been at the heart of the Judeo-Christian-Islamic cultural thread since their beginnings, these practices have yet to sufficiently permeate the fabric of its cultural identity. This identity now needs reinventing on a global scale. The need for a relational, humanistic, bioregional awakening that puts the Earth first will require an activation of the sacred Tao in our communities. This approach has been affirmed in the scientific fields of physics, ecology, and cosmology over these last 50 years. If there were any lingering doubts about the devastating effects of colonialism and exploitative capitalism, reductionism or materialism, science, as well as enormous bodies of documented mystical experiences, have made the case clear. The question of "how" still remains. How do we evolve into a compassionate, altruistic, and ecological culture? The exploration of this question will be the purpose and practice of the OSE.

Many of us are feeling the numinous creativity of the Tao entering our dreams and most intimate visions. Many of us feel this numinous quality down amidst the terror and grief in our hearts and bellies that stems from all of the social and ecological destruction taking place within our communities at this time. Both of these poles were a fundamental part of the universal life intelligence communicating to me through these two dreams. This intelligence feels like it is calling forth a revolution in how we relate to each other and to our wounded world. It can be heard in the voice of the trees, the song of the stars, and the guiding forces that pour into and shape our human relationships when we're open and listening. When we prioritize our personal soul connection to the Earth and become aware of our unique role (and limitations) in the greater ecology of the cosmos, when we see, as Thomas Berry did, the universe as a communion of subjects rather than a collection of objects, we begin to inhabit life as a true community. When we recognize that we are held within the continuous process of awakening to life in all of its numinous power, we can be filled with the inspiration and focus necessary to come together at a new level to face our challenges together. We may then integrate (and bracket) the worldviews, rules, and ethics of our parents, schools, institutions, and governments within a larger experience and within a larger story. To put it another way: Living in connection with the universe's intelligence doesn't exclude the rules and social norms that are given to us, but those things must be integrated into the larger, more truthful context. We may then have more room to explore within our communities what's really true outside of what's asserted as true. This practice doesn't require a Ph.D., a graduate school, or any particular genius. It only requires a community willing to give everything in the pursuit of its own truths within its connections to life's unfolding mystery.

In my meandering journey to soul discovery, I have come to believe that the necessary first step to awakening (as individuals and as a species) is the unraveling of fractured and egoic identities, self-imposed limitations, and all of the many numbing and suppressing tools that are currently consuming our inner lives and our culture. The evolution of our species depends on our ability to live in a way that safely supports the unraveling and releasing of these limiting patterns and cultural norms. This process involves discernment in choosing how to spend our precious time and energy. It takes courage to look deeply at ourselves. It takes courage to chose to live in radically new ways. It takes courage to explore what an eco-socially conscious life looks and feels like in these confusing times. It is often challenging to question our many comforting assumptions we maintain about ourselves and our world. Luckily there are many courageous people among us now who are listening and acting upon these calls to change.

My friend and mentor Matthew Fox called me at the end of the summer of 2014, about a week after I'd returned from Burning Man in Blackrock City. He told me about a dream that had awoken him the night before about a new kind of spiritual Order that honored creativity, difference, and a collective sense of the sacred in all life. I thought about the two dreams I had had. I thought about my experiences at Burning Man. I felt into the new levels of aliveness and freedom that are becoming more and more common as people wake up and live openly from their passions. I wondered if an emerging evolutionary consciousness is expanding throughout all of whom we are now. I wondered if a new global culture is forming according to new values that are changing the physiology as well as the psychological capacities of the next generations of our species. I pictured a postmodern network of healer-activists in community; people brave enough to bring together our different cultural angles of experience in service of this important common cause: to revitalize and reinvent the human-Earth relationship.

Our collective dreams came at a revolutionary time in my own life. I had been living in the most free and creative space I had yet known. Life was becoming a ritual of enchantment. I was learning to sustain a sense of deep happiness in my daily life and work (even amidst the usual struggles like paying rent in the Bay Area). I was moving into a larger sphere of acceptance for myself and starting to feel more trusting, more held by life, and was guiding others into this experience as well. I followed the signs and synchronicities guiding my inner and outer worlds toward aliveness and connection. I felt as if everything, including death, was a celebration of existence. I felt too, more clearly than I ever have, how the illusions of democracy and free-market capitalism were no longer holding up for the vast majority of people. I wondered, "Have they ever really worked?" I could see too the imminent and ongoing death of any notion of the American Dream. I had long seen that the modernist idea that the goal of life is to work within the system, at a job you don't like, so that you can buy what you don't need, and retire to do nothing, had to collapse. This so-called "American Dream" has been ending for many people for decades now as the ridiculous inequality among our population becomes more pronounced and countless species of life disappear on account of human destruction.

As I sit here writing in a small yurt in the Sierra foothills above the Yuba River, I can almost hear the beat of a continuos drum guiding me toward a life that works for all beings and the Earth as a whole. As the beat grows stronger, the pressure to fly this nest and live fully at the level of freedom that my soul yearns for is growing again as these words clatter up onto the screen. I take a breath and look out my window at the clouds moving slowly across the valley, their shadows moving along with them. I imagine you reading this, as the drum beats, again and again.

In the summer of 2014, I was feeling a magnanimous cultural transformation—in my own soul and in the world—when the vision of a new spiritual Order was evoked. I imagined warriors entering their inner wilderness alone and together. I imagined gatherings in which those dedicated to personal and collective awakening could support one another in wild and contemplative ways. This grounded transformational work is growing through a variety of practices and work that supports individuals to empower themselves and their communities to live from the inside out. Through seeing and mirroring each other's souls and vocations, through activism that simultaneously deconstructs and rebuilds every aspect of our cultural infrastructure, we will rise. We are warriors living at an exciting time in history where we have many kinds of tools and practices available to help us create our dreams together. I imagined rappers freestyling, hundreds of people practicing Qigong, and employees leaving their corporate jobs to build new local economies that serve the needs of all. I imagined billionaires and millionaires giving gifts and loans to all who wish to join in this renewal of an Earth-based culture. I imagined drums beating, poetry flickering recklessly amidst firelight, children laughing, food growing from walls and rooftops, and a diversity of trees and plants growing along clear rivers connecting cities and towns.

This vision felt so much more alive and free than the institutionalized dogma overflowing from universities and religious headquarters. Yet I felt an honoring sense of reverence for what has been. I felt a respect for the good intentions that have come from these institutions of the past. I felt grateful that they don't include all of who we are now because it means that a new way of life is on the horizon. A new spiritual Order is afoot—one which could include the wisdom inherent in these institutions and religions (which really are only structures of understanding) while welcoming those identified as agnostic or atheist and those who abstain from faith in anything other than the goodness of the Earth, Sun, Moon, and the human heart.

Matthew Fox and I met a week later to explore what a new kind of spiritual Order that's inclusive of, but not limited to, religion might look like at this time. This Order's intention could be to support the activation of mystic warriors in service of the Earth. This intention felt crucial then, and three years later it feels even more important.

The Vision

As more people awaken to this unique personal-communal-bioregional vanguard and we come to address the Earth and cosmos as conscious beings, a new intergenerational, ecological, and inter-cultural fabric can be woven into a new integral story that guides us along new intersecting paths. In this way, we might gather all of our wounds and teachings into a solid community container, allowing deeper levels of awakened consciousness to emerge, brew, and sparkle within a vessel that holds and empowers an emergent field of cultural creativity. Then life can start to take on a more cooperative shape, with more opportunities for consciousness to reflect and dance upon itself. Greater possibilities for collaboration can then arise with the more-than-human world. As we get outside of our human-centeredness, we approach life as a sacred being whom we love. We can open to the love that has created and is shaping our own intelligence. With this opening, we may have access to more of the living wisdom surrounding us now. Wisdom that our ancestors knew and contributed to, and which we now have the opportunity to contribute to as well. Only insofar as we can let go of our self-importance can we be in conversation with the full breadth of creativity and community that's emerging now. This is an approach to life that we must not only seek but allow ourselves to fall into. Rather than attacking life, we can enter into it through empathic feeling and open conversations.

In envisioning the Order of the Sacred Earth (OSE), the questions that I find myself continuously asking are:

How might we organize ourselves, our practices of attunement, communication, and collaboration within our emergent and ever-changing communities, and can an Order help to focus and support this cause?

How can we make ourselves and renew our relationships within the sacred limits of the Earth's resources without getting bogged down by scarcity and fear?

How might we organize ourselves within this postmodern time of ecological crisis in which all of our frameworks for understanding and functioning are continuously falling apart and changing?

Our goal is simply to continue to get better at living whole-heartedly and freely within nature's flow—which creates and renews us again and again.

If we are to engage in all that we are, we will need to face challenges including death—the death of our egos—our limited viewpoints, attachments, and desires and be willing to sometimes do without comforts and amenities in both large and small ways. These challenges can be seen less as enemies and more as a necessary part of growth and evolution. As Meister Eckhart noted in the 13th century, the soul grows through subtraction. We can hold onto our relationships, possessions, and childhood patterns developed in response to life's challenges or we can consciously move toward letting them go in order to enter into the subtle realms of soul where emptiness and form emerge from within.

This is where the warrior element of the OSE can serve. We have an opportunity to practice living courageously. It's an opportunity to let go, empty ourselves, and open to more of our common purpose. We have the opportunity to inhabit something deeper while becoming attuned to all of the ways that we are supported by the Earth. It takes a warrior to surrender everything to withstand the ambiguousness and uncertainty within the free-fall that often precludes evolving into ever-deepening levels of connection and wholeness. As my friend Lisa DaSilva puts it, we can approach life fully by feeding ourselves to the gods of nature. Through centering in the essence of who we are, we can practice offering everything away in order to live amidst the currents of our souls. In the safe container of a supportive community we can, as warriors, let it all go, give our gifts, and be open to the eclectic possibilities to play and work together that arise as a result.

Goals, Purpose, and Principles

The goal and purpose of the OSE can be summarized as: 1) The thriving of Gaia and humanity. 2) Carrying out "The Great Turning"[1] and "The Great Work"[2] to make ourselves and our communities into an Earth-nourishing presence. 3) A dedication to living fully while sustaining an open-hearted, evolving vision of ourselves and our world. 4) Shaping our lives according to Earth's self-organizing intelligence that moves through our eyes, hands, work, and communities.

1   Macy, Joanna, Johnstone, Chris. *Active Hope*. New World Library, 2012.
2   Berry, Thomas. *The Great Work*. Belltower, 1999.

Some of the principles and areas of focus for the OSE could be: intergenerational healing, sharing the deepest stories of what has shaped us, community, activism, eco-justice, sustainability, wholeness, cosmological orientation, omnicentricity, ritual, participation, emptiness, embracing death, reinventing education, rites of passage, working with the sacred wound, the evolution of consciousness, communal effort, commitment, participation, non-dogmatic spiritual freedom, sexual freedom, flexibility, co-creativity, practicing the healing arts, re-wilding, reconnecting with ancestry, and more.

I will describe each of these in more detail in the following sections. I will also take a look at religion, indigenous perspectives, and what it means to gather the tribes in service of cultural awakening. Of course I cannot paint a perfect and complete picture of what the OSE will be. **What I can offer are many fragments of my vision that have come from my life experiences—pieces of a puzzle whose final shape I cannot yet see. My hope is that some of these visions will resonate with your own puzzle-pieces of experiences and dreams in order to help you understand how you might fit into this vision.**

Intergenerational Healing

In our fractured culture, we have grown apart so much that it's as if different generations are speaking different languages. Ideally, we can bring together old generations with younger ones in order to re-establish pathways for connection and wisdom-sharing that our ancestors knew were so vital to our survival, but which are now greatly diminished or lost. Our culture is changing so quickly that the youth have much to teach older generations. At the same time, older generations are the gatekeepers to the wisdom and memory of the past.

Like any strong relationship, there needs to be reciprocity and a balanced sharing of resources between generations. We each hold something that the other needs. The youth offer vitality, physical and mental energy, a hunger for challenges and adventure, and an excitement for life. Older generations come from a time when Earth's resources were more plentiful and it was easier to accumulate wealth, and so—along with their stories and experience—they offer material safety, nourishment, and grounding to generations that can't so easily support themselves.

I have learned to see the youth as teachers. The youth are the leaders of the future. Although they often lack perspective, they can have fresh insights, technological expertise, and an immediate embodied engagement with new ways of being human. The more that I allow myself to postpone judgement the more I tend to see them as teachers who are researching the next phase of life. The more I appreciate what they are doing, the more they share with me. This often helps them to feel seen and interested in sharing openly with me. Only when I am willing to be changed by the interaction do they feel its real and want to bridge the age gap.

The Stepping Stones Project is a nonprofit organization that I've worked with over the past seven years. It was an initiative that started about 15 years ago at the Spirit Rock Meditation Center near Fairfax, California. At Stepping Stones, we bring together two young-adult leaders with an elder to take small groups of adolescents through a three-year process of individuation. There are also times when the whole organization gets together to do personal, interpersonal, and intergenerational training through council, space-holding, ritual, and a variety of intercultural, psychological, emotional, and spiritual practices. This creates a field of community that the leaders and elders then bring into their groups, including the extended network of families.

The two most important things that this has taught me is that getting everyone to continually show up is the hardest part. And that presence itself—simply being together as an intergenerational cohort—is what heals, empowers, and initiates everyone involved. After witnessing many amazing experiences of healing over the course of relatively short periods of time, I know that this work can heal many of the emotional, psychological, and physiological ailments that we suffer from as a culture.

Intergenerational healing and Earth-human healing doesn't necessarily mean changing that much. As Owen Barfield said in his book *Saving the Appearances*, "There may be times when what is most needed is not so much a new discovery or a new idea as a different 'slant'; I mean a comparatively slight readjustment in our way of looking at the things and ideas on which attention is already fixed." We now seem to be in this process of fine-tuning (as well as overhauling) many of our "modern" ways of being and thinking in order to adjust to new aspirations for how to be an Earth-nourishing human presence on this beautiful and precious planet. This process may already be underway. It may be easier than is often stated. This process is, after all, being guided by the Earth herself. In putting the intention to be an intergenerational community first, we can reshape our individual fulfillments within the light of relationship. New possibilities may already be emerging as we continue learning about ourselves and what fills us with juice. We may pursue what gives purpose to the elderly and supports and guides the youth at the same time. We may teach each other what it means to be human, including the great powers of creativity that have been needed to get us to this point after about 10,000 generations of human evolution, four and a half billion years of Earth's evolution, and 14 billion years of cosmic unfolding.

In the postmodern world we tend to be very self-absorbed and so we gravitate toward those who are similar to ourselves whether in culture, life experience, interests, religious identities, sexual orientations, ethnicity, or age. It takes effort to connect across these differences to dance together in the lands of understanding. Like the Stepping Stones Project has done in the Bay Area, the OSE can be a bridge for this difficult work of creating and nurturing essential bonds across generations so that we may usher one another into the next level of community support.

Sharing Our Stories

Years ago, while living in the Mojave desert, I had a dream in which I was falling backwards in the dark. It's still perhaps the most visceral experience I've had of surrender. As I fell through the cosmos (for what felt like a lifetime), all of my future memories were arising into vision. I knew that I had no control and that I could only truly "see" when I entered fully into the freefall of experience while moving on my unique path. I awoke feeling vulnerable, clear, and changed. It was as if I had shed several layers of armor. I knew that I needed to go back to graduate school to study consciousness (veering away from my previous career in ecology and environmental restoration). I hoped that I would find a community whose passion for the sacred and for the earth and for humanity were as great as my own.

The dreams which I've shared have been my thresholds into conversations with the Great Mystery. They have revealed parts of myself and my path previously unknown. When I have had the courage and sensibility to allow them to guide me, I have found that life opens up in simple and profound ways with support and guidance coming from places that I couldn't have anticipated. These dreams point toward enchanted ways of being that arise alongside wonderment and love, wildness and freedom that I yearn to have more access to. They became doorways into greater and greater contact with the living world, and have directed my attention toward some of the most uplifting forces and guidance that I have known. *I offer them now because I feel the OSE could be a place for sharing the deepest stories of what has shaped us.* These emerging visions will then become more and more real.

For thousands of years, storytelling was a primary form of communicating and educating. Sharing our stories allows us to bring consciousness to them. When we become conscious of them we see how they have empowered and shaped us, and where their limitations are. Because all stories are incomplete. The more we share our stories with one another in vulnerable and respectful ways, the more perspective and inter-subjective awareness can be shared. The more pieces of the puzzle we can put together. Through deep listening and empathic mirroring we can integrate more and more of our humanity within this vast cosmic puzzle.

Sharing our stories can point us towards more intimate realities than have been commonly accessible in the modern world; realities that are starting to grow more common in the free-fall from self-absorption and modernity. Story shapes our world and our lives. Story is how we relate our values to each other and how we relate to our own journeys.

Community and Eco-Justice

The indigenous peoples of every continent have demonstrated an understanding of the importance of community and a reverence for it, specifically community that supports a connection to the cosmos. Australia's aboriginal people represent this reverence in the way they depict the Dreamtime in their paintings and songs. The Omaha people of North America did this when they would lift a newborn child up to the heavens asking for the blessing of all of life to guide and protect the child in her fulfillment.

Another quality for a new spiritual Order that we can adopt from indigenous cultures is a sensitivity to the Earth and cosmos that comes from approaching them as interconnected, conscious beings. We can practice new depths of humility as a community by creating a container that encourages the development of this sensitivity.

We don't have to be as strong and hard and individualistic as we've been conditioned to be. We don't need to pull ourselves up by the bootstraps. When we learn to ask for what we need now, we can heal the traumas inherited when our needs weren't met in the past. When we know we are held by something greater, we can sink into this knowing. In coming back to the humus/soil and soul, we can heal our communities while doing sacred activism that doesn't make needless sacrifices. With reverent openness to giving and receiving support, new conversations are emerging that bring with them new possibilities for engagement with the great environmental and social challenges (and battles) of our times.

This is what happened at the Standing Rock protests of the Dakota Access Pipeline. Thousands gathered spontaneously from around the world to bare witness to the value of clean water, land, community, and reverence for the sacred Earth. We stood up against the destruction of the oil industries and consumer culture at large, and a global culture of reverence is forming. We stood up for indigenous values, and Earth's healing is taking place as our human traumas are being integrated. One of Standing Rock's great achievements has been the rippling impact and felt presence to the common cause of protecting the Earth, and its people, and it has been a sign of a growing culture of Earth Warriors—people who engage in an active sense of hope in humanity and in life prevailing.

The inspiring playwright and statesman Vaclav Havel teaches that what makes hope different than optimism is that hope isn't the conviction that everything is going to work out. Hope simply reflects the truth that life makes sense, regardless of how it turns out. Standing Rock is an immediate reference point for this embodiment of hope and for the ways we can gather as a species in support of one Earth simply because she is beautiful and she prospers life that "makes sense." Havel also says this about hope:

> "Hope, in this deep and powerful sense, is not the same as joy that things are going well, or willingness to invest in enterprises that are obviously heading for success, but rather an ability to work for something because it is good."

This is an important distinction. This is what we saw at Standing Rock—people who stood up for the Earth, and an Earth-honoring culture, because both are beautiful, instead of investing in an oil pipeline because it will be financially lucrative. The Order will be a community of people who are willing and ready to work for what is good. *It will bring together a global culture to renew our spirits and to support our immediate bioregional needs.*

In living a more ecological story, we can distribute resources to those in need. We can aim toward sustainability. In vowing to move towards one another and toward the Earth now, I suspect new and previously unknown political and economic solutions will come into place through new conversations, new means of exchange and gifting, as well as technologies that increase communication, exchange, and efficiency.

Working toward what is good does not mean attacking what has been. The Order, by nature, is a community of peacemakers. Ghandi was a great example of this with his nonviolent protests, which aimed to embody the truth rather than fighting for it. Nonviolent communication is a powerful tool that stems from the realization that we can create change for ourselves and each other without fighting. The warrior does this simply through being present while modeling the way forward. We want to move out of the "us versus them" mentality and start taking responsibility for the whole together.

Embodying Wholeness Through Cosmology

The OSE would help us to move into new pathways for taking responsibility for the whole together. The purpose of the OSE would be to hold a space for developing and sharing enchantment, wonderment, love, wildness, and freedom.

The OSE encourages exploration of the larger story of which we are a part. An understanding of the whole affects the way we engage in the relationships of our communities. The OSE may benefit from keeping a cultural attitude of openness with dedication to understanding how we fit together.

The New Cosmology, as taught to me by author and Cosmology professor Brian Swimme, seeks to convey the scientific consensus that the universe is a 14-billion-year process of unfolding energy which has led to the present. Our present moment contains this whole sequence of unrepeatable cosmic events. These events have led to the creation of the Earth, atoms, elements, and life. This journey is something like a song that is still playing and that we are here to jam with. It is also expanding in complexity and breadth from within and from all places at once. The principle of omnicentricity describes how each place and each person is itself the center of this universal expansion. This makes every one of us an essential part of the whole and points to the truth that we are each a creator.

Each mind is a part of a greater mind, as Rupert Sheldrake points out; the realization of a greater whole is what actually creates the greater whole. The OSE then can be an extended network dedicated to creating wholeness through integrative practices that embody this new understanding of the whole. It will, after all, take time and practice to embody this new understanding of who we are and what we are part of. It will take time for the understanding that we are part of the cosmos creating itself to sink into our body politic and the way that we address one another and the Earth.

Community Rituals

Ritual can be a powerful way to come together as a community to create a conscious group field with an intention. Rituals have often been a way of accessing primordial powers that create and sustain communities and they would surely be part of the OSE. The West African spiritual teacher Malidoma Some offers that there is no community without ritual. Ritual is the way we can come to know our togetherness. It is the way that we bring ourselves into the greater context in which we are each a part. It is the way that we create a community mind.

We often brought Malidoma and others to assist in creating ritual spaces in the community that I lived in for four years in Elmwood/Berkeley, California. The community formed the rituals and became as a result more enchanted, and more uniquely itself. This brought us continually into a high level of aliveness and presence together and attracted many spiritual seekers, healers, visionaries, and cultural creatives to our home. No one in the community was seen as being "THE" teacher or guru. This allowed for a high level of participation and personal empowerment to exist in each of our own relationships to the whole within a loving communal space. The community was inspired by Auroville (the 2,400-person international intentional community in India) as well as a dedication to the evolution of self and culture. Ritual was one way that we practiced coming to wholeness together by holding space for Rites of Passage, differences of opinion, and for seasonal celebration. We held space for each person's individual proclivities within our community. The most simple structures for sharing communal space were employed. These included holding council, sharing dinner, holding parties, as well as holding community rituals of healing. We met formally once every two weeks for council. Because of the high level of ongoing attention given to the community, including communal boundaries and the practice of self-awareness and communication, a shared understanding and way of life could be maintained. Life most often flowed without strain.

Rituals can help us to integrate traumas when we consciously re-enter experiences of the past that were too intense to be fully present to at the time. By intentionally going back into the void through rituals involving meditation, drumming, dancing, grieving, and prayer, I have been able to come back to an unguarded and surrendered sense of ease and joy—*a joie de vivre*, or love of life—begins to flow again.

Rituals can help us remember who we are. They can help us let go of the places where separation and grief have solidified within our muscles. Rituals help lift our spirits again. They can renew our lives by accessing and reconnecting the deep recesses within our psyches and within the larger cultural psyche to make meaning. In this way we can renew our energy when it's been depleted. Rituals can also bring us in touch with our individual callings and common purposes.

Ritual has become an essential part of my vocation as a postmodern priest and wilderness guide. The rituals of the So'tae'taneo'o Cheyenne and the Lakota people have been particularly helpful in bringing me in touch with all of the relationships that sustain me. Through countless lodges, I've felt what it's like to be fully surrendered in the womb of the Great Mother. Through the medicine wheel, I've felt the thread of connection between my inner world and each of the directions—including their powers and the archetypes through which I relate to these powers. Through extended Vipassana retreats and ceremonies with sacred plant medicines like Psilocybin mushrooms, Ayahuasca, and San Pedro cactus, I've entered into conversations with other nonhuman conscious beings who have helped with integrating fractured parts of myself, my relationships, and my life story.

My experience of integrative community rituals like the Cosmic Mass, the Sundance, Yom Kippur, funerals, weddings, and Burning Man, is that when the power of community presence is contained and directed toward specific universal experiences of grief, joy, communion, the sacred, the shadow, our primal nature, compassion etc., transformation and healing can take place at miraculous levels. These ritual shapes are temporary, intermediate spaces to practice coming alive fully to our life's work in order to participate more fully with life together.

Matthew Fox and I went up to the Sungleska Sundance ceremony of his late friend Buck Ghosthorse in the Pacific Northwest a few years ago. This is one of hundreds of Sundances currently taking place in the U.S. Although this ritual has been practiced for over a thousand years by many Native American tribes, it was illegal in the U.S. until the late '70s. I'm assuming that this was because it was so powerful and threatening to the Western mind. It could also be because people didn't understand the incredible intentionality of it and thought it was barbaric. In any case, it was the deepest and most powerful ritual that I have experienced. For four days we danced and sang prayers of gratitude and healing. The dancers dance around a tree (symbolizing the axis mundi or center of the cosmos) in the center of a semi-circle clearing (open to the rising sun in the east). As the sun rises, it fills this ritual container with divine energy. They dance for four days living only off of this energy, the energy from the prayers of the community, and their own intentions. They don't eat or drink, and sleep very little. This is quite exceptional, as most humans cannot go more than three days without drinking water if they're sitting and conserving energy, let alone dancing at the hottest point of the year. It's palpable that the prayers keep them going. The dancer's need for those prayers clearly invokes extra-strong prayers from the community. The level of sacrifice and gifting of time and energy of the community is immense. All of the intentionality and prayers infused into the altars, prayer ties, and the sacred tree in the center of the arbor create a field and a portal of magic that is palpable and grows as the days go on. This center of the cosmos is the focus upon which all of the rounds of dancing rotate. Each round symbolizes different aspects of life (they even have a trickster or Haoka round). Many of the dancers pierce themselves and hang from the tree to symbolize humanity's embodied connection with the Creator. The length and central focus of this ritual upon the cosmic center supports the ritualists in sinking into a state of nonordinary con-sciousness—a trance state of embodied union with Earth and cosmos. It is profound.

The Cosmic Mass is another powerful ritual that focuses on a cosmic center within the ever-expanding journey that we are on together. For the past 20 years, it has aimed to include and honor most of the world's wisdom traditions, shamanic traditions, and postmodern art (transformational and psychedelic visual art/projections, electronic music etc.). It aims to co-create a transformational experience by going into the four paths of wholeness that are part of the Creation Spirituality tradition. These include joy and wonder, grief and contemplation, creativity and communion, and finally compassion, justice, freedom, and transformation. In going through these archetypal experiences of expansion and contraction together, we create a community field of healing that is palpable.

Burning Man is another powerful postmodern ritual that has some similar elements to the Sundance and the Cosmic Mass. The week-long ritual centers upon self expression and the transitory nature of life and culture. The climax of the ritual is the burning of a giant effigy, which the village is built around. Many take this effigy to be a symbol of all that we wish to let go of in ourselves, our culture, and in the world. The temple is the home of a central altar for the whole event and symbolizes the sense of the sacred and is a place to grieve, meditate, ground your energy, or connect to something larger. The temple is usually the last structure to be burned on the last day.

These rituals could influence the culture of the Order of the Sacred Earth as we invent new rituals to embody more and more of who we are. We might do this by opening to a diversity of creative and mystical expressions. For example, the Cosmic Mass has inspired the growth of the Ecstatic Dance culture, which has now spread around the world. Burning Man is also becoming more directly conscious of its cosmological and spiritual significance, shown in this year's theme (2017): "Radical Ritual." Spirituality had been previously present but not explicitly part of the culture. It's a good sign to see Burning Man moving in this direction, especially because it draws 70,000 people to the *playa* dust-bed of Blackrock City and has influenced satellite rituals all over the world. Tickets to these festivals often sell out immediately—a sign that more and more people are becoming hungry for the transformation that happens when radical, divine freedom of expression and contact with community and something larger than ourselves are focused upon. We are hungry for ritual.

Both the Cosmic Mass and Burning Man celebrate principles like: Radical Inclusion; Gifting (the Cosmic Mass is donation-based and Burning Man charges a fee but doesn't allow the selling of goods in the festival); Self-Reliance; Radical Self-Expression; Communal Effort; Leave No Trace (which becomes an ethos of sustainability and permaculture practices that is brought back into the urban world); Civic Responsibility; Participation,

Immediacy, and Omnicentricity (meaning that everyplace is the center of the whole as well as a unified part).

The Cosmic Mass and Burning Man mirror the cosmic principle of omnicentricity by building the power of the group field around a central object, symbolizing the cosmic center of the community (similar to the central tree in the Sundance). A circular form of interactive participation democratizes the role of a shaman, priest, or rabbi. The group field, and the active participation of everyone, is the new spiritual teacher, as well as the vessel through which the cosmos is becoming more human (and the human is becoming more cosmic). Both rituals focus on being at home in the celebration of life.

The Order can surely integrate these principles while creating rituals that honor nature's rhythms to bring about cultural transformation within a diversity of communities and ecosystems.

Emptying and Embracing Death

As Barbara Ehrenreich reflects in her book *Dancing in the Streets*, the Western mind has the uncanny ability to "resist the contagious rhythm of the drums, to wall itself up on a fortress of ego and rationality against the seductive wildness of the world." Only when we surrender our resistance, and let go, can an ecological mode of consciousness come to meet us. This was the way of our ancestors, it was the lesson from my dream of falling into awareness, and may be a smoother path toward cultural healing for us now. The transpersonal connection to the cosmos that comes from surrender can feel both larger than life and completely normal at the same time. It is part of being a child again. When we let go of our self-importance, the weight of the world that we have been carrying can be released. Again, as we stop holding ourselves apart from the world, we can come home to our chosen communities—the ones that see us and nourish us in the real ways that our souls need. When we realize that we are the ones we've been waiting for and that we are already in a very well-designed and intelligent world, then we can let go in order to meet, mirror, and initiate ourselves into the universe's self-organizing intelligence.

I see a central part of the OSE being about supporting this process of letting go. We can do this by taking retreats and breaks from food (fasting), breaks from the consumption of information, recycling extra energy, giving our extra boxes of stuff away, and engaging in mindfulness meditation where we hold space for the excess of thoughts and feelings that have built up through our busy lives to dissipate. It's about clearing out all that is not essential to who we are at the deepest level, to avoid unconscious accumulation of that which we don't need. This is something that the Western world can learn from the East as well as from the indigenous cultures who often live so fully with so few possessions. It is clear that the acquisition of excess stuff is hindering our creativity while crowding our psyches. This way of life is also clearly locking up the ecological flow of energy while polluting the Earth. It can be deeply gratifying to allow this build-up of thoughts, matter, and energy to unravel and slow to the point where we can feel our essence again: that which dwells in us at the deepest level.

Repressed grief is often at the bottom of the pattern of overconsumption. There is so much in the world to grieve today. Grieving is an essential form of emptying ourselves. It's only when we hold space for ourselves and each other to fully feel the entirety of difficult emotions (like sadness, anger, rage) within a safe space that we can be free to experience life from the fresh edge and freedom of our pure essence again. Only after looking at and feeling our deepest disappointments (and even despair) can we be ready to be filled with hope and joy again. Only when we stop forcing our lives into place; when we stop repressing that which isn't what we want, can we let the chips fall where they may and show up fully to be present to new possibilities for sharing and collaborating from our hearts.

Grieving together feels like another important part of what the OSE could support. There is obviously much to grieve and let go of and the

Order could help to hold space for this process so that those initiated can have the energy and strength to support healing the pattern of suffering in places where grieving is feared and repressed. For example, much of the New Age community focuses on love and light and positive thoughts, while denying the shadow. This is often an unconscious way to coat over some much deeper traumas, which won't go away with positive thinking alone.

Matthew Fox and I have been producing the Cosmic Mass together for the past five years in many places around the country. Matt co-created this intercultural ritual 20 years ago as a way to bring a spiritual experience to young people (as well as older ones) and to empower them as leaders, to inspire and re-fire elders, and to build intergenerational community. Many have said that the most powerful part of the ritual is the grieving portion. Matt has everyone get down on their hands and knees and let out tones (from the third Chakra) that build into screams, growls, and weeping. The process ends with harmonic toning and beautiful music to bring everyone out of the darkness.

Though we have facilitators standing around the room holding space, we have never once had anyone get completely lost and not be able to come back to a space of love and light. It's quite something to feel a thousand people weeping together and to all feel held at that level of intimacy with complete strangers. It's especially powerful to see men letting go and allowing their feelings to wash over them. This ritual is evidence that there is nothing to be feared about going into the darkness. Our habit of repressing grief and anger comes from a collective fear that if we let ourselves feel the depths of our sadness we will never come out of it. The significance of this part of the ritual is that we do indeed come out, as the songs of ourselves expand, and feel all the better for it, rather than lost and depressed. This shows the value and necessity of communal grieving.

Another way to process our grief is by telling the stories of our small and large transformations and deaths. By doing this we build courage and depth in order to occupy more and more aliveness. In facing death head-on, we can approach life more fully. As Tyler Durden says in the popular American film *Fight Club*, "It's only after we've lost everything that we're free to do anything." Our dominant human presence is now endangering the life of the Earth. We're now being asked to let go of much of what we've grown attached to in the modern era, which we will experience as so many little deaths.

Facing death as a psycho-spiritual practice took a new shape for me several years ago when my grandmother Mima died on her 88th birthday. She and I were very close. Mima was a Sufi teacher who had lived in India and Nepal. She also visited sacred sites in Israel and Palestine in the 1970s. She literally never missed a day without practicing yoga and meditation. She had me baptized by her teacher Pir Vilayat (who also died on his 88th birthday) and I spent time in upstate New York at his retreat center. Mima taught me meditation, yoga, the arts, and shared her passion for seeing and representing natural beauty.

I had a gut feeling that she was going to pass on about a week before she did and so I flew from San Francisco to Florida to be with her. When I arrived by her bedside, she smiled, looked me in the eyes with loving recognition, then closed her eyes and immediately started to let go. It took some time, but when she died, I flew with her out into a very light space. She was giggling and ecstatic to be out of her worn-out body. We flew to where I couldn't go any further and waved goodbye as she continued, and I came back into my body. Once she was gone, I had the visceral sense that her essence had penetrated everything. I also began to feel her presence from within, whereas before, my psyche related to her presence in a more external way. This was an awakening for me, and the message was: There is nothing to fear in death. In fact, death can ultimately be an ecstatic process.

There are other ways in which coming into contact with death can wake us up, thereby giving us greater perspective and appreciation for the ways that we go back and forth, up and down, around the spiral of awakening and dying and awakening again. Sufi mystic poet Jalaluddin Rumi has a beautiful poem about this that he recited nearly a thousand years ago:

> *The breezes at dawn have secrets to tell you*
> *Don't go back to sleep!*
> *You must ask for what you really want.*
> *Don't go back to sleep!*
> *People are going back and forth across the doorsill where the two worlds touch,*
> *The door is round and open*
> *Don't go back to sleep!*

I recited this poem at my grandmother's funeral while feeling into the ways in which awakening and dying go together as part of a single movement. It's a fact that we are all going to die sooner or later. In bringing ourselves close to this knowledge now, we can bring a more awakened reality home. We can only then fully be in the present as our authentic selves.

In my near-death experiences, time has slowed and I have entered a state of increased presence and oneness that I now use as a benchmark to guide myself and others into fuller relationships with all of life's shapes. Close encounters with sharks in Florida, elephants in Africa, and with bears in Canada, North Carolina, and California have also brought me in touch with a greater sense of presence and respect for the dangers of being alive. It is quite a humbling experience to be hunted. It can also be exciting and enlightening when it sharpens your senses.

I have also come into contact with death through two bad accidents in cars, one on a snowboard, and another on a surfboard. I've felt my awareness leave my body and have learned to pray with all of my heart and soul. The duality of self and world disappeared. Through these close calls and serious injuries, I've learned an appreciation for the limits of my body and mind and the way that consciousness exists both within and beyond me. These experiences have guided me toward the edge of life and death while making it very clear what's important. They have been teachers in helping me to see beyond the day-to-day stories in which I can easily insulate myself from life's primordial powers. They have also helped me to see how precious a gift life is and how important it is to make our time on earth count. I can't imagine a healthy culture that doesn't know how to face death consciously. I see the Order supporting people in processing and moving through all of the many deaths that are inevitable to life.

Reinventing Education

There are some major changes we need to make to how we practice education if we are to develop into an ecologically oriented society. Future generations would benefit from education that is affordable, practical, fun, and heart-centered with schools that honor and consider the individual rather than homogenizing and objectifying every student that passes through their doors.

Waldorf and Montessori programs are both good models to pull inspiration from, both for the OSE and for reinventing education at large. Judy Dempsey was my Montessori teacher on and off for the first 14 years of my life. She recently published a book entitled *Turning Education Inside Out: Confessions of a Montessori Principal*. In it, she describes how a child's learning journey is best assisted by allowing her to follow her own passions for learning. The Montessori pedagogy is a good one to look at as a reference point for a new Order because it takes the individual's soul into account as well as spirituality and cosmology when guiding students in the classroom (which was often outdoors).

I didn't fully realize how influential Montessori education was in my life until I was talking to Matthew Fox as I prepared for a talk that I gave to the Jungian Society of Sarasota a couple of years ago. He asked me: "When did you first become aware of your interest in the human soul and its relationship to the cosmos?" Memories from Montessori came flooding back. Memories of playing, self-guided exercises, reflection time, meditations, creative writing, Native American stories of origin, art, and field trips to places rich in natural and cultural history. It was then that I remembered just how important Montessori was in shaping and supporting my sensitivities and core passions.

Montessori gave me permission and the space at a young age to explore a lifelong inquiry into my own unique nature, and the ways that I fit into the earthly and cosmic systems in which I am now consciously connected. In coming to know these origins of myself, I have discovered and rediscovered my own context, wholeness, and purpose while developing sustainable and life-enhancing ways of being human through the integrative practices of ecology, psychology, and cosmology. Montessori watered the seeds that grew into my fascination with life's evolving creativity, the Beat generation, and the human potential movement.

This brief conversation about my education with Matt ended up informing the speech I gave later that day, as I presenced the fact that psychoanalyst Carl Jung focused too heavily on the cut-off parts of the psyche of the individual and the shadow and did not incorporate the celebratory side of existence nor the cosmological perspective to create wholeness.

The OSE would hold space for the process of reshaping ourselves from the inside out to gain the skills necessary to confront the unfathomable challenges of our times like climate change. Reinventing education involves honoring the role of the unique soul of each person to guide the learning process. It means trusting that this process will co-create people who care about the whole. Reinventing education in the name of developing ecological and socially-minded consciousness is what schools like the California Institute of Integral Studies, Schumacher College, and the Fox Institute of Creation Spirituality are aiming toward. These are examples of graduate schools that include cosmology and the healing arts to balance the mental aspects of learning through differentiation.

The benefit of the OSE would be that it could hold space for the learning process without needing to carry the weight of an educational institution.

It would be free to hold many types of gatherings organically with different focuses in different places run by different people. The OSE could use empty facilities rather than own a building in order to stay light, inexpensive, and able to change quickly according to the needs of the participants.

Rites of Passage

Rites of Passage Rituals are our oldest form of education. They were an essential way that values and knowledge were passed down for millennia. They built individual and communal coherence through making important human developmental processes conscious, encouraging deep psycho-spiritual maturity. Rites of Passage are practiced in every pre-modern culture to presence change and instill values at important developmental times such as birth, puberty, marriage, entering one's vocation, bearing a child, dying etc. Sacred rites can be a way to integrate and honor core developments in life. Rites of Passage work by linking gifts and passions with core wounds. I see the OSE bringing Rites of Passage back into focus to connect us in both old and new ways.

I've often felt that our global ecological crisis wouldn't have arisen at the current level had Rites of Passage been more deeply considered in the modern era. Put another way: Had these practices been sustained at the depth of transformative power that was historically common, we would know ourselves better than to diminish the ecological integrity of this planet.

Through Rites of Passage we can link vocation with compassion because the whole community is needed to create a healthy context for the work of the individual. In focusing the energy of a community upon the individual, the latent potential that comes when one realizes one's most essential purpose and is guided to act upon it is then brought forth. Only by being seen can the individual grow into the vision of her vocation over time. Rites of Passage could very well support the awakening and the maturing process of our species now to avoid completely destroying the planet and ourselves.

We can step up together within a ritualized container of supportive and constructive challenge to move into ourselves and our individual callings in new ways that support the Earth.

Initiatory rites have always been an interest of mine since I got lost in the wilderness at 13. Since then, I've traveled to many places around the world looking at how other cultures support the individuation process within their communities and have come to the realization that although there are some really powerful techniques out there, to a large extent, we are all always learning and changing. No one fully knows what it means to be human. Our elders are doing the best that they can, giving everything to the next generation in the process, and yet there is more work to be done and more awakening to be had.

We experience periods of initiation over and over in our lives. Not just at birth, puberty, or marriage, but again and again in each of the little deaths needed to stay present to the ways life is changing us. We can also consciously be in dialogue with these changes in order to create the supportive structures needed at vulnerable times. The circumstances are always different, but the core principles and structure of Rites of Passage are consistent: crossing a threshold, leaving your community, letting go, opening to the mystery, discovering purpose, integrating the journey, and giving your gifts back to your community. These aspects are archetypal and unchanging over time and culture. We are in need of new rites now that appeal to the next generation while supporting the global conscious culture that we are becoming. This will help us to take responsibility for our impact and potential.

The core value used to guide the evolution of the field of Rites of Passage in the future is to hold space for the uninitiated to explore the question (possibly for the first time): "What do I believe in that is larger than myself?" Personally, venturing into the inner and outer wilderness of psyche and nature again and again has been the most potent place for me to explore this question and begin to answer it. As a boy, nature was the sole place in which I felt my inner spontaneity could arise and flourish fully. Camping as a child, I felt free and open to the larger-than-myself mystery. As my seat-of-self was still forming, I was often absorbed in the world about me. In nature I became profoundly open to the astounding sensory experience of the earth, from the rough but soft textures of particular kinds of bark that I gripped with my feet while climbing trees, to the moist smell of the air hours before the rain fell, and the three-dimensional depth of a glowing star-covered night sky.

Uncovering the Sacred Wound

As with many people, my first conscious individuation process was traumatic. Perhaps it was more traumatic than it needed to be because, like most Western adolescents, I didn't have a ritualized container. This trauma has very much shaped the arc from my core wound toward my life's work. My childhood contained a polar combination of deep nurturing love and chaos and abandonment. My parents separated when I was 11. This was a sensitive developmental time for me as I was just reaching puberty (with all of the wild fury of hormones and confusion that comes with them). I often felt overwhelmed by emotions of anger and sadness. Without a way to express these emotions fully within my family or social circles, I channeled them into sport and at times repressed them. I excelled and became a champion in gymnastics, soccer, swimming, and diving yet these accomplishments felt empty and I eventually pushed my growing body beyond its limits, injuring myself. This exacerbated my depression and nothing, including counseling, got at the core of my existential isolation and yearning for wholeness—until I went into the wilderness.

When I was 13, I went to Ontario with Andy Smyth, an old boy-friend of my mother's from her hippie days living in a teepee without running water in Woodstock. Andy was still a wilderness guide in Canada in the summers, and in a way he was an elder for me knowing, as he did, such a deep and intimate part of my story at that point in my life. We canoed more than 500 miles over 37 days on crystal clear rivers and lakes, portaging our supplies around rapids and waterfalls. It was beautiful and dangerous. We drank water without filtering it, as we were deep in the wilderness. We saw a bear, many moose, and a giant timber-wolf along the river. We cooked on an open fire and watched shooting stars and the Aurora Borealis. My psyche began to open to the wonderment of the cosmos and the wild languages of the Earth.

As we paddled day in and day out, sometimes to the point of exhaustion and real hunger, my attunement with nature grew, and with it an authentic and deep openness led to enhanced psychic awareness in which I could often tell when and where we would stop to camp long before we reached the camp-spots.

One morning, I awoke before dawn with the determination to check out an old trapper's cabin we had passed about a mile before we made camp. I ran along a beach with deep mud and on the way back, decided to hurry through the forest to avoid the mud. I missed the camp and got turned around. I was completely lost. I looked for much of the day and soon the forest seemed to close in upon me. I yelled out for help, I cried, and I thought that this would be the way that I died.

A search party eventually found me and led me back to camp before nightfall. Food had never tasted as good as it did that night! After dinner, as the light was fading, I paddled out onto the lake for some solitude. I soon began to feel the heaviness of my emotions and a flood of tears began to pour over me. Images of my father walking out on our family, leaving a note, and my mother sobbing on the floor. The subsequent unraveling of our family began to press back into memory as the night held me. I remember looking up and crying out to the universe: "What's my purpose?" and "Why am I here?" "Why do I feel so alone amidst my family and society?" Then silence came from below and softened my heart. I looked up again at the first stars appearing against a deepening purple sky and a shooting star shot across toward me at an angle as if the Creator was making a clear statement that I had been heard, felt, and seen. Deep gratitude welled up in my heart as tears of joy gently slipped down my cheeks. I knew that I wouldn't forget this moment despite still not knowing the answer to these questions. I was on my path now and felt a new sense of my soul and its place within the ultimate movements in which I am a co-creator.

I went on more wilderness trips each summer and dedicated myself to exploring the world while learning to listen. I began to guide others from the space that opened up in me amidst that twilight of soul and stars. Guiding groups of middle and high schoolers, college students, and adults on wilderness adventures and ecological restoration trips eventually turned into leading Vision Quests and Rites of Passage. Over time, the yearnings of my soul, combined with my life experience, and my core-wound, was shaped into my vocation.

My intention continues to grow into new ways of helping others uncover their inner-healer and lover and to explore their most authentic shapes of being in order to find and give their unique fulfillments to the world. I do this work through *Wild Awakenings*, an organization which offers many types of transformational experiences, both in town and in the wilderness. In entering the wild mysteries or the still presence of silence, we can help each other illuminate our inner worlds. Sharing in these intimate circles continues to nourish me while giving me the strength to face the brokenness, confusion, and pain of the world again and again. I realize now that these experiences of communion with life, coupled with deep pain and existential longing, are part of my dharma, and part of what the OSE offers: *A bridging of the polarities within every individual and in the collective human experience.* It is only when we integrate our light and shadow, our gifts with our wounds, our opposites within, that we can become the mystics and warriors the Earth calls us to be.

A Global Shift in Consciousness

We are now at a tipping point where enough people are awakening to our power and responsibility to show up for our vocations and purposes to nourish the web of life of which we are a part. I, and others, have sensed this shift happening for some time. The amount of information and the variety of cultures we are exposed to in the internet and social-media age are changing the ways we relate to old dogmatic religions and hierarchical institutions. We are connected and informed more thoroughly than ever before, allowing social, environmental, and technological change to speed up at perhaps the fastest pace in history.

Many have awoken to this need to muster the courage and discipline to uproot the destructive and unconscious cultural patterns that have dominated our species since our beginnings. With the shift into awakening, we will be able to organize ourselves into a mature and open spiritual tribe. This practice of community-bridging between the human and more-than-human worlds unites and builds capacity for understanding and compassion. These worlds become one through conversations, meditations, intimate journeys, rituals, and rites of passage that bring awareness to the patterns that bind and shape our togetherness. My hope is that we continue to orient ourselves and our communities from these ancient and new practices that increase freedom, reverence, playfulness, and understanding in this ever-expanding cosmos.

The most important practice the OSE will encourage is the practice of being present together to the Earth. It seems then that the core of this practice is listening and responding in support of the life systems that continue to shape and sustain humanity and all of the plants and animals that co-inhabit our incredible home. This involves responding to what the Earth is calling for now and what we are being invited to let go of in order to show up for this most important task. Letting go may not feel like too much of a sacrifice when filled with the purpose of creating sustainable work and technologies. And letting go might not feel so hard when we recognize the Earth as our true mother and our only home. This is what Thomas Berry has called "the Great Work" and what Joanna Macy refers to as "the Great Turning," both of which require our evolution toward an Earth-nourishing human presence. Our times are epic and great joy comes with taking on great challenges and making life work for all.

Billions of years ago, life developed a protective membrane around the cell, which created the necessary environment for cells to evolve into more complex life forms and eventually to evolve into the mammals that we are today. We know that the time has come for a great awakening in part because many have already awoken to the crises we are in.

We have come to a time now where we need a new protective cultural membrane to form and create a container of support, including the necessary environment for this next evolution of consciousness to take place in spite of the resistance to change that is present. This support is what the Order will provide.

The evolution of the horse and the bison is another example to relate to our current evolutionary state. Both, the horse and the bison, developed from a common ancestor, yet, over the course of millions of years, different communities of them learned to respond differently to their predators and pressures of life. What became the horse developed longer legs because it ran from predators—gradually getting better and better at it. The bison, on the other hand, faced and attacked predators as a herd and therefore developed a big bulky head and body that's built for ramming rather than running. This example shows how life continues to evolve physiology and intelligence in direct conjunction to the pressures upon it. A cheetah wouldn't be fast if it didn't have to catch a gazelle! Similarly, we humans wouldn't grow more conscious unless our environment required it.

Despite this knowledge that challenges are important for growth, so is protection and support. The more supported we are, the more risks we can feel confident taking and the more we can feel comfortable taking on challenges. The more we can know how to fall and get back up—the more we can jump and play and learn how to fall—the more we can bring our hearts out onto our sleeves and onto the streets and dark corners of our communities. The OSE would be a way to gather the community necessary to support a larger shift in culture by supporting those willing to climb out onto this scaffolding of what's now forming. The OSE can also be supportive in providing strength and focus to our individual and collective energy while we work as explorers of consciousness in support of the continued development of an Earth-honoring movement of mystics, healers, and activists. We might help one another to cut through the chaos and confusion accompanying cultural entropy and the overstimulation of our times. The support that the order could provide will probably look more like the work of a massage therapist or a yoga teacher rather than a paramedic or engineer in that these healing arts practice an intentionally indirect approach by supporting the conditions for healing to take place rather than attacking the problem. A massage therapist does this by softening the muscles to create space around an injury so that more blood can flow and energy can move again unobstructed and the body can learn to heal itself.

Creative and empowering movements are spreading around the world, from urban centers to wild rural villages. Take the rise of hip-hop for example—which has spread from the ghettos of New York City to the rest of the world—becoming a movement for liberation through a tradition of cathartic expression within the structured container of rhythm. Hip hop has also entered the wilderness including rural villages I've traveled to in Africa and Canada. On a canoe trip in Ontario, I saw the name of Los Angeles-based rapper Dr. Dre spray-painted on an Ojibway school that I came across in the settlement of Fort Hope. The settlement was a mess with trash strewn everywhere. Alcohol and substance abuse had become widespread and the people had lost much of the ways of life that had sustained them on physical as well as psycho-spiritual levels. Hip-hop was a useful healing art for them by flipping the perspective on the problems that have weighed them down. It has been a way of representing, accepting, and composting hardship while renewing the youth who have lost their identity. Hip-hop shows how the wilderness has moved back into the cities and the cities have moved into the wilderness. As we bring aliveness back into the ghettos around the world, we can build upon the *Occupy* movement while creating a spiritual vision of a world that supports the thriving of us all. The Order can be a place for this to occur through the cross pollination of creative cultural practices from hip hop to the Sundance. Our times require gathering and sharing the diverse array of cultural wisdom accessible now within a global understanding.

Grounding Medicine Ceremonies

There is a diversity of cultural wisdom practices that involve the use of plant medicines. From *Kava Kava* in Fiji to Ayahuasca in the Amazon and Peyote in the deserts of the Americas, it's clear that plants (and fungi) have been used to gain a depth of connection with the Earth and with ourselves that can be powerful. They can create powerful openings for our consciousness to receive new insights and make old connections conscious again within the community and with the more-than-human world. The great variety of healing ceremonies and nonordinary states of consciousness that have been developed in virtually every culture around the world can be a great resource for helping to shed light on imbalances and stress that can accumulate in our busy lives. When used with care and with respect for the cultural ceremonial guidance that accompanies them, sacred medicines can provide an immediate path to healing.

With the immense openings possible in ceremony, it becomes the responsibility of the individual and the community to integrate these experiences into day-to-day life. For me, yoga, meditation, and counseling have been essential tools for understanding and connecting to transpersonal experiences that have created big psychic openings that have sometimes felt overwhelming. There can be a large amount of personal and interpersonal work necessary to bring these peak experiences into one's routines and relationships. Without a commitment to this work, disconnection and neurosis can build up and can leave a gap between self and world, psyche and cosmos while reaffirming fear-based patterns of survival.

Given how disconnected our culture is from the Earth and from community, it's no surprise that it has oppressed these spiritual tools out of fear. If we are to offset these modernist projections, we will need new containers to hold space for the many layers of healing available to us. In order to push the medicine path forward, the insight and wisdom gained needs to be put into practice within a network of communities that regularly practice mirroring and understanding the lessons learned on the medicine path. The OSE could prove to be this kind of container if it can sufficiently ground the wisdom gathered in ceremony and help put it into practice.

Commitment, Participation, and Flexibility

The Order is an invitation to commit, first to one's self then to the work of expressing and focusing each of our unique purposes in the world. The Order includes making a vow and discerning commitments to live by. Making a commitment to waking up and to service constitutes a genuine Rite of Passage. It lays the groundwork to live with compassion and will help catalyze and focus an unknown amount of energy (the way a cultural commitment to equality catalyzed the Civil Rights Movement). As focus and presence are directed towards a common goal, they are amplified exponentially according to the people present and the power of their intention. This Order could be powerful in developing projects and ways of being that are aligned with the Earth because this is such an important integrative focus at this time.

A commitment can also conserve energy by helping us to know what not to do. This boundary is also energizing because it can empower us to follow through on the actions needed to push through resistance in order to show up for the creative process of reinventing our culture. As Howard Thurman suggests, to give one's self to one's passions is the greatest gift that we can give to our communities, to the world, and to ourselves. I've seen what the power of a central value (embodied by a central altar at rituals like the Cosmic Mass, the Sundance, and Burning Man) can do in terms of manifesting a reality together. The visceral sense of togetherness that develops through a collective understanding (with common reference points) is powerful in that it can expand a reality of interconnection to the point where newcomers can experience this reality (in ways otherwise not possible) because the collective field of understanding is so strong. A culture whose primary commitment is to practice being in sacred service of the Earth will create itself in that image and that reality. Our communities, and the myriad networks that make up the Earth community, will thrive with the new vitality that comes when we greet the world from this common depth of commitment. With greater and greater levels of uninhibited expression and openness to help from the more-than-human world, we can become channels for healing and connectivity.

I'm imagining that this Order is similar to a cooperative or a worker-owned organization that avoids hierarchy by laying out a living framework that supports ever-evolving manifestation of itself. The Order would support and encourage participation in ways that hierarchical governance are unable to, by encouraging bioregional community living. At least at this stage of our evolution, when most of our communities are so big, and so insular that we can no longer relate to one another, the qualities of the heart like intimacy and authenticity are clearly very difficult to sustain.

I do feel that the Order will only be rich and interesting if it has the ability to pull together many tribes or bioregional communities. One of the gifts that modernity and postmodernity have given us is differentiation, including the permission to be unique individuals. But this is currently at a dysfunctionally high level, which is why the Order is needed as a platform to encourage individual nuance within a connective culture of radical acceptance.

In recognizing that the Great Mystery has so many ways that it can manifest according to how each of us participates, we don't want to come up with any overarching laws. Flexible principles, however, may help us to move into ways of being that enact greater possibilities so that the most free ways of enacting reality together might emerge. This flexible approach is necessary for the dynamic process of shape-shifting and gaining the speed needed to shake off any stagnant and oppressive habits from modernity. The Order can provide dynamic feedback for itself, shape-shifting as needed according to the Earth's continued call.

Co-Creativity and Practicing the Healing Arts

We are recognizing and putting awareness practices like meditation and yoga, sweat lodges and Sundances, rites of passage, and other rituals to work in our lives. We are digesting the meaning within the stories that move us as we put them together in our own ways—according to our own experiences of togetherness. We are creating our own journeys through this mysterious life according to what is alive for each of us in this moment. The intelligible beauty of life organizing itself can leave us breathless, humbled, and connected to something more expansive and personally relevant than outdated, egoistic, and fear-based codes of conduct (like the ten-commandments) from the past. The monotheistic, patriarchal deity of the past is now subsiding into a panentheistic or pantheistic experience of the web of life as the conscious powers of collaboration and interconnection become more accessible within our practices. Our creativity surpasses our gaps in understanding when we engage from our hearts to bring the intelligence needed to reinvent ourselves and our culture.

Many are now ready to change their relationships to the "Messiah" and "Guru" and "President" archetypes in order to focus on the revelatory idea

of the "Network" and the "We" within community and "I-thou" relationships
where we take turns playing the role of leader without holding onto power.
We are now ready to find and enact our inner power to support those in
need by listening to the subjective experiences of the oppressed and taking
responsibility for everyone's well-being without taking any of it too personally. In gaining perspective on the pain of the past, we can be free to
feel it fully within the light of compassionate understanding and thereby
transmute it and free ourselves from the ways we have to identified with
it. We can recognize our collective wounds and show up to listen and hold
the pain of oppression together without getting weighed down by them.
The practice of dialectic conversation, council, and empathic listening are
our greatest tools for hearing and feeling others' perspectives even when
we disagree or don't understand. We may now be ready to move beyond
the "either/or" and the "black vs. white" dualisms that leave us feeling separate. This is the message within the Black Lives Matter movement. Through
bringing awareness to oppression, we can create new pathways of healing
and understanding. Many are recognizing that discomfort isn't always a
bad thing as it often means that we are expanding our collective capacity for
empathy. Through the practice of bringing awareness to injustice and sys-
tematic hatred, we may come across new ways of being that are more nuanced and open to our togetherness within the implicit order of life itself.

As we continue outgrowing religion, ever more nuanced and person-
alized forms of individual and emergent spiritual practices and values are
maturing and diversifying in practice and function. As more people awaken
to forms of spirituality that are alive for them, a kind of unstructured structure may start to emerge as people come together in ever-greater varieties
of interpenetrating shapes. Central to this new movement is the integrative understanding that everything is changing and falling away and that
no structure, religion, institution etc. will last. The Earth-based spirituality
supported by the OSE allows for this humble reckoning as we approach
new levels of existential maturity. Presence to death and the more-than-

human world go hand-in-hand in providing the Rite of Passage needed to free us from our narcissism in order to really celebrate the constant flow of endings and beginnings. Only then can we come to terms with our own end so that we can fully be here while we are here on Earth as we attempt to pass on what's essential. Only then can we become more than human.

Re-Wilding and Reconnecting with Ancestry

Since the agricultural revolution around 10,000 years ago, human contact with the Earth and her more-than-human voices has deteriorated, and left many in dark and disconnected places. A wild ethic, meaning the trust that wilderness is inherent to life, not something to be controlled or mediated, might be closer than we think, as millennials are growing up already knowing many of the cultural changes needed now (like living with less stuff, with more resources and sharing tools—like Craigslist—more readily available to us than previous generations were accustomed to).

Wilderness is home. It continues to symbolize the mysterious wild side of our existence that is the deepest source of creativity for our species. It brings light to the fact that everywhere is wilderness. Every city and town is impacted by the wild forces of nature.

The word "wilderness" was first created at a time when humans were settling into robust modes of disconnection from the intimacy of hunting and gathering (which has shaped our journey for most of our existence). Wilderness has also been used to point toward that which cannot be controlled or managed by humans (which is almost everything). It is the mystery out of which we have come and for many, it represents all that we wish to push away with walls and with distractions of all kinds. Being out of control is terrifying to the uninitiated modern mind! But the indigenous perspective is to have gratitude for life through embracing this chaos by forming nonlinear connections with the more-than-human worlds. We have been formed in the wild intelligence of a vibrant planet and can now gain an immense source of healing and inspiration by making contact with the practice of living close to the plant and animal worlds again.

Religion and our educational system at large have also remained so human-centered and industry-based that they have left us with little sense of how to participate with the more-than-human world. No movement thus far has been successful in redirecting our attention toward the biology of our wholeness. The stakes are building against us as mirrored by global warming and the population explosion that continues exponentially toward 8 billion.

A return to a premodern connection with the ancestors is now needed if we are to survive as a species. While West African teacher Malidoma Somé was teaching at my community house in Berkeley, I remember him asking us to imagine all of our ancestors at once. It would take the biggest stadium imaginable to hold them all. Now imagine that they are all cheering for you to succeed. They've done all that they could to pass on life to us and they succeeded through 10,000 generations! This image has stuck with me for years now. All of those who have gone before me doing whatever they needed to do to survive and pass on their wisdom so that I can put it into use now...wow! Each of us is here now as a result of thousands upon thousands of tremendous accomplishments, orgasms, and the perseverance needed to live, create, and pass along life. There were also traumas passed down, of course, and this integrative process of remembering who and what came before us is paramount to working through these traumas so that we can avoid making the same mistakes.

Indigenous and Mystical Perspective

We are now ready to bring ourselves into a mystical and relational way of life that integrates David Bohm's illuminations on "Wholeness and the Implicate Order," Thomas Berry's elucidation of "The Great Work," Matthew Fox's vision of the "Coming of the Cosmic Christ," Joanna Macy's hope for "The

Great Turning," Jorge Ferrer's "Participatory Vision of Human Spirituality," and the "Eagle and Condor Prophecy" from Amazonia. Teilhard de Chardin also gave us inspiration for this effort toward a global shift in human consciousness. Teilhard was a spiritual and scientific master who, like Einstein, wanted to know how God thinks. And yet, his love of matter and the Earth guided his eyes and heart toward the ground and the rocks in order to gain vision and insight into the big picture of cosmogenesis. Although he was a Jesuit priest, his nature was of a more indigenous or mystical bent in that he saw divinity or the source of energy in matter rather than as a purely transcendent force. He was also a champion for visionary and revolutionary communities well before the 1960s. As quoted at the beginning of this essay, Teilhard reflects: "There is almost a sensual longing for communion with others who have a large vision. The immense fulfillment of the friendship between those engaged in furthering the evolution of consciousness has a quality impossible to describe." These sparks of inspiration and possibility are popping up in communities all over the world right now. They grow stronger through felt experiences of coming together to face diversity. As the arms of oppression continue to lengthen and become more pervasive in their means of control, this tension is catalyzing a breakthrough. We can face the hard and difficult aspects of our descent from modernity by focusing on our passions rather than our competitive or capitalistic habits.

The tendency to awaken appears to be inherent in the process of cosmogenesis itself and in mystical experiences where life just flows, guiding us into deeper levels of complexity and relational communion with ourselves and with the world. At first this experience of being present to more and more of life can be overwhelming and can oscillate from being full of wonder to being more than our individual sense of self can hold. Brian Swimme and Thomas Berry finish their book *The Universe Story* with the realization that "Our individual self finds its most complete realization within our family self, our community self, our species self, our earthly self, and eventually our universe self...Nothing is itself without everything else. Each member of the Earth community has its own proper role within the entire sequence of transformations that have given shape and identity to everything that exists." There's no way to stop these fires of passion, inspiration, and transformation from exploding forth as this is our nature and the context in which the OSE finds itself as it co-creates a more sustainable culture.

Thoughts on Sexuality

Sex is good. Sex can be sacred or profane, depending on how we approach it and relate to it. Who are we to judge our urge for intimacy if we are not harming anyone? Some people are asexual and that is also good.

The sexual impulse can ignite creativity and set our imaginations soaring. As Kahlil Gibran eluded to in his poem, "On Children," the act of creating children is Life's longing for itself. (Life's longing also applies to forms of sex that cannot create children). Sex can be a spiritual experience of communion when it is approached with reverence, mindfulness, and openness to the other.

Sex requires maturity, discernment and some precaution as it is a powerful act that can change relationships, spread disease, and bring life into this world. This question of harming others is where it can get a bit complex however, in a culture that honors sexuality as a natural part of life, it can hold space for the necessary learning and healing to take place around sexuality. It's time for sexuality to come back out into the light and be honored as the integral part of life that it is. Only then can we be free to fulfill our sexual preferences in healthy ways that nourish our bodies, hearts, and communities.

Thoughts on Religion

While my critiques of religion are many, I respect the traditions of the past for the simple reason that they've worked, at times, in carrying forth the wisdom necessary for our survival as a species. For thousands and thousands of years, religions have worked to soften the reptilian and subsequent instinctual and competitive mammalian impulses within humans to attack and kill one another. They've also helped to reduce suffering by creating some very useful common goals, practices, and values to gather communities around. These practices often encouraged more subtly attuned modes of collaboration and organized life to emerge from the perceived chaos of the wild and often dark world of human confusion and violence.

For many, the experiential dimension of self-world exploration (including the adventure of being lost) can do more for the soul's development than predigested notions of "Truth" or another's view of what's best. Postmodernity is a time of deep questioning, unraveling, and falling apart. Our relationships are changing. Many recognize that religion has failed to this point in awakening humanity to ways of being that work for all. In order to make simplistic maps or to hold onto power, clarity has been lost and Truth denied. Relativism has shown how Truth isn't applicable or understandable to all, nor is it coming from one viewpoint only and calling it the whole pie. The experiences of Jesus, Buddha, Mohammed, etc. inherent in religions of the past can continue to inspire, yet they are less helpful when taken in place of our lived experience of tastes, sensations, and movements from within the creative immediacy of the pulsing, wild Earth herself.

The Order must not be simplified into another religion or a cult with particular dogmatic instructions or pressures to be one way or another. It must remain outside of religion and can be related to from either a secular place of nonbelief, a place of faith, or as a nondual place of being the change that we seek. In this way, we can integrate our inner and outer worlds while healing the Cartesian dualism involved in cultural separation and suffering.

Although I have traveled through many terrains of belief, I have found them all to be too small in accounting for the wild world and my place in it. I have practiced Sufi and Christian traditions as well as those of the

Cherokee, Cheyenne, Lakota, Iroquois, and Seminole nations only to find that I needed to more deeply explore nature and the cosmos for myself. Through tasting and touching, leaping and looking, my sense of wholeness has deepened as I have been able to return to the practices that most serve me. Still, I respect the multitude of wisdom traditions that have pointed my way toward right relationship with the numinous dimensions of life.

This developmental, self-organizing world is now asking us to pay attention to the ways of life that are the most alive with cooperative fluidity and ease of connection and collaboration. This is what is being developed in younger generations now: moving past the need for religious structure and into an ability to be in direct contact with more and more of the numinous powers of presence and aliveness that are creating the pulsing world from within and all around us. This ever deepening experience of the cosmos is guiding and sensitizing us to what is needed to respond and dance with more of what's being made available now in a deeper way than our great religions have been able to communally embody.

The OSE accepts all religions but is not religious itself. It accepts the faithful and the faithless, the orthodox and the secular, the spiritual seeker and the nonbeliever. It accepts all people now who are simply willing to be in service of the Earth.

Other important spiritual principles that I've touched upon in less detail, but are also essential, are: immediacy, presence, simple living, sexual freedom and responsibility, permaculture, civic responsibility, self-expression, self-reliance, decommodification, gifting, radical inclusion, contemplative practice, self love, love of the sacred, psychological awareness, and self understanding.

Gathering the Tribes

My hope is that the OSE can function as a grounded bridge between many of the groups and individuals working now to make life more liveable and free for all beings. The festival culture that has mastered the art of aliveness and celebration, the civil rights and black lives matter movements, the sustainability movement, the feminist movement, the eco-social justice movement, the bioregional movement, LGBT movement, the consciousness and contemplative movements, the plant-medicine movement, the indigenous empowerment movement, and the re-wilding movement (to name a few) because all of these movements have their roots in the art of community making and can gain depth in their relationships with one another. The OSE can serve to ground peak experiences, heal from traumas gained on the front-lines of protests, create rituals and Rites of Passage to assist individual and cultural connection and development while deepening our collaborative networks within all that is Earth.

Our need to evolve our culture is upon us now like never before. The intense pressures to grow up and evolve require inner work and forms of integrative training to connect open hearts and minds to something greater and deeper than our current culture. Population explosion, global warming, and extreme levels of pollution of our air and water are part of creating a birth canal for the ecological human to be born. If we are to band together in order to create lasting change, we will need to do the inner work necessary to participate with one another at a new level of collaboration. A movement that incorporates contemplation and ritual as well as activism and reengineering commerce. The Trump presidency is a sign of the cultural unraveling now underway. The unconscious instinctual drive for power and the anger around misplaced responsibility and government impotency is becoming increasingly transparent. My hope is that the wounding and re-wounding taking place won't surpass the learning and empowerment that is available to us now in which to help reshape our lives and our local economies. Divisions, borders, and differences have been the focus of modernity (and the focus of Trump's campaign) largely due to giving power to the reptilian brain (which acts and reacts from the fight-or-flight instinct), as well as the regressive mammalian impulse to compete and to dominate.

In placing rationality over intuition, difference over connection, we have forgotten how nourishing it is to be in a heart-centered space of acceptance and openness that comes when we are present to the one human family in which we are all born into. When we are supported by, and supportive of, an Earth-honoring culture, it is easier to understand that there is nothing to fight, repress, or make wrong. Those ready to live in a new way will need some help and some protection from the oncoming storm.

The need for an order, which acts as a clarifying protective membrane that buffers us from the toxic physical and psychic cultural patterns of modernity, could allow new cultural forms to develop, strengthen, and mature more quickly. It is now time to synthesize as well as embrace our polarities by accessing the center of ourselves and our communities. The renaissance of heart-centered ways of being carry with them new routes for relating to everything again and again. They can become a great source of hope and inspiration for developing a truly compassionate and sustainable way of being human. The OSE will provide a nourishing yet expansive container to dance with the spirit of community and to reach just beyond our common comfort zones. In stepping into a vow and a practice that is at the edge of our comfort zones, we may find something more fulfilling together.

Why not try to bring together a loosely held, diverse group of people into authentic relationship in order to self-organize around similar core values that support our evolution into an Earth-honoring culture? The OSE could be the supportive container needed to move away from the anthropocentric habits and fantasies of the modern era that have brought immense destruction to our planet while inflicting pain upon ourselves. A community centered around a sacred pledge, to be the best lover and defender of the Earth that we can be, will help to bind and focus the energy and inspiration within young and old, transgender, homosexual, and heterosexual, indigenous and western, religious and agnostic alike while encouraging a multitude of ways to nourish wholeness and fulfillment. The OSE can be a bridge toward the next phase of evolution. This vision will help to encourage the inner changes necessary to empower our personal and collective passage into a more integrated and self-aware culture—with new possibilities for participating with life.

The alchemical axiom, "As above, so below," guides us now more than ever in looking toward the biological ground from which we have come to understand where we are going and what solutions will allow us to enhance life. If we can take responsibility for our own lives and the well-being of others (human and nonhuman alike) then we may be able to move toward ways of being more alive with heightened new sensitivities of empathy, mindfulness, compassion, and integration in support of our progression toward Earth-human symbiosis.

Could the OSE help us to better understand and attune to the larger patterns and movements of the Earth and cosmos? We won't know unless we try! Unless we commit to participating in the emergent, self-organizing dynamics of the universe, we may not have the focus necessary to consciously change and may never know our own potential and what humanity might create in the next millennia.

When we look into what moves us and where we are being pulled, we open to the implicit order pervading all of our seemingly opposed cultural identities. When we enter into the real and uncut dimensions of life to feel, to grieve and to take space for ourselves to sink into the full feeling of the suffering and destruction of life on our planet, only then can we have the strength and courage to aim for our dreams in supportive ways.

Something like the OSE will support an awakening that activates new capacities and solutions for our important time on this planet. Let's take the plunge! Let's surrender into the arms of our own evolution. Let's be taken by the wild gods of nature again and again as we find new ways of being together. As we expand and deepen our commitment to be lovers and protectors of life, we may become more than human. Through surrender, we can open to the process of unraveling the cultural systems harming life. Only together can we stand up to the corporations that are making life less liveable and less free for the majority of beings on this planet. Through embracing collapse, grieving together, and releasing ourselves to something larger, a new ecological postmodern era can come to meet us. This was the way of our ancestors. It was the lesson from my dream of falling into awareness. And it may be a path toward cultural healing, integration, and evolution for us now that the patriarchal path is becoming more fully illuminated.

The OSE is an embodiment of a simpler way. It is like the support of loving and accepting parents, brothers, and sisters, and it asks us to be like children again while exploring the world with beginner's minds. As we inquire into the hardened places within our own bodies and within the collective body, we will hold space for these energetic and cultural blockages to soften, become conscious, and to be integrated—at their own pace—into a fuller dance of being and becoming. When we let go of our self-importance, the weight of the world that we've been carrying can be released. We can then show up with more energy for the work to support other's (human and nonhuman) and thus to flesh out pathways of long-term happiness. As we face death, we might enter unity. As we stop holding ourselves apart from the world, we can practice coming home to our chosen communities—the ones who see us and nourish us in the real ways that our souls need and desire. When we realize that we are the ones we've been waiting for and that we are already in a very well-designed and intelligent world, only then can we surrender control to meet, mirror, and initiate ourselves and one another into the universe's self-organizing intelligence. What fun we can have!

THE ORDER OF THE SACRED EARTH
Jennifer Berit Listug

"Until one is committed, there is hesitancy, the chance to draw back, always ineffectiveness. Concerning all acts of initiative (and creation), there is one elementary truth, the ignorance of which kills countless ideas and splendid plans: that the moment one definitely commits oneself, then Providence moves too."

W.H. Murray, author of above quote, was a daring Scottish mountaineer who travelled to India in the mid-19th century, and climbed the Himalayas. He is describing here the palpable power that radiates, simply from making a commitment when one is facing what seems to be an impossible obstacle. He discovered on his adventure that it was his committing to go, purchasing his boat passage, that signified the powerful beginning to the rest of the journey. Yes, there were still supplies to gather, gear to pack, seas to sail, and mountains to climb. There was all of the work and the fun and the challenge and the wonder inevitable in travel, and yet all of these elements fell into place with ease and grace once he had committed, simply committed to listen to his heart and go. When one makes that sort of commitment, Murray continues, "all sorts of things occur to help one that would never otherwise have occurred. A whole stream of events issues from the decision, raising in one's favour all manner of unforeseen incidents and meetings and material assistance, which no man could have dreamed would come have come his way."

What an epic and impossible task it must have seemed, reaching the peaks of the Himalayan mountains, when envisioned from the comfortable safety of his humble living room in Scotland. And yet, he asserts, with his commitment, Providence—which is to say, the generous support of God or Nature, or the Higher Self—opened the world up for him in exactly the way that was necessary to complete his mission.

This is the value of commitment. This is the value of taking a vow. This is the power of saying "Yes" to the great unknown.

The Order of the Sacred Earth is a community of people, self-selected, who have committed, *taken a vow*, to honor the Earth as a conscious being, and celebrate all life as sacred.

We now have a much bigger task ahead of us than climbing the Himalayas. If that mountain range seemed challenging to Murray, the mountain of crises we have co-created over the ages seems to me at times, well, insurmountable. Matthew and Skylar have done a thorough job explaining in detail the contours of our postmodern problem mountain: climate change, and the denial of it (and most recently in the United States, the Trump administration's withdrawal from the Paris Agreement), outdated educational institutions, bigotry and hate toward one another. Looking through the lens of all the world's problems one would see no end to human, animal, and earthly suffering. Fortunately, there are many other lenses we can look through too—the lenses of love, compassion, activism, beauty, and wonder, to name a few.

I am, though, reminded of the imminent flooding of the coming spring in the foothills of the Sierra Nevada mountain range where I live. We are faced with the double threat of the rain continuing to pour (more volume this year than since 1896, by the way) and the beginning of the snow-melt, months of water built up and stored as ice, ready to release itself on our already flooded waterways. The structures we have built around us (our institutions, our bureaucracy, our corporations and economy) can no longer contain the downpour of violations, the ones committed daily, and those that have built up over the season of humanity.

Am I wrong to compare human failings to the mountains and the rivers who are so beautiful, wild, and essential to our ecosystems? I only mean to stress the enormity of what we are being called to do: to rise up together, to navigate and surmount our crises before they bury or drown us. And perhaps in drawing this comparison I have too unconsciously illuminated another truth of our situation: that humans too, even with our flaws and misused power, are beautiful, wild, and essential to our ecosystems. And what we call "problems" are in fact in divine alignment with the natural order of our evolution, as time and progress will eventually show.

The question is, how might the Order now mitigate our "problems," and plant the seeds for solution? It would be impossible for this new Order to undo the many specific social, economic, and political problems we face, on it's own. Rather, the Order, and the people who join it, will seek to *illuminate* and *heal* the underlying *dis-ease* that every one of our "problems" is rooted in. We have already articulated this fundamental worldwide issue as "an absence of the sense of the sacred." Philosopher Rick Tarnas, in his book *Cosmos and Psyche*, calls it "the profound metaphysical disorientation and groundlessness that pervades contemporary human experience...the widely felt absence of an adequate, publicly accessible larger order of purpose and significance." We are missing a *larger order of purpose*, that unifies us, inspires us to make decisions about our lives and our world that are in support of equality, justice, sustainability, and love.

The value of the Order of the Sacred Earth will be in creating a community around the great task of revolutionizing and respiritualizing (or re-sacralizing) our world. If Providence works in favor of the single explorer who has made a commitment to climb a mountain, imagine what it will do when thousands, hundreds of thousands of mystic warriors commit to waking up, to protecting and celebrating each other, all life, and our common home, the Earth.

I have seen the lengths we humans go to in search for our missing connection with the sacred. In the summer of 2016, I went on a pilgrimage, the Camino de Santiago, a thousand-year-old journey following a 500-plus mile path through Spain, to the tomb of the apostle St. James, one of the last people known to walk the Earth with Jesus. With hundreds of other pilgrims, I walked endless days, let my feet grow callous and my back ache, reached Santiago de Compostela, and found that it was not St. James who held the secret to our healing (nor did I ever expect it would be), but was rather the freedom and purpose we felt on the interminable path, and the heart-to-heart connections we made with one another, walking side by side for six weeks, on the same virtuous mission.

So it was in a Chanupa ritual I participated in not long ago, led by a Shaman from the Native American Church. Dozens of people gathered in a ceremonial yurt, and one by one we took turns speaking our deep, beautiful, wretched prayers. We cried, and moaned, yelled, laughed, and hugged, and in the end we passed around the peace pipe, took a puff of the sacred tobacco, and sent our prayers out with the smoke, spiraling up to the heavens. These grieving people were not sick, dying, starving, or homeless. These were people who, an hour before, mingling outside the ceremonial space, projected images of happiness, confidence, and general well-being.

What I want to show, what was so obvious in this ritual, and on my pilgrimage, is simply that every being suffers—the privileged, and the oppressed. The orthodox Christian, and the atheist. The newborn child, the elder on her deathbed, and everyone in between. (And though I am aware of, and sympathetic to, the gross inequality in societal treatment of the different ethnicities, genders, sexual orientations, nationalities, and classes, it would not be right for me to judge whose suffering is more justified than whose). We all suffer for the collective, for the history and present state of oppression and violence in our species. We suffer for the animals we have driven to extinction, and the beautiful lands we have developed and industrialized. We suffer, most of all from the great affliction of being disconnected from our sense that this world is sacred, and so are we.

And while our valiant efforts to reconnect—our pilgrimages, fasts, dances, songs, and prayers are worthy of our efforts, and certainly temporarily sustain our yearning for connection, there is a more lasting medicine to humanity's great disease. We need only look at the ancient origins of the words that have become so charged, and even taboo in the postmodern world, so that we might reinvigorate them. Let us reclaim the original meanings of Religion and Spirituality.

Religion comes from the Latin *religare*: to bind. I read this not as to *restrict* or *hold back*, but to bind, as in to connect, to interweave like the sewing of many different colored threads to create a great tapestry. Our new religion then, is the path to bind ourselves, our lives, and our purpose, to that which is sacred—the Earth, our brothers and sisters, the four-leggeds, the swimming and winged ones, the crawlers, the plant nation, the stone nation, the infinite sea of stars, and all the space between.

Spirituality comes from the Latin *spiritus*: the breath. What gives us life. And so our spiritual practice is nothing more than to acknowledge and appreciate that which gives us life—the air, the water, our food, the Earth-our-mother, and all her beings who contribute to life's diverse and expansive spiral.

The Order of the Sacred Earth provides a context for these new forms of Religion and Spirituality. It is a community of people, and a network of communities, who believe that the end of suffering (of humans, all life, and the Earth herself) will begin when we acknowledge and embody our intricate and inextricable connection to every other being in this cosmos. It is a community of people who have committed to living, to the best of their ability, in this web of all our relations. After all, the origin of the word "church" comes from the Old English plural for "Christian"—meaning that the church was not a brick-and-mortar building or institution: it was a gathering of like-hearted people coming together in worship. So this new Order exists first and foremost in the very heart of each person who makes the commitment.

The Order of the Sacred Earth

Understanding the purpose and power of making a commitment and taking a vow, I turn to the subject of our vow—the Earth. Considering the endless and diverse social and political (which is to say, human) problems, why is our vow to love and defend the Earth? It seems a self-evident moral imperative to me, to honor and sanctify our home and mother, and yet it is not for so many: the lobbyist who prioritizes oil and industry over sustainability, the justice activist who (nobly) believes that salvation of humanity must come first, the average human who goes about his life, seeking happiness and success with little thought for the impact that his decisions and actions have on this planet or other beings. We all have it backwards. True prosperity, lasting justice, deep happiness and success, begin with the creator of these things: the Earth herself. This is not, by any means, to say that our collective efforts toward ameliorating our many human problems should be postponed or disrespected. (Indeed, activism and social justice are a core part of the Order too.) But I want to emphasize that *how we treat each other* and *how we treat our planet* are intimately intertwined. We are taught from a young age to "treat others the way we wanted to be treated" but this moral code breaks down when we start selecting and categorizing which "others" deserve our equal and fair treatment. The Order is now trying to teach to the postmodern mind that the "others" we are morally responsible for treating with compassion and justice, are *all* others— humans of "other" ethnicities, genders, political identities, and religious beliefs, animals of "other" species, insects, trees, and flowers, our ocean, the mountains, all "other" life.

I believe that the salvation of humanity and of the Earth will naturally happen together, or not at all. We are all interconnected in the great web of life and we humans are a beautiful and essential member of the kingdom of Earth; so the Earth's healing *is* our healing; its thriving, *our* thriving; its salvation, our salvation. And when we talk about loving and defending the Earth, we are talking, also, about loving and defending all of her life, including one another. Robin Wall Kimmerer, author of *Braiding Sweetgrass*, puts it this way: "Because the relationship between self and world is reciprocal, it is not a question of first getting enlightened or saved and then acting. As we work to heal the earth, the earth heals us."

We are not unguided in our great task. The Earth herself is everywhere providing us with pristine examples of how to create the world we envision. We no longer need to look to gurus and heads of state, deities and messiahs, and other so-called authorities for guidance; we need only refocus our reverence and respect on the Earth and Cosmos who are our greatest teachers. We can listen and learn by turning our attention to the most ancient of wisdom, life itself, and the stars where it is born.

What can we learn from the birth of the star? Simply described, a star is born when atoms of light elements are squeezed under enough pressure for their nuclei to undergo fusion. The centers of the atoms literally fuse together, and the bi-product is a light and energy so great that it gives life to a new-forming world, as our star, the sun, did for the earth. So we see, the pressures of destruction we feel upon us now are not barriers but catalysts for our evolution. They become creative rather than destructive when we, the elements of light, let our cores, our heart-centers, merge together to create new energy, new vision, new life.

What about the life of a tree? In the fall, a tree sheds its leaves in order to conserve its resources as it enters a time with less nourishment from the sun and soil it depends upon. The tree effortlessly gives up what its instinctual wisdom tells him he cannot sustain. Why can't we? Imagine what our world be like if every season we humans collectively shed the systems and institutions and ideologies that we cannot sustain (and which no longer sustain us), trusting that from their compost we will nourish ourselves, and, in time, new leaves and blossoms will emerge.

What we need is the courage and context to come together, to fuse our core visions, and the insight to shed what we no longer need so that we might compost it into new life. This process is not difficult or unnatural. We were made to cycle and renew in this way. It is our birthright and a cosmically endowed gift. The ecological and social pressures upon us are greater than they ever have been, and the detritus of unsustainable institutions is sapping us of resources. This must mean, in the natural order of life, our time has come to cycle into rebirth and new growth.

The Earth is now creating the conditions for her own salvation, and we humans, who have caused so much destruction, are a key element. We have the unique power to be the speakers for the Earth and all her life. This is not to say that we are in some way *more* powerful than any other entity in our world. In fact, shifting out of our anthropocentric perspective is an essential step, and a crucial commitment for the Order of the Sacred Earth.

Another inherited perspective we learn as children (which most of us never question) is how to categorize everything we perceive or interact with, and where we stand in relation to it. Think about the children's game "Animal, Vegetable, Mineral" in which we point to an object and categorize it—in which we are really saying, "Alive, Sort of Alive, Not Alive At All." A dog is alive. A flower is, sort of. A pile of sand is not at all. And what about a fire? Is a fire alive, the way it dances and licks the air with its flaming tendrils? And the squirrel, noisily running up the tree outside my window, is it less conscious than me because it doesn't know how to kneel and pray?

But even these three distinctions fall under one umbrella categorization, which is at the root of our anthropocentrism. In his book, *Becoming Animal*, cultural ecologist and environmental philosopher David Abram calls it "the bifurcation of matter from spirit." It is the inherited belief that *matter* has no consciousness, and we humans, with our awareness and intelligence, are the only beings who are awake in this world.

We teach this and profligate this idea, if not directly, then indirectly, in every aspect of our modern world: when we herd cattle and genetically modify their digestive system so we can feed them what is "cheaper" for us to grow; when we blow mountaintops to smithereens and mine their remains for coal. Is this how we would behave if we believed the cattle and the mountain and the corn to be as conscious as us?

In our human-centered or human-dominant thinking, we have reified, as Abram asserts, "the great chain of being—wherein those phenomena composed entirely of matter are farthest from the divine, while those that possess greater degrees of spirit are closer to the absolute freedom of God."

And yet, anyone who has let themselves get lost in watching the airy purple leaves of a Japanese plum tree flutter in the wind, anyone who has gazed at the flat surface of a stone, and seen its spiraling colors wind their way back in time to the moment it was formed, knows that our perception of the nonhuman as static and spiritless simply isn't true.

When, as Abram says, "we begin to question the distinction between matter and spirit," or, to put it another way, when we see, acknowledge, and celebrate the sacred spirit that endows all things with life, this hierarchy of being, with humans at the top, begins to crumble. Then we see the truth, "a diversely differentiated field of animate beings, each of which has its gift relative to the others. And we find ourselves not above, but in the very midst of this living field, our own sentience part and parcel of the sensuous landscape."

And so it becomes clear that our responsibility to be the revolutionaries and change-makers of the world is not a righteous position for us, the supreme beings at the top of the food chain. We are not the chosen ones, with the god-given right to carry eminent domain over the Earth, nor to be its only savior. We are ones of the many, in the kingdom of all life, with the unique gift and task of being mystic-warriors, lovers, and defenders of the Earth that births us all.

The Order of the Sacred Earth, I hope, will provide the container we need to incubate each of our visions for our healing and evolution. If this still seems insurmountable, like the peak of the Himalayas seemed to W.H. Murray from his house in Scotland, let us look once more to the wisdom of the Earth for guidance, and contemplate how a little seed becomes a strong and thriving tree.

A seed falls from a living tree, perhaps is carried on a wind or in the belly of an animal to a more distant land. It is buried in fertile earth and in its first phase of growth it sprouts roots and feeds itself from the nutritious soil. Only then, after it has rooted itself in nourishing land, will it be ready to grow its first stem that will become the sturdy trunk and canopy of leaves over centuries.

So may the Order of the Sacred Earth, our seed, plant itself in the fertile soil of loving and dedicated minds and hearts, sprout its roots of ritual, community, and activism, and grow and spread its branches of prolific and sustainable new culture, society, and life for all.

I write these words at a tender time, when (for the first time in my life) a new being is growing inside of me. It is an extraordinary thing. I have always sensed my creative ventures as lifelike beings that grow from within, birthed in the form of a poem or a song. But this creature, this human growing in me now uses and creates more energy than my most divinely inspired prose ever has. And the big question looms ahead of me in a foggy and uncertain future: What world am I co-creating for this child? What will this boy grow up to know about life, and the earth, and all of its beings? That the world is a kind, just, and wildly beautiful place? Or will he live in a world, still, where men and women assert themselves as the omniscient all-powerful creators of things, and societies, and philosophies and ideas, where we each stand alone in the forest, trying to absorb the most water and nutrition and light from the world around us?

I may not have any power over the trajectory of our human condition, or the tides of the sea, or the hour of the setting sun. But I do have power over my energy, my century or so of life on this beautiful planet, and what I devote that time to. As do you. As do we all.

Clarissa Pinkola Estes says that asking the proper question is the central action of transformation. So the question is, what kind of world do we want to create? What do we value? What do we stand for? And how might we come together, to reorder ourselves and our perspectives in a new way that will thrive and prosper all life for generations to come?

PART II

IGNITING OUR CREATIVITY
Brian Thomas Swimme

Dear Reader,

I want to begin by saying how moved I am to learn of the Order of the Sacred Earth that is being created through the initiative of Matthew Fox, Jennifer Berit Listug, and Skylar Wilson. In my opinion, there is no spiritual order—anywhere—that is more comprehensive, more profound, more timely, than the Order of Sacred Earth. I find the articulations by Matthew and Skylar to be both brilliant and explosive. I feel only the deepest gratitude to all three of them for bringing forth this vitally important movement in our time. As I write this, the OSE does not yet even exist, and yet already I feel certain I will find a home there for my own life and work.

As a way of making a small contribution to the launch of OSE, I am responding to a question I have been asked by Matthew, Jennifer, and Skylar: *"What might a new, inclusive, spiritual Order contribute to our world?"* I am happy to offer my speculations, but only with the understanding that this is just a guess; the actual contributions to our world will only show themselves over time as the members of the OSE pour forth their gifts to the larger community. And no one, not even God, is capable of knowing what that future will look like.

My angle will be to look at the universe itself and see how its dynamics are involved in the work of the OSE. I want to focus on just one of the many amazing aspects of the universe's wisdom. In a phrase, I want to highlight the way the universe gives birth to itself by assembling communities with the capacity to awaken the creativity of their members.

The archetypal story concerning this dimension of the universe begins with the hydrogen atom. In the previous era of humanity—by which I mean the modern industrial era, which is presently in its death stage—scientists were convinced they understood the hydrogen atom in all its details, and thought of it as indestructible and inert. Then they discovered something that took them by surprise. They learned that in the center of stars, hydrogen atoms are transformed into carbon, nitrogen, oxygen, and all the elements that make up our bodies and the bodies of every living being.

Here's the feature of this discovery that relates to the OSE and that I ask that you think about. *An individual hydrogen atom can NOT transform itself into carbon, nitrogen, or phosphorous.* An individual hydrogen atom will persist as it is without change for billions of years. At the most, it might disintegrate into an electron and a proton. It will never create anything new by itself. But, the amazing fact is that if a hydrogen atom finds itself in the intense and interacting community called a star, it discovers that it has the power to participate in crucial ways in its transformation into the elements that give birth to life. In the community called a star, an individual atom becomes the gateway into the next era of the universe's story.

This process whereby the universe constructs communities that ignite the creativity of its members has been at work for 14 billion years and at every level of complexity. It now operates in the human world. It will, I predict, be operating with a new intensity within the Order of the Sacred Earth.

Creative and sensitive humans alive today yearn to make a difference in the world. They can feel the creativity that surges within them. They know they have an important gift to bequeath. What they need is a way of activating these creative powers. That is what the OSE is. Matthew Fox and his colleagues will draw from the wisdom traditions all around the planet to create a community rooted in the work of mutual empowerment. A person will enter the OSE and over time will see the emergence of a creativity one has always suspected was there but is now become powerfully present. The entire Earth Community is thrilled by the prospect of what the OSE will release upon the world.

Sincerely yours,
Brian Thomas Swimme

THE LUMINOUS DARKNESS
THAT CONNECTS US
Mirabai Starr

For as long as I can remember I have been both irresistibly attracted and practically allergic to every single one of the world's great religions. When I was 16 I had an English teacher, who also happened to be a rabbinical student, who hoped I might embrace my ancestral roots and find a relevant road back into Judaism. Unable to hold my own in conversation, I wrote him a letter in which I tried to explain that I was neither Jew nor not Jew (though I had been born Jewish), not Hindu (though I had an Indian guru and had been named after a Bhakti poet), not Sufi (though I had been initiated into three Sufi orders) nor Buddhist (though I practiced Vipassana). I was, I declared, a bridge-builder.

It's not that my teacher was evangelizing. He was riding an emerging wave of consciousness that honored existing religious institutions while imagining them in a fresh and more inclusive way. But even this—the seeds of the Jewish Renewal movement—was too organized for me. My Beloved was too wild to contain in any one tradition. It was dawning on me that my path was to navigate and facilitate the spaces between the traditions, and that I was somehow not given to linger in any particular holy house.

It is important to acknowledge that I developed this interspiritual sensibility not in spite of but as a direct result of the way I was raised. I grew up in the counterculture of the 1970s in which established social norms—such as religious belief systems and a culture of over-consumption—were being actively subverted. My educated parents uprooted us from suburban Long Island and replanted us in the mountains of northern New Mexico to go "Back to the Land" and live more intentionally, in conscious communities, primarily drawing on indigenous wisdom, with a generous splash of Eastern philosophies to guide them.

That's when I first encountered the Lama Foundation, an interspiritual community in the mountains near Taos where Ram Dass had written his iconic book, *Be Here Now*. Lama was connected with the alternative school my siblings and I attended and, as a result of this association, we were exposed to a vast array of teachers and teachings from multiple traditions: Vedanta and Yoga, Zen and Tibetan Buddhism, the I-Ching and the Tao Te Ching, some Persian poetry, a bit of Kabbalah, and of course local Pueblo Indian culture. The one faith missing from my eclectic spiritual education was Christianity. I think the counterculture was so busy recovering from the wounds they felt had been inflicted on them by the prevailing dogmas they had rejected when they took the risk of "tuning in, turning on, and dropping out" that they accidentally threw the beautiful baby of Christian contemplative tradition out with the stale water of divisive doctrines. I took it upon myself to reclaim that baby later.

By the time I fell in love with the 16th-century Spanish mystic St. John of the Cross, through his masterpiece, *Dark Night of the Soul* when I was 20, my heart was already open to the perennial wisdom at the core of all spiritual traditions. John's ecstatic poetry sounded to me exactly like the Sufi poet Jalaluddin Rumi. The language of love-longing, of the secret rendezvous of lover and Beloved in the Garden, the imagery of fire and wine, resonated in my own love-drenched being and drew me into a lifelong relationship with this Christian mystical master. This bond with John of the Cross eventually led me to his mentor, Teresa of Avila, which then opened gate after gate to many other great Christian mystics: Francis of Assisi, Hildegard of Bingen, Julian of Norwich, and archetypal wisdom figures such as Our Lady of Guadalupe and the Archangel Michael. Through the Christian mystics I came to know and love Christ. Free from the baggage of institutional dogma many of my friends and elders carried, I found myself able to access the heart of the tradition in a more direct and transformative way.

My decades of work as a scholar, translator, and commentator on the mystics has not been purely academic. In fact it has hardly been scholarly at all! The fragrance of love emanating from the contemplative heart of multiple religions has led me to the altars of many houses of worship, where I have prayed with diverse communities. I have experienced peace and connectedness almost every one of these sacred spaces. My point is that this experiential approach comes naturally to me, given the ecumenical quality of my upbringing.

As I enter my 56th year, having navigated my spiritual path for over four decades with singular devotion, four essential features of the landscape have emerged: the common heart that beats at the center of all religions, the interdependence between contemplative life and activism, the transformational power of not-knowing, and the vital importance of the feminine face of the Divine.

I have already spoken at length about the ways in which my alternative religious education instilled in me the tendency to recognize the perennial wisdom wherever I encounter it. Another gift has been a felt experience of the interconnection of all that is, coupled with a sense of imperative in activating this subjective truth in service to the world—to the human beings who abide on the margins and to the Earth Herself. Over its 50-year history, the Lama Foundation, where I moved on my own as a teenager and on whose board of trustees I continue to serve, has always modeled the seamlessness between cultivating the inner life and responding to the cries of the world. This deeply ingrained value, intermingled in my psyche with my family's commitment to social justice and sustainability, makes it impossible for me to consider a spiritual life apart from the whole of humanity, other animals, and the air and the water and the soil we share.

If I were to identify the single most transformational song I have heard echoing from every one of the mystical teachings it would be the power of not knowing. This transmission comes through the Christian mystics in the form of the Cloud of Unknowing and the Dark Night of the Soul. In Sufism it is *fana*, the blessing of annihilation. In Hinduism she is the Dark Goddess Kali, who consumes anything that stands between her children and their total liberation, and Shiva Nataraj, who dances in a circle of fire. At the heart of Buddhism is the beauty of Beginner's Mind and the liberating doctrine of *sunyata*, the emptiness that is plenitude. Each of these wisdom ways affirms the necessity of dying before we die, which, to me, means dropping our preconceptions and letting ourselves down into the unknown. In the naked encounter that unfolds from such surrender we are able to meet the sacred face to face and discover that the darkness is not dark at all; it is unutterable radiance. Pure light is blinding to our ordinary vision until we develop new eyes with which to perceive it directly. This radiant mystery connects us all, and not knowing becomes a starting place for our spiritual lives, and also the ground of our activism.

For it is only when we look upon the suffering of the world—the violations of human communities and the ravaging of the climate—with a willingness to jettison our opinions and solutions and instead embrace the brokenness with tenderness and humility that we may skillfully participate in mending it. Knowing that we know nothing, we practice simply showing up to offer our loving witness, extending ourselves to touch the luminous heart that underlies the darkness, and act from love rather than fear. Then our actions are energized by authentic wisdom and the limitless power of compassion.

Finally, I have come to see that the voice of the feminine is one of the most significant missing ingredients in our collective religious story. To my amazement, I too had a significant dream when I was endeavoring to write this essay and asked my Beloved for guidance. I dreamed that I was being forced to sleep with a man's dead body in my loft bed. Three days had gone by and it was starting to stink. A young woman lived with me, but she was not strong enough to help me remove the cadaver. I managed to roll the body off the bed and lift it into my arms. I lurched out of the house with the putrid face pressed against my face, and was swept up in a line of people walking down the road. A young man walking ahead of me must have noticed my struggle and turned to ask if I needed any help. My eyes filled with tears and I nodded. He lifted the corpse from my arms and easily carried it for me.

When I woke I realized that the man's dead body represented the religious patriarchy I have inherited, which is devoid of life. But my younger sisters and I cannot dismantle this system by ourselves. We need the emerging family of men—who also know that the existing religious institutions are obsolete and toxic—to lend their strength and assist us in shifting the paradigm toward the feminine model of cooperation, compassion, and creativity. It is, of course, the balance of the Sacred Feminine and the Holy Masculine that will restore wholeness to the soul of the world. We may hope to strike this harmonious chord by placing special emphasis for now on the feminine attributes that emanate from the goddesses and women mystics of all spiritual traditions.

It is with great joy that I discover this vision of the Order of the Sacred Earth, flowering from Matthew Fox's decades of spiritual activism and groundbreaking theology, nourished by the fresh insight and extraordinary dedication of the youth who are drawn into his sphere. Everywhere I go now, as I travel and teach, I am seeing these seeds bursting through the ravaged landscape. The youth I meet are hungry for meaningful spiritual practice and are wary of organized religion. They embody a beautiful blend of intellectual rigor and openhearted vulnerability that fills me with hope. I want to be part of this revolutionary effort to build a holy container in which to access and express the deepest truths of love echoing from the heart of the world's wisdom communities in honor of "Our Sister, Mother Earth," who sustains us.

A NEW ENLIGHTENMENT
Dr. David Korten

Reading the papers by Matthew Fox, Skylar Wilson, and Jennifer Berit Listug proposing the Order of the Sacred Earth brought to mind the 18th-Century Enlightenment. The intellectual advances of that defining historical moment birthed a human narrative that has since shaped our common understanding of reality and our human nature, purpose, and possibility. The consequences present us with a profound imperative.

The Enlightenment narrative unleashed extraordinary advances in technology and governance that transformed how we live, work, play, and organize society. These advances roughly doubled the global human lifespan, unleashed an explosion in human numbers and aggregate consumption, and connected us into a seamless global economic and communications web. The consequences now play out in extravagant material abundance for the few, material deprivation for the many, and an accelerating depletion of Earth's capacity to support life.

The essence of our situation is captured in two statistics. We humans currently consume at a rate 1.6 times what Earth can sustain and the wealth of the world's eight richest individuals equals that of the poorest half of humanity—3.6

billion people. Caught up in the thrall of a partial, dated, and often demonstrably false narrative, we support a global economic system that drives growing environmental and social imbalances to ever more intolerable extremes.

We humans are a species of many possibilities that organizes around shared narratives. By our choice of our shared narrative, we choose our common future. Our hope for a viable future resides in an emerging living universe narrative that draws from all the many sources of human understanding. This is my short summation:

We humans are living beings born of and nurtured by a sacred living Earth, itself born of and nurtured by a sacred living universe evolving toward ever treater complexity, beauty, awareness, and possibility. We now face a defining choice: prosper in the pursuit of life and its possibilities, or perish in the pursuit of money and its illusions.

The insights of this narrative draw from indigenous wisdom, the teachings of mystics and religious prophets, the findings of science, the lessons of history, and the insights of daily experience.

A product of science, the narrative of the first enlightenment advanced our recognition and understanding of coherent order in creation. In its denial of conscious intelligent agency, however, it stripped our lives of meaning and purpose—and of responsibility to and for Earth and our fellow humans. It subordinated the teachings of religion to the teachings of science—thus undermining the credibility of science in the eyes of those who see the beauty, wonder, possibility, and meaning in life that science denies.

The resulting tension plays into the hands of climate deniers and political demagogues ready to exploit it for their own ends. There is urgent need for the second Enlightenment now emerging.

My academic degrees are in psychology, business, and organization. The latter is the foundation of my fascination with the contribution the life sciences are making to our understanding of how living organisms and communities of living organisms organize to create and maintain the conditions essential to their own existence.

Take the example of the human body in which our individual conscious self-awareness and agency resides. Each human is a composite of more than 30 trillion individual living cells engaged in a constant exchange of energy, water, nutrients, and information under ever changing conditions. Equally essential to our health and wellbeing is an even greater number of microorganisms, such as the enteric bacteria and yeasts of our gut that manufacture essential vitamins and help metabolize our food. Each cell and microorganism is an individual, self-directing living being joined together in a self-organizing, continuously self-renewing alliance that functions as, and by all outward appearances is, a single being.

Throughout its lifespan each multicellular organism renews its physical structures through cell death and replacement. In the human body, approximately 3 billion cells die each minute—each reliably replaced by a living cell of like kind. This is no machine.

The wonder of these infinitely complex and purposefully adaptive processes confirms the existence of mechanism and order in creation. Yet it defies purely materialistic/mechanistic explanation and demands an additional assumption of integral conscious intelligence.

That each cell of our body is constantly making choices that balance the needs of both self and the whole on which the self's existence depends, suggests a nuanced moral code consistent with Creation's intention. It also brings recognition that the well-being of the whole, without which the single individual cannot exist, must always be primary.

And just as quantum science points to a reality that matter is defined by relationships rather than particles, the observations of the life sciences suggest that life also is defined by relationships and exists only in communities of organisms that self-organize in response to the needs and abilities of both individual and community. Within this frame or paradigm, competition is a subtext of a larger meta-narrative of symbiosis that defies purely mechanistic explanation.

If we assume that conscious intelligence is synonymous with spirit, the premise that all being is a manifestation of spirit aligns with the premise of Creation Spirituality that the spirit is both immanent and transcendent. It also aligns with a living universe cosmology that recognizes intelligent consciousness as the ground or origin of the energy field that following the Big Bang gave birth to matter—and to all that now is.

We may discern Creation's purpose from how it expresses. Science now gives us a quite detailed description, with a stunning parallel to the sequence outlined in Genesis. That expression began 13.8 billion years ago with the bursting forth of an energy cloud that formed into ever more complex particles that formed into atoms, and then molecules of growing complexity that clustered into stars that gave birth to planets.

At least one of the planets—Earth—gave birth to a simple single cell living organism that, as it multiplied, became ever more varied and complex. Two cells joined to become one. These more complex ones joined to create multicellular organisms that over many generations became larger and more diverse, complex, conscious, and self-aware.

A mere 200,000 years ago from today, this evolutionary process gave birth to an extraordinary self-aware species with the ability to choose its future as sacred Earth's dominant species. We call ourselves human.

This is the story of a great spirit seeking to know itself and its possibilities through becoming—the greatest of epic journeys of self-discovery. It is the story of a spirit imminent in all that it creates from the quantum particle to the grain of sand, to the mountain, to the living Earth, to the human being. All are manifestations of the Spirit seeking to know itself through becoming.

For humans, meditation is a practice that reconnects us with our deeper self to reaffirm our true nature and the purpose of our being as the spirit expresses itself in our human form. In the practices of meditation we renew and discipline our warrior spirit as we exercise our individual agency to fulfill our contribution to Creation's continued unfolding.

The deepest moral and spiritual issue of our day centers on the defining choice evoked in the biblical admonition that no one can serve two masters. We must choose between God (the spirit of life) and money.

In his homilies, Pope Francis has observed that money itself is not evil. He admonishes, however, the *idolatry* (worship) of money is profoundly evil. His Encyclical Letter Laudato Si' calls all of humanity to accept our responsibility to care for Mother Earth—to care for life.

Captivated by a science narrative that denies Earth's living essence and an economics narrative that values Earth's air, soils, and waters only for their market price, we have made a potentially fatal choice. Measuring economic performance by growth in GDP, we treat the making of money by destroying life as wealth creation—an act of collective suicidal insanity and arguably the ultimate evil. It is an evil now deeply imbedded in our most powerful institutions.

A viable human future requires our transition to an Ecological Civilization grounded in the emerging living Earth narrative of a Second Enlightenment that recognizes and honors the true wonder of creation's order, complexity, intelligence, and purpose. This civilization will rest on the foundation of an economy that measures performance by its success in providing every person the opportunity for material sufficiency and spiritual abundance in balance with the generative capacity of a vibrantly healthy living Earth.

I welcome the opportunity to find a spiritual home and intellectual identity in an Order of the Sacred Earth in fellowship with other spiritual-intellectual-activist seeker/doers seeking a deeper truth beyond the partial and outdated cosmologies of established religious dogma and political ideology. Within a narrative frame that recognizes our nature as living beings participating in an epic journey of self-discovery by which the spirit seeks to know itself and its possibilities, we can find strength and inspiration together as spiritual warriors of our time confronting the forces of institutional evil as loving protectors of all beings.

TEMPLE OF THE HOLY EARTH
Geneen Marie Haugen, Ph.D.

Blue damselflies hovered and darted over clear pools in the creek bed. The tiny nest of a hummingbird clung, at eye level, to the canyon wall. I peeked at the pair of jellybean-sized eggs inside. The scent of wild roses intoxicated. My nostrils flared with tremendous inhalations.

I was drunk on the world, drunk on the spring rapture of this sandstone canyon where I walked while dreaming aloud. The stream bed was stone—patterned, textured, and colored like the back of a tortoise, like a glimpse of Turtle Island. It was an effort to be mindful enough while walking not to fall in to the stone basins that suddenly appeared beneath my wading feet. I wandered, awestruck and delirious, from one marvel to another.

As sometimes happens when wandering in wild ecstasy, I heard words that seemed not quite my own—as if issued from the canyon itself—as if the stone pronounced: *Temple of the Holy Earth.* Oh yes! Of course this canyon—with its stone basins brimming with clear water, with its incurved walls stained the colors of sunset, with its dripping springs nourishing monkeyflower and maidenhair fern—is a rapturous expression of the temple of the holy Earth.

Hardly anyone would miss the felt-sense of an Earth temple is this canyon—at least that's what I supposed. How does it change us to make pilgrimage in such a place? The Temple of the Holy Earth took root in my embodied imagination, and I wondered if I had heard an invitation or an instruction.

* * *

Matthew Fox and Skylar Wilson had concurrent dreams that led to what they call the Order of the Sacred Earth—a vision that arrived via the liminal threshold of night dreams, and a vision stunningly resonant with my own felt-sense of the Temple of the Holy Earth. The waking vision of the Temple arrived (like the Order of the Sacred Earth) through the liminal, or imaginal threshold—in my case, via nonordinary consciousness in wild nature, some years ago.

Earth, I believe, speaks to us through images, intuitions, dreams—waking and night—and other impressions. It is possible to cultivate greater receptivity to Earth's longings by cultivating a wilder, more liminal, porous consciousness—and then deeply attending what shows up in the imaginal world. In my work as a guide for the Animas Valley Institute, I offer many practices that help open human awareness to the array of intelligent presences with whom we share the world—practices such as moving across the land in an attitude of pilgrimage, where every encounter is met with curiosity and reverence, or going forth each day with elaborate praise spoken to the world, directly, *as if* the other-than-human beings are responsive and listening. Such participatory acts often have an effect on consciousness: suddenly the world comes alive to us in a way we may not have previously noticed. And then we might find surprising images, voices, intuitions, or impressions presenting themselves on the horizon of our awareness—presences that may be the world speaking to us through what Goethe regarded as the "organ of perception" of imagination.

* * *

For a spell, I wondered if I had been summoned to build a physical temple, like a church or other constructed sanctuary. It wasn't remotely clear how I would ever accomplish such a thing. It wasn't clear, especially, how I—or anyone—could build a temple that reflected and emitted the felt-sense of that particular canyon, or the felt-sense of any of the other holy Earth temples to which I make wild pilgrimage. I have been a pilgrim for dozens of years to places of extraordinary planetary expression—places whose elemental qualities deeply resonate, as if a hidden chord vibrates between us.

But of course the Temple of the Holy Earth is everywhere—or *was* everywhere, and perhaps could yet be recovered. As Wendell Berry writes, "There are no unsacred places; / there are only sacred places / and desecrated places." For people in lands ravaged by war, poverty, famine, or toxic industry, desecrated places may be all they know. For privileged others, desecrated lands ask for our attention and care.

I believe that every human being benefits from intimacy with a place where the original wild temple is still present as a felt-sense, not just a gorgeous view. We have psycho-spiritual receptors for an experiential, embodied, mystical sense of the sacred Earth; we have an innate genius for communion and ceremonial participation with mysteriously potent places. All creatures, as well as the planetary body, benefit when human beings recognize, honor, and participate with the holy Earth. This may be a most important "right" of human beings, along with the right to a nourishing, curious, playful childhood. And, we are yet a long way from such a world.

But now, with the emerging Order of the Sacred Earth as envisioned by Matthew Fox, Skylar Wilson, and Jennifer Berit Listug, we are closer to an articulated vision of what such a world might be. We are generating new communities who practice and participate in a profoundly meaningful, mystical relationship with our shared larger body, Earth.

To honor the Sacred Earth in the wild place where I live, I go outside with a drone flute that was carved of holy yew from an ancient churchyard in England. I play for the green beings now emerging from the ground in spring, I play for returning hummingbirds, for old pinyon and juniper, for clouds and canyons, and for all the beings who long for sacred reciprocity and communion.

THE CASE FOR A NEW MYTHOLOGY
Joran Slane Oppelt

In the car this morning, I asked my five-year-old son a few questions.

I asked him what he loved about the Earth. He listed things like "clear water" and "lime green grass." I asked him what he thought was hurting the Earth. He narrowed his eyes and with a frown he described things like "garbage" and "smoke" and "cutting down trees." So, I asked him what he thought we could do to help the Earth. Then, his eyes lit up and a smile came across his face and he said we could "pick up the garbage" and put a "lid" on all the chimneys so that the smoke couldn't get out, and that we should "watch out" for the "builders and their axes" when they come to chop down the trees.

It's clear that the mind of a child can comprehend the interconnected nature of man's place in the world in its most simplistic form. When do we lose that awareness? What are we taught or told along the way to make us numb to or forgetful of the image of ourselves as not only part of our environment, but as protectors of it? What role models do we have that ensure we become the kind of person who will "watch out" for others bent on destroying or exploiting the Earth?

In our sacred faith traditions, we have stories about our world (how it was created, and sometimes even why) that have been told and re-told for thousands of years. Sometimes it is difficult to read or retell these stories through the lens of the 21st century—hearing them as if they were written in the language and postmodern culture of today. In the age of pollution and skyscrapers, satellites and online banking, the stories of Brahma floating on a lotus in a sea of milk or of Adam and Eve alone in a garden paradise can make little sense.

It is necessary, then, to open our ears to the new mythologies being written in our day, by new generations—stories like *Star Wars* and *Harry Potter*.

Joseph Campbell famously said that *Star Wars* was a new mythology for our time. It is a story of good versus evil, darkness versus light, and a heroic journey full of both technology and mysticism. It pits the protagonists not only against the temptation of the "dark side," but against "the state as a machine"—at the same time painting an image of the cosmos as imbued and unified by something called "the force."

The *Harry Potter* series was a worldwide phenomenon, and was a familiar story of a child born into the world to battle evil, overcome darkness, and eventually die in order that he may live forever. The mythology of the *Harry Potter* universe recently spilled over into the streets of Washington, D.C. as people dressed up in Potter cosplay for the recent 2017 Women's March on Washington, holding aloft signs that read "The Order of the Phoenix will rise!" This is today's version of the Rebel Alliance rising up against the Empire and the machine state.

Frank Herbert's *Dune* has been hailed as the greatest science-fiction story of all time. It is the story of war and political dynasty in a world where the planets act as a living ecosystem. The first three books of Dune have been described by author and poet Joey Lusk as "one of the most comprehensive analyses of human relationships to power" and the last three books as "a set of tools to do something about it."

Jeff Vandermeer's *Annihilation*, John Skipp and Craig Spector's *The Bridge*, as well as many other "man versus nature" tales have woven grisly yarns about what happens when we ignore environmental warning signs and the planet finally decides to stand up and bite back.

When will we finally hear what these stories are trying to tell us? When will we realize that these protagonists, sacred warriors, and heroes are versions or dimensions of ourselves?

It used to fall to the church (usually under the guise of "faith formation") to provide commentary about how to understand myths and relate them to our own lives, but as the excluded and disillusioned have fallen away from the church, we have lost touch with the art of storytelling and our ability to find ourselves (and each other) in story.

In 2015, Angie Thurston and Casper ter Kuile—both students at Harvard Divinity School—published a report of their findings following a U.S. study of the religious "nones" (those who are religiously unaffiliated, and those who identify spiritually as "nothing in particular"). The "nones" have been labeled everything from "spiritual but not religious" to the "spiritually independent." Yet, these names are labels assigned to them by a society (and academic institutions) who struggle to understand the phenomenon. Like a quantum field that collapses into a single point when you try to measure it, there is too much breadth and depth within this new (and growing) demographic to simply label them and move on. From "hard" to "soft" atheists, agnostics and humanists, and even the formerly religious (who have been turned off by organized religion and yet continue a personal practice)—the only thing these people have in common is their refusal to check a box on a form. For some, there really is no name for what they believe or what they do.

In their ongoing study (available for download at *howwegather.org*), Thurston and ter Kuile identified six key themes common to sacred and secular communities. The study makes it explicitly clear: Religion in America is changing. It also describes the role that interfaith and secular communities play in filling the gap created by shrinking churches, where the younger generation is finding religious life outside of its institutions, and what innovative leaders can do to reconnect with them.

The six themes (common to sacred and secular communities) identified in the study are:

1. **Personal Transformation**—"Making a conscious and dedicated effort to develop one's own body, mind, and spirit"

2. **Social Transformation**—"Pursuing justice and beauty in the world through the creation of networks for good."

3. **Community**—"Valuing and fostering deep relationships that center on service to others."

4. **Purpose Finding**—"Clarifying, articulating and acting on one's personal mission in life."

5. **Creativity**—"Allowing time and space to activate the imagination and engage in play."

6. **Accountability**—"Holding oneself and others responsible for working toward defined goals."

Mainline churches manage to do three of these (Community, Personal Transformation, and Social Transformation) very well. They remain skilled at providing safe and sacred space for fellowship and worship, distributing the spiritual tools necessary for personal development, and plugging members into programs or opportunities to give back.

However, when it comes to Purpose Finding (identifying your own vocation or calling), Creativity (thinking outside the box, or from the neck down through music, art, dance, etc.), and Accountability (either organizational transparency or using metrics to check in with community members and their progress on the spiritual path), most churches fail miserably. And so, according to the study, the "nones" have turned to things like spiritual study or discussion groups; interfaith dinners and potlucks; co-working and makerspaces; yoga, meditation and exercise programs; volunteering directly with local organizations; sustainability or permaculture programs;

and even the Sunday Assembly or "atheist church" that gathers in local bars for sing-alongs.

The HDS study offers insight into those who have grown up without church, but also what we have seen as people "mature" out of traditional church structures (joining more liberal organizations or opting out altogether). It gives us a glimpse into what the future may hold for religion, if it is to survive at all.

The next generation does not need permission to love their neighbor or their planet. They do not need an intermediary or a chaperone. They are digital natives, who turn inward and to one another for meaning. They have the world's body of wisdom at their fingertips, in a global society that is immediate and hyper-connected. They are raised on the Internet, multiculturalism, religious pluralism, and gender fluidity, and they can smell inauthenticity (or bullshit) a mile away. They have heard about or seen the patriarchy (and corruption) within religious institutions firsthand and want nothing to do with it. It doesn't "work" or it's not inclusive enough when it comes to science, philosophy, sexuality, ethics, race, culture, or gender.

It is necessary for the future of our planet that our spirituality abandon the "either/or" thinking of the past and move toward a "both/and" approach. This applies to science and religion, masculinity and femininity, mysticism and the way of the warrior, the left- and right-brain, mythology and history, transcendence and immanence, individuals and communities, contemplation and action, particles and waves, the pulpit and the lectern!

It's not enough to renounce binary pairs of so-called "opposites," we must know that all things as Spirit-in-Action exist along a spectrum and that we embody that spectrum fully.

It is necessary to create a new mythology using new language to tell our story. It is necessary to rethink how we "do" religion, embracing new forms of prayer and worship, convening more circles and fewer "lectures."

We need a new interspiritual order. One that exists outside of the current (or failing) institutions and that encourages us to, in the words of philosopher Ken Wilber, "show up, wake up and grow up." One that instructs us to lift one another as we climb. One that is sworn to protect the planet and all of creation.

We need new sacred vows. Like the Jedi who took an oath to uphold peace, knowledge, and harmony, we need sacred vows separate and distinct from our rituals, initiations, and rites of passage. Vows are embodied intention—a personal contract with Spirit. They re-sanctify the body, mind, and soul and reframe our commitment to "watch out" for ourselves, each other, and the world. They remind us that the situation or circumstances may change, but "I" have been transformed.

It is my prayer that the future of our planet, that Mother Earth herself, is protected by those who are willing to take these vows—those committed to a new level and degree of spiritual awareness and authenticity. It is my hope that, in the meantime, this new order serves as a mark of identity—a form of tribal war paint—so that we can see each other more clearly, honor those who have been "called out," and recognize where there is still work yet to do.

Only then can we become more human and less alone. Only then can we transform the world with accountability and reason, with purpose and imagination.

Only then can we, as a species, live to tell a new story and find each other inside it.

EARTHHEAVEN
Carol P. Vaccariello

"Deep Mystery, who art in heaven."

Heaven? Where's that?" I look up and see a cosmos of wonder and awe. Is that Heaven? Orion, my old friend, smiles and draws his bow. Still chasing those seven sisters is the tale that I hear. For the eternity of ages the "Heavens," the Cosmos, has been a place of wonder and awe. All there for us to gaze and wander through with our deepest imaginings, our most profound longings. Humans named and labeled the constellations, finding comfort and a place in the magnitude of it all. Our small radiant planet, a bit of dust, finds her home amidst the magnitude and wonder.

Speaking of wonders, we humans have invaded, in some small way, what is so vast. We have pierced the "Heavens" with the Hubble telescope. Through Hubble we have ventured billions of light years into the "Heavens" and there is still so much more. Our imaginings have gone from billions of stars to trillions of galaxies, each with billions or trillions of stars. Now that has been quite a work out for my imagination. With all this stretching,

I can't help but wonder, "Are there trillions of Universes with trillions of galaxies with billions of trillions of stars?"

Important for me, as my imagination is stretched in myriad ways, is the realization that there is no "heaven" to be found out there or up there. There are glorious wonders of nature filled with the presence of Mystery and every bit a total gift.

The night sky has always been "home" to me. I go out and sing to Grandmother Moon and dance with my heartfriend, Orion. My soul feels deeply connected to what we have labeled Pleiades. I could be easily overwhelmed with the immensity around Earth and experience life here as puny, but for me it is quite the opposite. One way of thinking about this is the experience of first meeting and experiencing the power of superhero cartoon character Mighty Mouse. No one expects a little mouse to be so clever and mighty and possess so many extraordinary gifts. That little cartoon character exceeds all probable or possible expectations. The expanding Universe has been like a fairy tale discovery for me: highly improbable and definitely impossible.

Living on our beautiful blue planet is a total gift from a generous Universe. Native Americans often sing chants to Mother Earth. I tend to think of Earth more as a Grandmother. She loves me. She provided my amazing parents and all manner of love filled experiences for me: picking apples in the fall, swimming each morning in the prayer pool, friends to be with, to sit at table for meaningful table talks each day, glistening white blankets of snow just right to make snow angels, the power of lightning, thunder, and storm-filled waves on Lake Erie, the grace of tall grass and wispy flowers, the kiss of wind, the joy of nature's humor, and so much more. A Universe that is forever giving, sacrificing, growing, and becoming, for me.

Recently I am drawn to search realms that no Hubble telescope can probe. These realms, so close and yet so far, so profound yet by my side, also hold Deep Mystery and awesome wonders. I sit in StillPoint, seeking the no-thing that is everything. The immensity of no thought opening my soul and consciousness to awareness beyond imagination. I long for the union of the mystics. At times, I am blessed with a union that is truly divine. The Angels have found a welcoming home in my heart. As these experiences continue to grow in me, I find myself, much like Hubble, seeking to peer more deeply into the depths of my cosmic soul. Is that where heaven is? Is it within me? Jesus seemed to think so. (Luke 17:21)

Living in an age where technology can transport my awareness to magnification of both large and minute detail. I took in a *Powers of Ten* Video on YouTube (Powers of Ten, uploaded by Eames Office). marveling at what we know and realizing that we don't know. This is my cathedral; this is the place of awe and wonder; this is so much more than I know how to dream; this is DOXA. Doxa, the condition of ultimate blessedness, glory, majesty, beyond words, and wonder: The Cosmic Christ.

When I began my doctoral studies, my childhood concept of God was challenged, and for a time I wobbled a bit as the ground, of what I thought I knew for certain, was shaken from beneath me...a psychological, philosophical, emotional earthquake of sorts.

Everything morphed when I began to take in and receive without the need to understand. I know that this Cosmic Christ is in me while I am in it. I know that divinity isn't in some far-off "heaven" looking down on my insignificance. I know that I am connected to divinity just as I am to my parents. I carry my ancestors' genes, I carry divine genes. The Hindus say that we are the stuff of divinity, a spark of divine Light. Divinity fills my being and I fill that which is divine. One of the important consequences of this knowing is that Divinity finds my being essential to its search as it continues to know itself. In a similar way, I find Divinity essential to my search as I continue to know myself. There was a time when I thought this was language that I would never embrace. Now I have been given tremendous insight into realms that I never thought to transverse. I know I am just beginning to explore this portion of life's amazing journey.

My life is a wonderland of awe. I live in a home in Medina, Ohio. When I purchased this home, it didn't matter much to me what the house was like.

I bought the home because of the Grandfather tree in the backyard who welcomed me to this place, literally with open arms. There is the Cedar tree and its healing presence on the west side of the house. The praying mantis, the first one I had seen in 40 years and I have not seen since that day, who clung to the back, northwest corner of the house, reminding me of childhood, inviting me into the magic and mystery of this holy place. The spirits of this place, this sacred Earth, danced excitedly when I offered tobacco and cornmeal as an Earth honoring gift requesting that I be welcomed to share this place, to co-habitate with those in spirit who already lived here. At that time, I promised the spirits of this place that I would make the grounds beautiful for them. I experienced the spirits' joy when I planned, designed, and filled the new flowerbeds with soil and mulch in preparation for the blooming flowers and the sage and herb garden.

Water is extremely important to me. Every morning, prior to doing water aerobics, I meet with spirit companions for prayer in the resistance pool of a neighborhood facility. This is where together we set the day's intentions in motion. I ask for spirit help required for the day ahead. Frequently I am given insights, a song, a memory, a new project, ideas that I never entertained before. I used to think that I was experiencing visions, but now understand that I am not experiencing visions, rather, I believe that the spirit world is parallel to ours and we can exist in both simultaneously.

Most recently, my lifetime angelic companion aided me in writing a book of our experiences together with the intention of helping others in their walk with Spirit. The next phase of this unfolding is also mind-boggling. As people read the stories, which are touching their hearts and opening them to new ways of understanding, especially the Angelic Realm, they are contacting me with their new awareness and the depth to which the stories are touching them. I didn't think the impact would be this moving. Adult men and women are approaching me, eyes glistening with tears, as the awareness of spirit presence is awakened in them through the reading of these stories. I am very appreciative that the Universe, which includes the realm of spirit, has invited me into a more complete experience of our shared reality. This is exactly what Archangel Ari'El was helping me to understand. He wanted this book of stories in print so that those who are ready will learn to open to the presence of divine messengers, the angels, and seek their help and presence in their lives.

As I visit these mystical moments, the newfound depth and frequency of spirit-filled events, I realize that it is a very lonely journey. There are so many who either don't understand these experiences, are afraid to permit the Holy into their lives, or simply don't believe these encounters are possible. I seek others who are open, on this path of caring for Earth, honoring Creation, the Cosmos, and Beings of every shape and size.

When Matthew Fox mentioned his dream and the task set before him regarding the formation of the Order of Sacred Earth, I immediately thought that this could very well be the support group that each of us needs for this important and amazing journey.

The Order of Sacred Earth, or the OSE, could be the safe space necessary to pursue experiences of awareness in the evolution of consciousness. The more we open to Earth in her relationship to Cosmos and to the awareness that Heaven is right here, the more passionate we will be about caring for her as she cares for us. The OSE would be a powerful vehicle to raise the awareness of Earth's sacred presence and her life-providing call. Without her there is no life. Heaven is right here when we open our eyes to a more complete reality.

As our consciousness evolves, we catch up to our Ancestors in understanding that we live with the spirit realm, not separate from it. These Ancestors on whose shoulders we stand also stand with us and walk with us. The Angelic realm is only a thought away and long for us to reach out to them. They need us to help them help us. After all, we are in physical form and they are not. If the Angels want a book written, they need to enlist one of us to help them do that. If they want an Order of Sacred Earth created, they come to one who is open to co-creating.

The importance of the Order of Sacred Earth at this time in history is monumental. Our world is changing and growing more rapidly in conscious awareness than ever before. Science and technology have provided volumes of information along with the possibility of high speed processing new ways of understanding, communicating, and knowing.

One day I imagine our progeny looking back at where we are in this evolutionary moment just as we look back at the cave dwellers as they discovered how to harness fire. We are on the brink of tremendous awareness that needs the OSE and those it draws together, who will be like-minded pilgrims, companions along the Way.

A NEW STORY
Theodore Richards

We live in an age of unraveling and unmooring, of re-imagining and rebirthing.

In Buddhist cosmology, it is understood that sickness and cure co-arise. In this worldview, because we are inextricably interconnected, each action ("karma") impacts the entire universe and gives rise to other actions. The brutality of white supremacy, ecological devastation, and Donald Trump have brought forth something of an awakening in the West. The youth have—at least in some cases—put down their smart phones for a moment and taken to the streets. From Occupy Wall Street to Black Lives Matter to Standing Rock, people, especially the young and marginalized, are rising up in response to political, racial, and ecological violence.

But we are witnessing something more than mere political unrest. This is a time of apocalypse. A time for both destruction and revelation. This means that we are called upon to do something more than just develop new technologies or engage in political action. We need, as Thomas Berry suggests, a new story.

I refer to these times as apocalyptic not to be hyperbolic, but because I believe that a true and deep understanding of what the apocalyptic tradition actually describes is the best way to understand this moment. Human beings understand who they are through mythology and cosmology. The world is not merely an object, but something we co-create, spiritually, through our myths and symbols. That is, we tell stories that place us in relationship to community and cosmos. When these stories no longer make sense, or when they have been lost, cultures and communities unravel. This is the experience of apocalypse. The ancient apocalyptic tradition developed not because of a literal end of the cosmos, but because the cosmology through which the ancients understood themselves was coming apart. This unraveling is experienced, psychically, as the end of the world.

Today's world is unraveling on an unparalleled scale: ecological destruction threatens our existence and the existence of all life on Earth, and yet, even as we understand this *factually*, we remain unable to do anything about it because we are so wedded to the dualistic cosmology of industrial capitalism and consumerism.

In many ways, in spite of all the left-wing handwringing, Donald Trump provides us with the logical culmination of this cosmology: who better to lead us over the cliff than a billionaire reality-TV star?

The time has come to look at modernity and challenge its values. Apocalypse, after all, means "unveiling." The destruction contains within it the seed of revelation and re-birth. We must ask ourselves what new story is revealing itself.

And a myth, a deep story, reveals to us the answer to the most fundamental question: "What is the sacred?" There is no more important question we can ask at this moment. For when we think of the sacred through a dualistic, consumerist lens, we find ourselves putting species and peoples into categories of saved and damned. We believe, above all else, that we are primarily *individuals*, capable of being separate from Mother Earth. But when we rediscover a notion of the sacred that is rooted in a cosmology of compassion and interconnection, based upon the insights of our wisdom traditions, indigenous peoples, and the Universe Story, we realize not only that we would not want to separate ourselves as individuals, but also that it really isn't even possible. We are living in community, whether we like it or not. We are entangled in a beautiful web from which there is no escape.

This apocalyptic moment, I believe, is revealing to us the deep and urgent need for a new story that allows us to re-imagine what is sacred. And the birthing of the Order of the Sacred Earth is doing just that. To give birth to a new myth, we must not only use different language, we must also learn to think differently about our institutions. That is, the form matters as much as the content. Perhaps more.

Religion—at least the religion that we have grown accustomed to in the modern era based on books and lists and big, cumbersome institutions— no longer serves the people or the planet. Nor does the old clericalism and its hierarchies. Postmodern religion—perhaps better to call it *spirituality*— must be freed from the dualisms of modernity. These dualisms, in the case of traditional religion, separate our religions into institutional boxes.

But New Age movements can be just as dualistic, in a different way. New Agers tend to think of religion as something they experience as individuals, devoid of cultural or cosmic context. The Order of the Sacred Earth, I believe, is seeking to create a movement that has this context without the baggage of the old institutions.

Specifically, this order—in focusing on the sacred Earth as its basic context—can bring forth a sense of the sacred that draws from our indigenous traditions and our non-dual mystics. The universe, according to what science now reveals, is a single event, a single and continuing unfolding. Creation is one. With this as our basic context, all is sacred or nothing is.

This does not mean that evil isn't real or that there isn't work to do and injustice to fight. The sacredness of our planet calls on us to be not only lovers of the Earth—mystics—but also warriors for her.

This requires not only new approaches to spirituality, but also new approaches to education. We have to relearn how to be human. A school, or any learning environment, including a church, teaches not merely through curricular content. It provides a metaphor for the world. When we treat the youth like criminals, and our schools like jails, we teach them that the Earth is something from which to escape. When we treat the youth like products, and our schools like factories, we teach them that the Earth is a collection of resources to exploit. When we treat the youth like consumers, and our schools like businesses, we teach them to conflate the *value* of the Earth with the *cost* her "resources" bring in the marketplace. In all these examples, the Earth has lost its sacredness. No matter what we might teach about climate change in the science curriculum, our civilization will continue to destroy the planet as long as our schools convey this narrative of our place in the world, of our relationship—or lack of relationship—to the Earth.

In 2009, I founded the Chicago Wisdom Project, an organization dedicated to re-imagining education. This endeavor largely came out of the work I'd done with Matthew Fox in Oakland to get YELLAWE, another youth program, off the ground. Rather than focusing a test scores or a job in the global economy, the fundamental focus of education for us was to re-imagine the story. We saw marginalized young people as an asset, a source of wisdom. But they needed to be empowered to tell their story and to recognize that they were more than the shrunken-down consumers they'd been taught to be. This meant that they had to see themselves as part of an ecological web of relationships, interconnected to the entire cosmos. And this required that we used more than just one modality in our process—the entire self and entire community had to be engaged.

Community. This is a word I find myself using more and more. There is no such thing as a human being without community. Our survival has depended not merely on having big brains to solve problems; more importantly, our capacity to become a part of a community, to trust and care for each other, is the unique evolutionary trait the human possesses. The

Order of the Sacred Earth can provide not merely new ideas and practices, but also a community in which to grow them, to nourish them. Just as plants require soil in which to flourish, ideas and practices require strong communities.

I have seen this, over and over again, in my work at the Chicago Wisdom Project. Our work succeeds when we can create caring communities in which young people are free and trust one another. In other words, the specifics of the curriculum, radical as it may be, are easy to convey when people love and trust each other, because learning is not an individual process but a communal one. We lift each other up and learn together. This, perhaps, is the most radical part of our pedagogy: We are part of a learning community rather than an individual in competition. To paraphrase Sir Ken Robinson: In most places they call it collaboration; in schools it's called "cheating."

So the work of the Order of the Sacred Earth is deeply revolutionary, for it challenges our most fundamental assumptions in capitalist culture. There is nothing harder for humans to do than to re-imagine a core narrative. It is an apocalyptic endeavor. But I believe it can, and will, be done, through the commitment to creating, through the order, a new kind of caring community.

EFFECTIVE LEADERSHIP FOR THE 21ST CENTURY: THE MYSTIC WARRIOR
Deidre B. Combs, D.Min.

"Walk the mystical path with practical feet," Angeles Arrien

"We are all mystics, we are all prophets," Matthew Fox

We live in interesting times. Climate Change confounds our optimism. Autocratic leaders around the world threaten or steal basic human rights from citizens. We are in uncharted territory in terms of global population growth and ecosystem stress. It is easy to be terrified and disheartened if you pay a bit of attention to the daily news. We are currently in heightened conflict with our environments, with our existing political and organizational structures, and with each other. These are interesting times indeed.

Meanwhile, human beings have been gathering in communities and thus working through societal conflict for at least 25,000 years according to prehistoric research. We have learned a myriad of problem solving strategies over the millennia. Our hidden, hard-won wisdom on how conflict works and how to overcome it can be found throughout lasting cultural traditions. Ubiquitous and effective conflict resolution practices like fostering gratitude, holding detachment, and understanding your opponent are described across sacred texts. Common mystical practices teach us, regardless of culture, how to expand our perspective so we can foster innovative solutions, another core conflict resolution technique. As Albert Einstein once said, "We cannot resolve a problem with the same thinking we used to create it." To also fight well around the globe, we would also be sent to each culture's warrior tradition. Theologian and activist Rev. Matthew Fox thus urging us to act as *mystic warriors* in these interesting times makes perennial cross-cultural sense.

Mystics listen to the Greater Whole, emptying themselves so they can be a channel. They tap into the vastness of the Universe and recognize the endless possibility available through the Divine spark within their hearts. They share forth immense love and compassion, which seems to be a natural result of this deep listening. Yet, mystics across traditions caution to never rest in knowing, but instead in a sea of uncertainty. As Meister Eckhart once said, "I pray to God to rid me of God."

Warriors meanwhile are called to sharply pay attention to the here and now, surveying the battlefield, opponents, and our own capabilities. Where mystics connect to the heart, warriors are called to focus the mind—to research and act. They train to be strong and to then use their resulting power honorably. Our individual performance is our legacy as warriors. Through discipline and self-control we hope to act heroically. Warriors are expected to serve as we see in the oaths typically pledged. As management theorist Margaret Wheatley summarizes, "A leader is anyone who wishes to help at this time." Leadership is warrior work.

Integrating mystic with warrior energy, however, fosters truly *effective* leadership. Leaders we want to follow combine a warrior's strategic thinking with the mystic's compassion, efficiently overcoming challenges while simultaneously nurturing those around them. They bravely step forward to lead, yet hold that they are simply tiny atoms of a vibrant whole. Jewish philosophy advises that in one pocket we carry a note that says, "I am unique in all the Universe," while in another, we guard the words, "I am nothing but dust." The wise leader know which statement to read from moment to moment knowing both are equally true.

The mystic warrior leader listens to heart and head simultaneously. We need to care for both relationships and tasks, but instead we often drive for results and then regret our behavior, or fail to get things done for the sake of friendships. Only when we wrestle with the internal mystical warrior paradox do we progress along leadership's transformative path. It is a search for the Holy Grail as you bravely enter the forest to achieve the impossible, even though you are unsure and your vision seems unattainable. If you aren't broken along the way or believe you have it all figured out, you aren't truly paying attention. The archetype of the warrior boldly takes up the sword or the pen or the placard and steps into the fray while the mystic holds our innate interconnectedness, uncertainty, and insignificance. Siding only with head or with the heart will lead you astray and, worse, will put others at risk.

In the ancient Bon tradition, from which Tibetan Buddhism flows, mystic warriors have hearts so open they feel a mosquito land on it, yet are so strategic that they are undefeatable. The true mystical warrior path is found when we are paradoxically groundlessly grounded. Buddhist teacher Pema Chodron describes this as where we no longer know and become able to respond well to whatever arises, seeing it as fresh and interesting. Taoism explains this orientation as the integrated dance of yin and yang. To sustainably lead, we must combine the mystic's yin—or magnetic quality of non-action and uncertainty—with the warrior's yang—action orientation of shooting a confident arrow of truth and integrity into what is false to our essential natures. Hold leadership's innate conflict: When do I rest? When do I act? How do I listen? When do I speak? What does it mean to know, or to give up knowing? If the path is clear far into the future, it is not the path, or at least it's not yours.

In the Western traditions we have the symbol of the mandorla, which is the center almond-shaped intersection of two circles that mirrors the yin/yang.

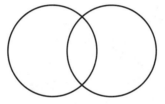

Mandorlas grace the medieval windows of Chartres cathedral, sacred wells of the British Isles, and Roman ruins. To stand in the mandorla is to hold the opposites within you. The mystic warriors Jesus, the Virgin May, and Buddha are depicted within mandorlas as models of holding both Heaven and Earth, Male and Female, Eternal and Temporal within them. None of these leaders were considered bland compromises, but instead ascended masters who learned how to be paradoxes.

Poetry emerges from the mystic warrior's journey. Holding the opposites, we begin to understand what "patient impatience" looks like as an activist, or "compassionate accountability." We model "selfless selfishness." We see the beauty in the dog poop on the carpet or, as poet and artist MC Richards once shared, "Everything that arises becomes welcome and useful in fighting the good fights."

Jungian psychologist Robert Johnson, writing about the mandorla, explained that if one intersecting circle is white and another is black, the resulting mandorla is never gray but instead is *pavanis* or the color of pea-cock's feathers. To be mystic warriors, to take in all the myriad of perspec-tives on an issue like Climate Change or Globalization, add visions and dreams that arise, and the knowledge that we are each just one among bil-lions and let all this information mix within us. To stand in the mandorla is no small feat. F. Scott Fitzgerald captured this challenge as he wrote, "The test of a first-rate intelligence is the ability to hold two opposed ideas in the mind at the same time, and retain the ability to function." Yet the possibil-ities that emerge when we are able to do so are extraordinary. In Africa, there are caves or spaces where it is believed that we can be suddenly trans-ported into new realities. Sometimes we return to ordinary times, and other times we don't. We can create mandorla wormholes for ourselves and our communities if we follow the mystic warrior path and keep saying to friend and foe, "Tell me more."

Mahatma Gandhi in 1913 spent one year, on the advice of his mentor, taking third-class trains and walking across India posing one question: "What does India want?" He asked Brahmins and Untouchables. He asked this question of Hindus, Sikhs, Muslims, Christians, and Jews. Gandhi was both a British barrister and an Indian activist. We know that he listened to his dreams for guidance. By taking all this seemingly contradictory infor-mation within him, he became India's mandorla. After a year of listening, spending time each day in prayer, and allowing the opposites to dance, he developed innovative non-violent campaigns like walking to the sea for salt and calling for a unified religious holiday across all of India's traditions that shut down work across the country. By becoming a mandorla, Gandhi transformed the world.

Mysticism and the warrior traditions are rich with how to lead and live well over the long haul. Both remind us that we are simply lightning strikes in the long body of time, yet we are part of an illustrious lineage. The ances-tors or saints before us create the foundation upon which we can stand and speak with courage. Our work can then serve as a source of fortitude or ideas for those who come after us. Every mystical or warrior tradition I have studied shares that we aren't expected to "fix," but instead to be a solid link in a golden chain or thread through history that conducts the good from the past well into creative future solutions.

In the summer of 2013, I taught an intensive environmental leadership course to a combined group of undergraduate and graduate students. With class from morning to night, I watched the younger students wallowing in our Earth's current struggles as they had no choice but confront the facts. Their despair permeated our course. My open heart, too, was aching with general misery as we rested in the loss of species and habitat. I asked myself, "Was the pain I was nurturing even necessary? Would teaching this course make any difference?" While I swam into the dark waters with my students, a more seasoned environmental humanities graduate student shared how she kept finding hope. She didn't speak of blithe optimism, but what environmental activist Johanna Macy might call Active Hope, where we face the darkness of these times while simultaneously marveling how lucky we are to be participating in such an extraordinary part of history. Like an angel, the quiet graduate student shared a quote from philosopher Mark Talbott: "There's a hole in our boat. It's midnight, but the stars are out and it's a beautiful night. Bail." In that minute exchange, I was transported. She acted as a mystic warrior who effectively called another back into battle. By modeling "hopeless hope" the student inspired me to pick up the warrior's sword and shield once more…or at least a good bucket.

Mystic warriors face stark realities while trusting in unimaginable possibility. F. Scott Fitzgerald, after speaking to how hard it is to hold opposing ideas in our minds, added, "One should, for example, be able to see that things are hopeless and yet be determined to make them otherwise." Mystic warriors recognize we are but dust, but could be angels for another or an entire generation. As philosopher and activist Rebecca Soinit states in *Hope in the Dark,* "The future is dark, with a darkness as much of the womb as the grave." Your bailing may create the alchemy for forging a link of another in the golden chain a century from now. Who knows, your link might be just what is needed to call another to pick up her sword again, now or long after your work is done.

The invitation is awaits. It's midnight, Mystic Warrior, and our collective boat clearly has a hole or two. May you pick up a bucket strongly forged from your heart's endless flame, and wisely crafted, so you bail masterfully while enjoying the stars.

SHIFTING THE TIDE
OF OUR FUTURE
Broderick Rodell

Life is a reflection of its environment. Throughout the 200,000 years of their history, humans have responded to their environment in order to survive. Our history and self-sense has been shaped by our experiences under various conditions on this planet. In our migration out of Africa into the various corners of the world, we've had to adapt to the places we found ourselves. This planet, with its plentiful, colorful, and robust forms of life, has molded and shaped our humanity into its current manifestation. We are among the multitude of morphing expressions of the evolution of our planetary system, and we are at a critical phase in this process.

How shall we proceed along this process in the midst of the myriad concerns we face from global warming to poverty to political destabilization that threatens the existence of life as we know it? What must we do to make the evolutionary leap to a more sensible and sustainable coexistence on this earth? I believe we must find a means to build bridges and coalitions to tackle the global issues that we are faced with.

Below, I extend my thoughts on the matter, and share why I support Matthew Fox and friends in their desire to create a collective organization/movement that is Earth centered, spiritually centered, flexible, non-dogmatic, transgenerational, and inclusive of various domains of human understanding.

Throughout our tenure on this planet we have exploited our environment in order to survive. Yuval Noah Harari in his seminal work, *Sapiens: A Brief History of Humankind*, eloquently cautions our tendency to overly romanticize our history on this planet. We've left our mark wherever we've found ourselves and it hasn't quite been a harmonious, peaceful, loving coexistence with nature. In the process of meeting the demands of our own survival, we've fostered the extinction of many forms of life on Earth. I state this to remind us that the basis of our current actions are not that extraordinarily different from that of our ancestors. Throughout our history, humans have selfishly sought to maximize their own existence at the expense of others. However, we are at a juncture in the human evolutionary process where we can wreak havoc in ways our ancestors could not have imagined.

We have entered the Anthropocene, the phase in our evolution where we have become the dominant influencer on the environment and the planet as a whole. Throughout our history we have shaped the environment as it has shaped us. But now, due to drastic increases in human population and the advancement of powerful technologies, we can coerce the earth to our will on a much grander scale never before seen. And, consequently, we are not faring too well at this current juncture. We are dangerously playing a game of self-destruction. We are on a course of destroying ourselves, and most of life on earth, in ways incomprehensible to our forebearers.

Can we reverse the course and shift the tide? I think so. It will require reflection, re-evaluation, and a commitment to change. We must come together and bring together wisdom from various domains of knowing in order to transform our situation. I believe that my dear friend and mentor Matthew Fox along with Skylar Wilson and Jennifer Berit Listug are proposing a cogent contribution to our progressive culture by creating the Order of the Sacred Earth (OSE).

My appeal to the OSE stems from my commitment to mitigating suffering and maximizing wellbeing, love, kindness, and compassion in the world. I have spent my adult life attempting to make sense of the human experience in order to inspire the cultivation of those values. My original locus of attention was maximizing health and healing within the African American community. As an African American male, witnessing the suffering of poor health quality within my community had become unconscionable. I felt I had to do something about it. So, I began to investigate into the root causes of poor health and suffering. Over time, I soon came to understand that the well-being in the black community is inseparable from that of everyone else and the planet as a whole.

We are all in this thing together, and are in need of each other in perceivable and unperceivable ways. We are dependent upon and share this spheroidal ecological system we call Earth. What we each do influences the balance of this system, consequently impacting each other's experiences within it. We all depend on the same air, the same water, and the same earth for our sustenance and survival. The quality of the systems on Earth informs the quality of our lives.

From the resources of the Earth we have created comforts of consumption we've come to take as basic necessities of life. With this, we are reliant on each other to extract the Earth's resources, produce, and distribute the artifacts of our needs and desires. As our population increases and as individuals demand more, we will need more complex economic and social systems to meet those demands. The viability and sustainability of such systems necessitate cultural agreements by collections of individuals working in some kind of cooperative fashion.

Our current systems are at a critical juncture where we need to reexamine the cultural agreements that foster them. We are feeling the brunt of their failing from poor health quality to a general malaise; from material, intellectual, and spiritual poverty to wealth and income inequality; from political disarray to a burgeoning global ecological disaster. These issues of concern are messages encouraging us to reevaluate our current narratives about how we live. Are we listening? Are we grasping the gravity of these messages? Their resolution demands our collective involvement in many areas of society on many levels. We must engage our individual agency to overcome the perceived boundaries between one another that limit our capacity to find common ground in the face of these challenges. Yes, it is possible for us to do so, and nascent collective agreements such as the OSE attest to that fact.

We are responsive and adaptable creatures. Our evolution until now speaks to our extraordinary capacity to respond to our environment in order to prolong our existence. The complexity and immensity of our current set of issues will require sophisticated, coherent and well-integrated ideas to combat them. I believe we have the capacity to meet the demands of these challenges. It will not happen by simple wishful thinking. It will require our collective attention, intention, and action. We must adopt a worldview likened to that of a universalist scientist who makes observations from various modes of knowing, who collects and analyzes complex data from various mediums, and who can, from those observations and analyses, create a new story about how we are to live together on this shared Earth. This story must be sustainable, global, comprehensive, inclusive, durable, flexible, intelligent, and sophisticated.

A New Story

Our story about the world stems from and is bound by our worldview. A worldview is a collection of ideas that functions like a lens, filtering out sense data and shaping our perception of the world. The story that we hold, part consciously and part subconsciously, determines our actions. If we want to change our actions, we must change our story. We humans have long navigated our experience through story. From the stories of the great myths to the current story of science and modernity, we've invented tales to guide us through the uncertainty and variability of life. These stories were not randomly conceived out of nothing. To the contrary, they were intelligently considered out of real experiences constrained by a particular psychological frame of reality. As our minds developed further, enhancing our capacity to extract more subjective and objective data from our experiences, it enabled us to create more complex and inclusive stories. Well, new data is pouring in, and it is suggestive of a need for a better and more sophisticated story to navigate our experience sustainably.

Throughout our history old stories have given way to new. The old became the foundation of the new. Like now, our current worldview must be the foundation for the construction of a better, more sustainable worldview. Those of us who are troubled about our current state of affairs can easily succumb to a stymying cynicism, where everything about our current worldview and narrative is hopelessly flawed and irredeemable. Such a perspective leads one to totally disregard everything about our current construction of reality. I admittedly fell prey to this level cynicism and as a result disengaged from society. I ultimately found that this thinking undermined my capacity to mitigate suffering in a way that I desired.

It is indeed true that all worldviews have their pathological aspects, including our current one. And it is also true that every worldview has healthy aspects that promote goodness and beauty. I fervently believe that there is a significant amount of good about a dominant construction of reality that overwhelmingly embraces universal human rights. For instance, though imperfect, the current dominant worldview in the U.S. decries slavery and seeks to encourage universal human rights for all. In the not so distant past, the dominant worldview denied these rights to groups outside of white men, and justified slavery and the subjugation of women. This type of transformation into more inclusion is arguably a clear example of an evolution in worldview. It would behoove us to keep those positive aspects of the various ways humans have structured the world in place and build on top of that. Those parts of our worldview that support ignorance, unsustainability, divisiveness, hatred, insensitivity, neglect, and disregard of the other is what we want to disengage and transcend, i.e. get rid of the bath water and keep the baby.

We do not live in a world where we all see eye to eye. Some of us may adopt more or less the same worldview and still hold different viewpoints depending upon an emphasis of attention on different aspects of that worldview. For example, in the politics of the American two-party system, you may have a member of one party who focuses their attention on economic and individual freedoms while another of the opposing party focuses attention on the social welfare of all citizens. They both value human rights, individual freedoms, and the free market; however, each one will approach how they govern in terms of their primary interest.

On the other hand, you may have folks who inhabit very different worldviews. This poses a different set of challenges when attempting to work together to solve problems that threaten our common interest. For example, continuing the analogy of our two-party system, one member may fervently maintain that the world was created by a humanlike being in seven days around 6,000 years ago. This anthropomorphic being manages and determines the course of the world from the heavens. Another may inhabit the view that the world, as we know it, came into being 13.8 billion years ago from a big explosion out of nothing. To them, the world is managed by the process of evolution and the associative laws that came into being with this big explosion. Finding common ground across these worldviews may pose more of a challenge than the former example. Yet, we are all beneficiaries of the consequences of the concerning issues that threaten our existence. Therefore, we must find a way to common ground concerning the cause of sustaining our presence on Earth.

In order to address the issues that we are facing we need to adopt a new story that extracts the best knowledge from different domains of knowing from past to present. We need a story that honestly considers the information that we are being presented with now. And right now, we are being called upon to evolve our story into more complexity and sophistication. It needs to consider honestly the historical observations of our past. Our past has so much to teach us, and yet, we don't need to overly romanticize or denigrate it. We need to embrace what can serve us in our evolution and relinquish that which stagnates us. We need a story that recognizes our collective interest in working together. It should be a story that is able to both celebrate and transcend our differences while acknowledging our sameness. We need a story that embraces our connection to the Earth. It would recognize that the well-being the Earth reflects our own well-being. This story must be intergenerational where the wisdom of the elders is fused with the creative impulsiveness of the youth. It must embrace the best of science, acknowledging that scientific thinking and exploration has been one the most extraordinary achievements in our evolution. It must also embrace the truth claims of the various religious traditions, recognizing the value of thousands of years of exploration into the realm of Spirit. For those who are fervently against these traditions for various reasons, I strongly encourage an exploration into the tremendous amount of wisdom that they have to offer. As earlier stated, we must caution against throwing the baby out with the bath water.

The Order of the Sacred Earth

The Order of the Sacred Earth offers a promising path towards a more sustainable, healthy, and corporative future on our planet. It is based on a story that is Spirit centered, Earth centered, and community centered. It asks would be participants to commit to a sensible, sustainable, and viable future. It asks of us to transcend our differences and rally around our common interest, a livable planet. The OSE appreciates that our survival is dependent on our combined action. It suggests that the issues that threaten our existence are a plea for us to step into the next phase of our collective evolution.

The OSE calls on us to pursue the development of our higher potentials individually as well as collectively, celebrating the power and value of our uniqueness while also acknowledging the greater synergistic value of our mutuality. Accordingly, community is central to its formation. The idea of a community embraces the notion that the whole is greater that the sum of the parts. We are capable of more by working together than alone. At the higher stages of human development an individual sees itself intricately linked to others, and knows that isolation limits its own capacity to maximize its potential to add value in the world. Through community we are able to take advantage of each other's gifts and generate more power to act on our objectives.

The OSE calls on us to take full responsibility for our connection to this Earth. It recognizes that we are the Earth. It understands that care of the Earth is care for ourselves, and that its health reflects that of our own. The OSE invites us to explore together sustainable ways of living that allow for the greatest amount of well-being for all. It invites us to take a vow to collectively care for the Earth as a means to commit to our common interest. The OSE appreciates the sacredness of this Earth. The simple fact that we cannot exist without it suggests that the Earth deserves our reverence.

The OSE isn't dogmatic. It encourages us to explore and discover new ideas while preserving the best of what we already know. It invites us to seek wisdom from all sources of human knowledge from science to religion. It welcomes the atheist, the agnostic, as well as the religious. Regardless of our preference, it ask us to embrace the wisdom from the various religious traditions without falling prey to outdated dogmas that could constrain our capacity to experience the deeper dimensions of what they have to offer. It invites us to accept the gifts of science, while not succumbing to a dogmatic notion that it is the sole progenitor of and means to knowledge.

The OSE recognizes and embraces the power and validity of spiritual/ mystical experience. Owing to its subjectivity, admittedly there are a variety of ways to describe these types of experiences. Interpretations are dependent on one's worldview. For example, a Christian will likely interpret a spiritual experience in terms of a Christian ideological framework. A staunch scientific materialistic may even deny the legitimacy or subjective value of the experience, and may simply describe it as a mere byproduct of an extraordinary shift in biochemistry. Nonetheless, in my opinion, these different perspectives do not invalidate the value or relevancy of spiritual experience in human life. Mystics from various traditions and cultures, from past to present suggest that the essence of mystical experience is fundamental to our nature. Common qualitative descriptors for them are a feeling of bliss, boundlessness, love, awe, beauty, light, and wonder. These are the type of qualities that the OSE suggest we cultivate to support a more sustainable and loving world. The OSE acknowledges that no one has sole ownership on how to name or access these experiences. It therefore encourages exploration into the multiplicity of avenues that are available to us. We currently have access to a plethora of ancient and contemporary methodologies from all around the world. They are designed to maximize our capacity to tap into spiritual experience, as well as develop our ability to express the qualities they evoke in our daily lives.

The OSE offers a great opportunity for us to come together to not only solve the problems that face our existence, but to become more fully human. I believe that the more fully human we become, the more we'll embrace a manner of living that is sustainable, communal, affable, loving, kind, and compassionate. The challenges we are facing encourage us to move forward in our evolution. I believe that the OSE is the kind of collective movement that will contribute not only to our survival, but also to our capacity to harmoniously thrive together on this precious Earth for generations to come.

EARTH CENTERING
Kerri Welch, Ph.D.

A squirrel chatters at me from the live oak's branches behind me. A mourning dove coos from across the creek, gurgling through a hand-built rock dam. A cardinal calls, "pretty, pretty, pretty, pretty." Other tweets and twitters, recognizable, but unnamed, join the chorus as the rising sun's beams glide down the rocky limestone ledge opposite me. All these beings have opinions for this essay. My spot is noisier in the morning. Normally, I come sit by this ribbon of water in the evening or afternoon, but I woke earlier than usual this morning. I knew I needed this place's help to write about our relationship.

Reading through others' essays, I felt lost in the flow of words and abstractions, like we're all saying the same thing over and over again, and why add to the din? But even through the gurgle of words flowing over letter's humps, curves, and corners between the straight banks of margins, images reach out and touch my heart. I hear my experiences spoken back to me from other mouths and other lives.

This magic of mirroring is that of communion, both with people and with wild places. After all, our deepest selves, the selves we crave to know, do not live within the boundaries of our own skin, but rather are scattered in secret corners of the world, waiting for us to recognize them.

A mayfly just teetered onto the surface of the creek from a rocky ledge. It reached for the rock bank, but the current carried it away. Does it need help? Is the creek too forceful? And then, wings. Oh yes, wings, of course. I smiled at my lack of trust and self-importance, and at nature's capability for surprise. Sometimes I teeter on the verge of overwhelm and forget I have wings too.

I've been sitting with this land daily over the past week, working a ritual to reset my patterns in intimate relationship, asking Mother Earth to remind me what excites me, and then pursuing her as I want to be pursued. One of the surprises this time was the visceral experience of how it might feel to be pursued by Earth.

A gaping chasm in the earth rose to devour me, dark walls of a deep grave, the heaviness of earth, and a more palpable fear of death than I had ever experienced before. Is this what men's fear of women feels like—their own death, the return to the womb as annihilation? Our need of them is so great. Our fear of losing them becomes the devouring they fear, and we both lose.

Lessons from other rituals now reemerge, acquiring new layers of meaning. Squeeze too tight and what you sought to hold slips away—projectile love. Charged particles shoot through the curve of magnetic fields—physics' right hand rule. My lesson here was how *not* to be devouring, how to cultivate patience, Earth-like patience—content in abundant, flourishing resilience, whether anyone notices or not.

Three years ago, my vision quest death lodge gave me the mantra, "Like Mother Earth I will always stay centered." Patience is my own death-fear to face. I received the name Owl Earth Centering. Now Earth reminds me again to center.

Earth centers by spinning. So I spun inside the tight embrace of a circle of women under the redwoods six months ago. I spun to come back to myself, to magnetize and draw in right relationship. Like the two downy feathers that just now alighted on the surface of the creek in front of me, twirling down stream, with whirling dervish's hands—one facing up, one facing down. Owl Earth Centering, full circle, weaving four different rituals into one.

And as I stepped outside this evening, a screech owl, the first I had seen in several years, flew toward the east and landed in a live oak tree.

"Owl Earth Centering, remember."

And again, weeks later, taking a break from another round of edits for an evening walk, another whooshed silently by, inches from my nose.

"Owl Earth Centering, remember."

So much of our time in the modern world is spent in the deadness of the indoors, facing a screen, worrying and fantasizing. This is the mind's power—to travel in time and space—and it's peril—to lose sensuous engaged experience with the body and the immediacy of the world. People and nature both draw us into the aliveness of the present moment. I need these to remember my centeredness.

I feel high right now, recognizing all the ways my rituals connect, reinforce, and build on one another. My body is buzzing, my senses alive, and my mind marveling at the flow of interweaving alive in this moment. I am giddy with the perfection of it all. I wouldn't be surprised if people I love just started arriving out of the woods. In a sense they are—arriving in this essay as I recall the ways they have held me in ritual, and in their own writings for this collection of essays.

My relationship with places: West Coast redwoods, central Texas woodlands and waterways, and the piney woods of La Terre, Mississippi, are all contoured by the people who loved them before me. The indigenous peoples, my biological and intellectual ancestors, all deepened grooves of relationship, into which I slip. The land carries these memories, as do the traditions that meander over it, sculpting human experience with story, song, and ritual. Together we guide one another.

My rituals have roots in West Africa, the American plains, and the Amazon, as carried for centuries by the Dagara, Lakota, and Shuar. They came to me through people I am proud to call friends: Zayin Cabot, Elizabeth Husserl, James Inabinet, and Pluma Blanco, with other pieces carried by Kathy Anne Woodruff, Kelly McMenimen, and Jackie Richards. We came together through the gravitational pull of the California Institute of Integral Studies, and the Elmwood house community that coalesced within it.

Another Elmwoodian and dear friend, Skylar Wilson, is now collecting these essays to seed a wider Earth-centered spiritual community, the Order of the Sacred Earth. While my spiritual community centers around the San Francisco Bay Area, I now live in Austin, Texas. So I am now patiently coaxing tendrils of spiritual community here in my ancestral home.

During my first shot at this ritual, several months ago, I forgot to ask what excites me. Instead, I got inspired to gather people in nature, to observe and learn from nature together, to share music, stories, and teachings—I called it Earth Church. It hasn't happened under that guise yet, but what has been happening for several years now, here in Austin, is Moon Language Story Circle as spearheaded by Olivia Pepper and others. Every full moon we gather around a backyard campfire to share food, stories, poetry, and songs—both old and new—along the theme of that season's particular moon and astrological motions, seeking to honor natural cycles, social justice, and indigenous traditions.

These people and places are the wings that I sometimes forget I have. Whether human, mayfly, or owl, they remind me to return to center.

Like the mayfly's winged surprise, and like Skylar's essay's flying dream, I received a dream on the night of my vision quest where I rose into the air seeking wider perspectives for something I had lost. The feeling of rising through the air was so exquisite, I forgot what I was looking for and just kept rising until I burst into an orgasmic, blinding light. May all the goals we seek be sidetracked by the blissful surprise of the present.

By all the names we call it, earth ritual community is happening. May the Order of the Sacred Earth spread and strengthen us.

Aho. Ashe. Amen. May it be so.

FINDING THE CENTER OF HEAVEN AND EARTH
Mark Youngblood

Although noon would not arrive for several more hours, the sun already drew heat waves from the northern California grasslands. I didn't know it yet, but my life was about to change dramatically.

My head bent in contemplation, I walked mindfully down a dirt trail toward a transformational encounter in the appropriately named "Plato's Cave." I have always felt connected with nature. As an Explorer scout and then afterward, I gleefully traveled the grueling drive each summer from the marsh lands of south Texas to the mountains of northern Wyoming. I sought the beauty, majesty, and awe that I felt hiking in and camping among the mountains.

I experienced the Sacred in the mountains in a way that I never found sitting in a church pew. Although raised in a moderate Christian church, my questioning of dogma had rewarded me with the label "smart aleck" and resulted in being kicked out of Sunday school. I was 14 years old.

I found it difficult to reconcile the hypocrisy I saw in the church leaders with their preaching the very rules and principles they so readily discarded.

Not to mention that the teachings simply did not make sense to me. I was told, "God sacrificed his only son for our sins so that we could have eternal life." My response was, "Really? That's the best the 'Almighty Creator of All That Is' could come up with?" How about just forgiving us? Having compassion? Even a 14-year-old could come up with those alternatives. I figured that a god that lacked imagination wasn't all that special, and I went looking elsewhere.

In nature, I found a spiritual connection beyond words and human-imposed rules. Being in nature always brought me a sense of peace and revealed an implicit logic in the natural order that seemed sane and rational. I encountered a Creator that could not be defined, labeled, or put in a box. Neither male nor female, beyond human comprehension. And somehow I knew I belonged, that I fit in this order and was integral to it.

My spiritual seeking led me to books and teachers outside the Christian sphere and I encountered a philosophy that I related to—an explanation of our nature as eternal spiritual beings. And also a way to understand life and death and the continuance of consciousness.

However, the metaphysical teachings rejected our earthly nature in a way reminiscent of the moral posturing about "the sins of the flesh" in my childhood church. Our earthly nature was to be subdued and transcended. Heaven was UP and there was nothing below except a prison of attachment for the Soul. And this did not resonate with me either. "How could creation, which is the vibratory body of our Source, be a problem for us?" I wondered, "How could it be separate from our spiritual journey?" It didn't ring true to me or reconcile with my own sense of oneness when in nature.

Which brings me back to that hot, dusty trail on a beautiful California morning. The spiritual retreat was designed to put us participants in accord with nature as teacher and guide. As I strolled slowly, I sought to quiet my thoughts and let guidance flow freely.

After only a few minutes, I heard a voice clearly ask, "Where in your body do Heaven and Earth meet?" By this point in my life, I commonly received higher guidance so I was not particularly surprised or taken aback. But this felt different. This felt like a test, or maybe an opportunity for a profound opening.

As I considered the question, I thought at first the answer would be obvious. I assumed the center would be somewhere near my middle, perhaps my solar plexus chakra. But as I felt into that answer, it was clearly not correct. I thought, "Maybe my heart then? Nope. Ok, it's a long shot but how about my head? No, that's not it, either."

I hadn't expected to be stumped by what seemed like such a simple question. When I reached the end of my ideas, I grew quiet and allowed an answer to come to me. Then an intuitive knowing flooded through me that still gives me goose bumps.

The answer was, "All of me."

"I" am the center where Heaven and Earth meet. It is through me, through my whole being. I am the point where Divine consciousness experiences and delights in its creation. The downpouring energy of the "Divine Heavenly Father" and the rising energy of the "Divine Mother Earth" meet and blend within me. As a conscious, eternal soul integrated with a human body, I am like one of "God's taste buds." And so is every other human on the planet.

My spiritual life and existence suddenly took on a whole new meaning and direction. We are not here to transcend the earth, but to embrace it and consciously pass our experiences through to Source with appreciation, humility, and joy.

As these thoughts thundered and careened through my mind and my entire being, I looked up and found myself standing on the threshold of an immense opening in the earth. I gathered with my group to receive some last-minute instructions. When ready, we each found our way down into the depths of the cave to meditate and commune with nature.

For whatever reason, I was the last to make my way in and down. There was no trail to speak of, mostly just an endless jumble of stones and boulders leading down into the darkness. I found my way by depending on the dwindling light and intuitive guidance until the sunlight was a distant suggestion. Then I settled down to meditate in the nearly pitch-black darkness and breathless silence.

Without going into a lot of detail, I experienced many intense visions of the earth in the form of the Divine Mother. I confronted and cleared limiting beliefs and patterns that kept me separate and disrespectful of the Divine Feminine as symbolized by the Earth. The intensity felt like passing through a white-hot fire and coming through cleansed. I then had visions of participating in rituals that harmonized the energies of Heaven and Earth—the Divine Masculine and Divine Feminine—within me.

Afterward, I left the cave feeling reborn, cleansed, and "baptized" in a sense. I felt a regard for the Earth that resonated all the way to my bones. Since then I have felt a peace and sense of my place in the universe like never before.

I also cannot tolerate the smallest transgression against the earth. I recall dropping a small piece of paper on the ground as we returned to the van and feeling an overwhelming urgency to pick it up. It seems silly, but would you throw trash on your human mother? That's how the earth felt—and feels—to me.

So, when presented with an opportunity to participate in a new Order of the Sacred Earth, I said, "Oh, hell yes!" My name, Mark, means "warrior." And I see myself as a spiritual warrior using the weapons of love, compassion, courage, and wisdom to call people to remember and reclaim their divine heritage.

We must each come to feel our connection to the earth, and to understand our role as the center where heaven and earth meet. When we reclaim our divine heritage, as sons and daughters of the Heavenly Father and Divine Mother, we will inevitably treasure and celebrate the sacredness of earth.

We must lead with developing loving acceptance of, and compassion for, ourselves. Without it, we will not have love or compassion for others, much less for nature. Our emotional and psychological wounding—so evident in the strife and suffering in society and callous disregard for the earth—must be healed. Love for the earth begins with love for the self. Heal yourself and you will take a major step toward healing the planet.

Exposure to nature, spending time in the heart of beauty and wildness, is both healing and transformative. We can hear our true voice better in the desert silence, catch glimpses of the cosmic serenade in the Northern Lights, lose ourselves in awe at the expansive majesty of the Milky Way. We develop a deeper sense of ourselves and feel more connected with all that is when we spend time with nature.

And that can happen anywhere, not just in national parks or wilderness experiences. There are trees, parks, birds, fields, flowers, clouds, weather, sunsets, and moonrises everywhere—big city and remote canyon alike. We can experience nature everywhere and find the healing, connection, and reverence for the earth that we are seeking.

I HEAR THE EARTH BREATHING
Deborah Santana

"Another world is not only possible; she is on her way. On a quiet day,
I can hear her breathing."
—*Arundhati Roy,* War Talk

I clearly recall the moment I heard a woodpecker's steady drumming on a redwood tree whose tip touched the sky. I was on the downhill slope of my hike on King Mountain, lost in thought, inhaling the clean air, feeling the freedom of being alive. I stopped and looked up, scanning the limbs for the industrious bird, and found the black wings dotted with white, chest with brown markings, and a bright red feather cap, the tail curved onto the trunk of the tree. The percussive sound brought my attention to a sacred moment in nature.

This was years after I came of age during the Civil Rights Movement. There was little justice for those whose skin color was brown or black, and whose families had been enslaved in this country. In San Francisco, I did not experience the horrors of fire hoses turned on me, the lynching of innocent people, Jim Crow laws, or the right to vote being taken away, but being ostracized and maligned was palpable. In our church, we joined with others who wanted to eradicate racism peacefully. It was our mission, as people of color who followed Dr. Martin Luther King, Jr., to stop racist oppression through peaceful protest and working together to change policies of persecution. "We Shall Overcome" was an anthem we sang from the center of our souls. But we were not successful, and the fight for equality and justice continued.

The idea and vision to have a spiritual order to celebrate, heal, and protect Mother Earth is a gallant one. To dedicate ourselves to this community will require deep prayer and the practice of nonviolence as we witness the destruction of our planet. I look to Native wisdom for guidance and light. Oren Lyons, Faithkeeper of the Turtle Clan of the Onondaga Nation and spokesman for the Six Nations Iroquois Confederacy, suggests a map to follow: "In our way of life, in our government, with every decision we make, we always keep in mind the Seventh Generation to come. It's our job to see that the people coming ahead, the generations still unborn, have a world no worse than ours—and hopefully better. When we walk upon Mother Earth we always plant our feet carefully because we know the faces of our future generations are looking up at us from beneath the ground. We never forget them."[1]

Yet we are not taught Native ways. In early times, Native tribes' medicine people and societies made medicine and prayers for good crops and for success in the hunt. If the tribe was faced with going to war, the medicine people were consulted. In times of sickness or drought, prayers and ceremonies were made to the Great Spirit.[2] There was no action taken without prayer and the consensus of all.

With this understanding of healthy community, I joined activists when I was a teen to protest the Vietnam War. We marched through the Golden

---

1   Steve Wall and Harvey Arden, *Wisdomkeepers: Meetings with Native American Spiritual Elders* (New York, NY: Atria Books, 1990). 68

2   Wabun, and Nimimosha Sun Bear, *The Bear Tribe's Self-Reliance Book* (New York, NY: Prentice Hall Press, 1988). 5

Gate Park Panhandle carrying signs: "End the War," and "War is not healthy for children and other living things." In January 2017, I joined 600,000 lovers of our world marching in Washington, DC, along with millions of others around the world. We stood together to bear witness and cry out for human rights, environmental rights, LGBTQI rights, and to love and cherish the Earth and each other.

For decades, activists and scientists have warned about the dangers of forgetting to respect Mother Earth. Jeannette Armstrong is Syilx (Okanagan) from Penticton, British Columbia, Canada. She originates from the Okanagan Valley, where the ecology has very harsh and dry summers. The Syilx people practice a philosophy and system of governance that requires them to always be vigilant and aware of not over-using, not over-consuming the resources of their land, and they are mindful of the importance of sharing and giving. She writes, "…the land is a body that gives continuously, and we as human beings are an integral part of that body."[3] We are all responsible for our Earth. We are all responsible for our children and their children, for the future of creation and life. We are not helpless bystanders who can afford to throw away plastic cups, bottles, toothbrushes, baggies, food containers, and store-bought product packaging that cover the Earth and fill the oceans with trash. We must be attentive and mindful of everything we touch so that our presence on this planet does no harm.

In October 2007, I heard Wangari Maathai speak. She had been awarded the Nobel Peace Prize for her environmental work in Kenya and the world. What made her a shero and activist of monolithic proportions was her belief that poor and disenfranchised women could plant seeds to re-birth their rural devastated landscapes. She knew innately that working to heal the environment would heal people, too. "Planting trees came to me as a concrete, doable response," she wrote.[4] She founded the Green Belt Movement to educate and work at the grassroots national and international

3   Jeannette Armstrong, "Indigenous Knowledge and Gift Giving," in *Women and the Gift Economy: A Radically Different Worldview is Possible*, ed. Genevieve Vaughan (Inanna Publications, 2007).

4   Wangari Maathai, *Replenishing the Earth* (New York, NY: Doubleday, 1989). 31

levels to promote environmental conservation. She witnessed the climate become dryer and warmer and the glaciers on Mount Kenya and the snows on Mount Kilimanjaro vanish, Kenya experiencing recurring droughts and losing forests and vegetation.[5] Today, over 51 million trees have been planted worldwide because of Wangari's work to empower women to repair the destruction of their environments. Her belief was "to urge individuals not to wait for divine intervention, but to give themselves the energy they imagine, or pray that God will provide, and to recognize that God expects them to take action and rise up and walk!"[6]

I hear the Earth crying for people to rise up and act as if every decision we make will either destroy or protect the planet. The denial of climate change is loudest from the billionaire titans who profit mightily from oil and chemical industries.[7] We see the consequences of living without environmental conservation as the planet's surface temperature has risen 2.0 degrees Fahrenheit,[8] ice caps are melting, the Plains are flooding, and sea levels are rising.

In order to stand in unity with the Order, I must sit in silence, and in prayer. When I am quiet, the wind whispers loving songs through tree leaves, birds whistle sweet melodies that soothe my soul. The ocean waves remind me of nature's power, and each sunrise is a promise that I have been given another chance to make choices that preserve and replenish the gifts from Mother Earth.

The Order of the Sacred Earth is asking us to serve, give back, to become part of a spiritual order. They ask us to hope. I am not a joiner as such. I am an empath, one who feels deeply the suffering, joys, struggles, and growth of my sisters and brothers. I commit to defending Mother Earth and to being in circle with those who say "yes" to this vision. Sun Bear, Chippewa

---

5   Ibid. 65
6   Ibid.143
7   Jane Mayer, *Dark Money: The Hidden History of the Billionaires Behind the Rise of the Radical Right* (New York, NY: Doubleday, 2016).
8   NASA's Jet Propulsion Laboratory, *NASA Global Climate Change*, https://climate.nasa.gov/evidence/ (accessed April 29, 2017).

leader of a community of Native and non-Native people, wrote about common vision. "Members must be in agreement on the purpose of a community, its goals, methods, and priorities. This common vision is necessary so that our energy is not dispersed in conflicting directions, but channeled toward a specific goal."[9]

I have seen and heard many woodpeckers since that day on King Mountain 10 years ago. I have learned that they are socially monogamous and show displays of bi-parental care. The males build new nests each year in the cavities of dead trees such as willow, oak, and alder. The woman and mother I am loves this shared caregiving. The environmentalist in me loves that these woodpeckers are not endangered. The activist in me will continue to be in circle with voices guiding us to save our Earth and love each other.

---

9   Wabun, and Nimimosha Sun Bear, *The Bear Tribe's Self-Reliance Book* (New York, NY: Prentice Hall Press, 1988). 69

TREE PLANTER
Trevien Stanger

With a gleam of hilarity and joy in her eyes, she holds her tiny, dirty hands up to me and says, "When I grow up, I want to be like one of you guys. I want to be a Tree Planter...." She pauses, seems to turn over the idea in her 10-year-old brain, "But I've never met a Tree Planter before. Can I really be one? Is it like becoming a lawyer or a doctor?"

I let the question hang in the air for a few moments, as I notice that her three classmates—who are also on their knees and have hands full of soil and compost—seem to be watching the question flit about like an iridescent butterfly above our heads. How do we become Tree Planters? How do we become anything?

"Well, I'm not sure how you'll do it in the future; but for today, I can tell you this," I say, standing up now to grasp our baby apple tree's thin brown branches, "today, you *are* a Tree Planter."

And just then a call goes out from their teacher that it's time to wrap up and head back inside—but before they leave, I lean back toward my group of students and our new trees and repeat myself: "I mean it, kiddos, today you're all Tree Planters, and you can consider yourself a Tree Planter for all of your days under one condition."

"What's that?" one of the young boys asks expectantly.

"You keep planting trees…"

* * *

There is a tendency in our culture to define ourselves based upon what we do for work and how we make our money. "I'm a (fill in your occupation). And you?" And while this may serve us fine in the arena of small talk or when filling out a customs form, I've often wondered how much this simple act of self-definition might be contributing to the epidemic of spiritual and ecological apathy around us today. There is a power in naming, and there is a spiritual dimension to how we name ourselves. For some years now, I've made a conscious decision to define myself based upon what I do for my home, my watershed, my community, and my spirit: I plant trees. I am a Tree Planter. Let me explain.

Like many of my fellow millennials (I was born in '82), I grew up in what Buddhist scholar David Loy has called "the religion of the market." As organized religion failed to bear much fruit for our parents' generation, the fields of spirituality were left fallow for us. And while a few brave souls might have foreseen that an empty field does not stay vacant for long and began to cultivate some new/old spiritual ideas, most of us just assumed that those territories no longer mattered. On the contrary, the same questions and yearnings remain, but without Elders and a tradition to help us tend the ground, those fields were instead colonized by the invasive species of consumerism and the proselytizing pesticides of profit. In turn, many of the old-growth questions and the heirloom myths were then paved over, and what were once questions of self and community became matters of mere personal preference: my essence shall be an Axe cologne and my place of Sunday worship shall be the local mall!

Luckily, and due to some degree of privilege (young white male from the middle-class forests of New England), I was able to hack my way through these thickets and discover that an ancient, wise, playful, authentic, and altogether more wild sense of Self was possible—and for that I have many teachers (both human and more-than-human) to thank. "Out beyond right and wrong, there is a field: I will meet you there," Rumi invites and reminds us. But for many of us, visiting that far field of detached freedom and selfless serenity does not translate into a lasting peace nor a durable identity—be it through travel or sex or music or medicines, we find that the *state* of unitive consciousness wears off and that we have not actually reached a new and lasting *stage* of identity to inhabit. We find ourselves thrust right back into the muck and mayhem of the world, getting scratched and scraped by the injustices and the trivialities of this modern miasma. The spiritual field we inhabit most of the time is not Rumi's, but rather Nike's and Mickey D's, and theirs is a world that seems to bring mostly degradation and despair. The evidence that this field is withering is piling up like a brushfire, and it's burning hotter by the day. What are we to do? What sort of immune response can we summon?

Ethnobotanist, author, and Potawatami elder Robin Kimmerer asserts, "We need acts of restoration, not only for polluted waters and degraded lands, but also for our relationship to the world. We need to restore honor to the way we live, so that when we walk through the world we don't have to avert our eyes with shame, so that we can hold our heads high and receive the respectful acknowledgment of the rest of earth's beings." As we restore this honor to ourselves and others, we can begin to feel our own "impeccable warrior" rise up to participate in what Joanna Macy has so aptly called "The Great Turning." For Macy, to participate in the restoration of the earth community's body and spirit is to find ourselves engaging in any or all of the following dimensions: Holding Actions, propagating Shifts in Consciousness, and generating Structural Changes. I contend that every individual can participate in this Great Turning, and that one of the great challenges of our time is for each of us to figure out how and where we plug into this psycho-spiritual current. Perhaps the Order of the Sacred Earth can be a guiding community, helping us put our revolutionary passion into action.

I, for one, plant trees. Literally. When I look around at the apathy, the neglect, and the confusion amongst my generation and the ones coming up next, I feel compelled to act, and act I have. Between my work in stream restoration throughout New England, my time volunteering with Common Vision's "Fruit Tree Tour" in California (where I met the girl asking how to become a Tree Planter) and in my more recent work as an environmental studies professor at a community college in Vermont, I've had a hand in planting just shy of 100,000 trees over the past 12 years. I've planted trees alongside people on every stage of their journey, and this practice has carried me through from my wandering 20s and into my more recent attempts to root myself and allow my body to be claimed by a particular place (the Champlain Basin of Vermont). Consistently, and with little deviation, I have seen that this simple act of planting trees transforms the Tree Planter in ways that I'm only just beginning to understand.

But why trees, you may ask? Isn't that a little, well, cute? There is no doubt that tree-planting has lately been relegated to mere feel-good, green-washed environmentalism that does little to address the systemic nature of environmental injustice and spiritual degradation, especially when we remember just how many acres of the Amazon are being cleared as you read this (last check on Wall Street: 5,000 acres a minute). And while I could certainly retort with some significant reasons why trees are nevertheless so good for us and our communities (shade, fruit and nuts, erosion control, flood mitigation, clean air, green space, pollinator support, etc.), I argue that the revolutionary power of trees may also lie in the *act* of planting them, and that this act is best understood as living metaphor: the tree you plant will bear spiritual fruit, most often in the form of delicious and nutritious questions.

What happens when you plant a tree? What happens when you wield a shovel in one hand (a human artifact) and a tree (a provisional mystery) in the other? What happens when you dig a hole (a Kali-like destruction) and plant a tree within it (an act of creativity)? What happens when you learn about your local ecology not just as an observer, but also as a participant? What happens when you embrace the wildness of a tree-being and integrate it into the semi-wild streets and streams of your local community? What happens when you crack open your isolated sense of self and plant within your heart this symbol of our ever-branching inter-being? What happens when you consider your actions in terms of your ecological and cultural legacy? What happens when you move beyond your concerns of today and inquire as to what type of ancestor you will be? Nelson Henderson posits that "...one true meaning of life is to plant trees under whose shade you do not expect to sit." Under whose shade do you sit beneath today? Whose shade shall you help gift for tomorrow? I hope that the Order will encourage all of its participants to keep asking the important questions.

* * *

At the of the school day, with the fruit tree orchard install complete and our trucks all packed up, a few of my Tree Planter companions and I are reclining against the base of a massive Eucalyptus tree, the only large tree we see on the whole street. Foot traffic has picked up and with it comes an increase of people asking us questions through the schoolyard fence. "What's going on in there?" and "Y'all planting what now?" and "Ohhhh, my grandmother planted peach trees in the country when were kids. Can we really do that here?" and my favorite, from an old African American man with white sideburns the color of birch, "what are you young folks all about? Y'all some sort of eco-revolutionaries?" At this we all chuckle, as we watch the groups of school children load into buses nearby and wave at us and thank us as they pass. "Well, good sir," I say, "that be just about right. Want to join? We have more trees to plant tomorrow..."

THE ITALIAN CHALLENGE: SOWING THE SEEDS OF OSE
Claudia Picardi

As I turn the last page of Matthew Fox's, Skylar Wilson's and Jennifer Berit Listug's writing, my heart leaps with a sound "yes!" One year and a half ago, when I started contributing to the Italian Association for Creation Spirituality (AISC, *Associazione Italiana Spiritualità del Creato*), I did so out of a desire to bring the experience of the sacred out of the cage in which it has been convicted by both religious fundamentalism and materialistic atheism, and I intuitively feel that OSE may be just what we need to accomplish this.

By "experience of the sacred" I mean an ongoing experience of life, Earth, and Cosmos, which is profoundly aware of the interdependence of all things, of the correspondence between microcosm and macrocosm, and is therefore awakened to compassion toward all existence. Although I believe that most human beings have encountered this experience at least once in their life, many of us have lost a framework where it can get nurtured, cultivated, and hence bear fruit. Mystical awareness nurtures the experience of the sacred. Practice and commitment cultivate it. Prophetic action is its fruit—and as all fruits do, it seeds the ground for a deeper encounter with the mystical. OSE, as I understand it, is precisely such a framework: Its openness to all wisdom traditions, its independence from all dogmas, together with its being deeply rooted in what we all share—a life on this wondrous planet—can thus be the key to open the cage.

Joseph Campbell argues that one of the greatest losses of our time concerns our capability to let the symbolic speak, and to understand the language of symbols without resorting to intellectual interpretation. We lost—as a culture—our intuitive and imaginal sense of the metaphoric. "Half of the people in the world," he lectured 30 years ago, "think that the metaphors of their religious traditions are facts. And the other half contends that they are not facts at all. As a result, we have people who consider themselves believers because they accept metaphors as facts, and we have others who classify themselves as atheists because they think religious metaphors are lies."

I cannot speak for other societies, but this dualistic polarization has deeply conditioned Italian culture and politics since after World War II, and it is still very present on many levels of our society, including social activism. I have a first-hand experience of it. My mother came from a Catholic family, while my father's grandparents had been partisans and sympathized with Communism. I was raised as a Catholic because everyone at the time did so, but my family never attended the Mass nor discussed spiritual topics at home. After rejecting my Catholic upbringing because I could not bring myself to "faith as thinking in assent," as Matthew Fox aptly puts it in *Original Blessing*, I was left with no other option than to embrace a materialistic, atheistic view of life, where all metaphors were lies, intuition had no place, and the meaning of life got lost in translation together with both the sacred and the experience of it.

A consequence of this cultural rift is that, whereas in Italy there are many people involved with eco-justice, social volunteering, feminism, defense of the minorities' rights, etc., and many organizations exist that support varied forms of social activism, most of them stem from left-wing movements which have historically been at great odds with everything religious. This in turn can be mostly ascribed to the Catholic Church's meddling in Italian politics since World War II, often in a "theocon" alliance with right-wing movements.

The Church of Rome has dominated our religious and spiritual landscape for so long that it is very difficult for us to find other pathways when we decide to leave it behind, and to reconnect to a more primeval and original form of relationship with the sacred. Matthew writes, "We need to travel with 'backpacks, not basilicas' on our backs." You could say that we Italians walk with the whole Vatican on our back, rather than just basilicas!

Nevertheless, many are trying and seeking (and stumbling and falling and getting up), as I did after deciding that there had to be a third way beyond religious blindness and atheistic either/or logic. I personally discovered that I needed to find my own path to experiencing the sacred, no matter how tortuous or uneven.

I believe that, while we can support and cherish each other on the spiritual path, for the path to be real it needs to be personal, at least to a certain extent. While religions may be helpful when they provide maps to aid the seeker along the path, they become harmful when they try to establish one same road for everyone to follow, and when they confuse, as the saying goes, the map with the territory. Many independent spiritual seekers feel the need to make their own way, and imagine their own theology, imperfect and ever-evolving as it may be.

Hence a question for me—as a seeker, a scientist, and a teacher, but first and foremost as a person who is constantly striving for creative, spiritual, and intellectual freedom—is: How can we help our communities and our society to grow beyond the atheist/believer dualism, to recover the sense and the experience of the sacred? How can we plough the soil so that the seeds of OSE can be sown, rather than the seeds of discord that fundamentalism would like to spread? How can support each other in finding our mystical and prophetic vocation?

I had a firsthand experience with the power of ritual when, in the context of an AISC seminar, I encountered the symbolic gesture of bread and wine offering traditionally practiced in the Catholic Mass, something I had rejected long ago as meaningless. We were invited to partake of bread and wine in the circle, rather than by lining up in front of someone who had the special power of bestowing the grace upon us. When my turn came, I was suddenly awestruck, and I felt as if an inner door, previously sealed shut, had suddenly sprung open, liberating a great energy. Exploring further beyond that door, I re-encountered the archetype of the Cosmic Christ, which I had denied and repressed for many years. I also felt that the healing I experienced was part of a greater healing: we are all connected, and by healing our individual wounds we contribute to the healing of those wounds we share as a culture.

I believe that in order to "sow the seeds of OSE" in the Italian terrain, we need to start precisely from training and education. Many people are blocked, as I was, by their rejection of images associated to powerful archetypes; the cultural rift I discussed above, together with the fall/redemption theology that influenced many thinkers, even nonreligious ones, brought many people to choose one side and reject everything that was even remotely connected to the other one. The word "spirituality" is rejected by both: Many atheist intellectuals equate spirituality with religion and belief (sometimes they show a lukewarm acceptance for Eastern spirituality, which however they prefer to call "philosophy"), while many believers equate it with New Age wishy-washy philosophies.

OSE training could play an important role in overcoming these obstacles. By teaching us again to use our "other intelligences," and provide a context where the blocks that prevent people from experiencing the mystical can be loosened and ultimately removed, it can bring us back to an experience of the divine in our lives and in our world. The mystics of all times have taught us, through their paintings, their songs, their poems, and their writings, that when the divine is experienced we find common ground. When we walk the same terrain, the language in which the map is written loses importance.

Besides, Italy has a history of positive experiences in attempting different approaches to teaching, although these can be found mainly in primary and secondary education. There are several kindergartens and primary and middle schools applying the Montessori method mentioned by Skylar Wilson, as well as several others applying the principles proposed by Rudolph Steiner, the founder of anthroposophy, focusing on mind-body balance, creativity, and process-over-result. Two Italians, Luigina De Biasi and Valentino Giacomin, are the founders of the Alice Project, a teaching method—initially experimented with in Italy and then successfully applied in several schools in India—where students across different subcultures and religions are taught according to universal principles found in all spiritual teachings. To borrow their words, in their schools students are encouraged "to investigate and explore the fascinating world which lies beyond the rational mind, the world beyond the ego (transpersonal intelligence)."

The activities we propose at AISC may form the basis for a wider training program. We aim at creating connections with educators who share the OSE principles in order to integrate our proposal, presently tailored to adults, with other approaches, in order to talk to the younger generations. Also, we are studying how to apply this type of training to a wider range of topics beyond Creation Spirituality itself.

The OSE opens for us seekers a more open and more connected future. Italians are a creative but difficult people—we are travellers, poets, and dreamers, but we can also be very individualistic, sometimes utterly selfish, in our need to prove ourselves smarter than our neighbor. Still, by moving across the landscape of this populated country, I am often awed at the beauty that the intertwined hand of man and nature has brought forth when working in harmony. Yes, we may prove to be a hard and possibly malnourished terrain, but by looking at the vineyards thriving on the volcanic soil of Mt. Etna or Lipari island, and tasting their bright, mineral wine, I cannot help but smile. Difficult terrains, when tended with care, respect, and love, often give birth to the most juicy and surprising fruits.

ZEITGEIST NOW
Nathaniel Jaye

Human.

This one word includes us all. The spirit of our time inspires us to recreate the world with our human and cosmic unity in mind. This inspiration shares many names: global consciousness, the millennial age, The Great Turning, the zeitgeist. What they all describe is the connected, freedom-seeking, and inclusive impulses of our time.

Human means more than race, nation, and gender. It's more than culture, religion, and preferences. More than politics, profession, or class. Being human means we are cut from the same mold and belong to the same whole.

The zeitgeist now calls for a conscious human society. We each have a role to play. Our job is to remake the world and rise above everything that seeks to divide it. This won't happen on its own, and no one else will do this job. The future of the world depends on us.

The last age will resist. It was built on different rules, different values. It spoke of races, populations, abstractions, and systems. It was mechanical rather than life centered. It didn't see the human spirit and its interconnections. The zeitgeist now is about spiritual values. We need to articulate, live, and practice them—clearly, simply, forcefully. We are messengers of the zeitgeist. There are millions of us—in every corner of the world. This is the new community. It's global, it's local, and it's diverse.

And we have work to do.

There is inner work and outer work. The inner work is to experience the human in ourselves and every other person. To see beyond appearances, beyond personas and opinions—to each person's inner essence. To speak to and from that. Every day. In every interaction.

The inner work is also to recognize our relationships with the earth, with nature, and with the cosmos—being of service to each.

The outer work is to recreate our social structures. We are moving from one age to the next. The last age is already over—but we've only begun to build the new one. We live in the ruins of the past. That's why so much feels uncomfortable. Now everything needs to be reimagined. Redesigned. Recreated.

Let's learn how to live as unique individuals, together in community. Let's build a world that supports this. This has never happened before. We are the pioneers.

In both our inner and outer actions, we should hold one question in particular: *How will this help an individual unfold their uniqueness in balance with the earth and the cosmos?*

There are many answers, but this is the question. Because if not this, then what are we doing? An abstract idea like standardized education misses the point because it doesn't account for the individual human being. Abstract solutions are tools of the previous age attempting to solve the problems of the present. This will never work.

The zeitgeist now needs inspired solutions, focused on the deepest needs of each individual and the planet.

This requires a new way of thinking and acting, one we're rarely taught in schools. It requires seeing every being as sacred and on a spiritual journey. It requires holding this idea at our center and building around it. Our starting point can be the spiritual development of every person. This can become the prime motivation for our actions. Into this we can throw all our forces.

In every sector of life—as we redesign—let's again hold the question: *How will this help humans unfold our unique potential as spiritual beings and stewards of the earth?* In recreating community, government, economics, education, health and healing, music, media, architecture, art, farming, philosophy, science, sex, relationships, and so much more, let's search for, explore, and apply our answers to this question.

How do we do this? Gather people who are interested. Have them voice their expressions. We aren't looking for immediate answers so much as truthful ones. This takes receptivity and openness. We want to find directions that relate to our deepest human impulses. Put them into practice, even if only on a small scale. Evaluate the process. Is it working for people? Is this serving and sustaining the needs of people and the planet? Refine as needed. Share with others.

Imagine what is possible. Imagine education that sees each child as a unique human being and tailors itself to each child's growth. Imagine government in the service of every citizen, existing to protect the rights of all. Imagine an economy that wisely utilizes the offerings of the earth and the gifts of its inhabitants.

Imagine relationships that unveil our deepest and greatest selves. Imagine healthcare that knows how to strengthen the human spirit, rather than merely fix its body. Imagine community that cares, supports, and uplifts each of its members.

The future of the world is not an update. It's a newborn baby. Let's be inspired by the most—and best—we can imagine. Let's push ourselves to try, succeed, and fail—and keep going. The future of humanity is waiting for us. All that's required is our full participation in creating it. This is our task. But it is also our reward. This is what we asked for. This is what we wanted.

This is who we are.

We're here to do this job.

POSTMODERN NEW MONASTIC FRIARS AND DEFENDERS OF THE SACRED
Adam Bucko & Rev. Chelsea Macmillan

These days, it seems that we are living in a world that makes less and less sense. Black kids are being executed on the streets of our cities by the very people who purport to be protecting them. Mother Earth is crying out as we go on with "business as usual," refusing to address our dangerous addictions to comfort and consumerism. Poverty is on the rise and, everyday, more and more children are denied access to opportunities for basic survival, let alone for the life they deserve. Our broken political systems continue to fail all of us, and fear, racism, and misogyny are no longer hidden in the shadows. Where do we fit into all of this? What is the correct spiritual response?

It is this broken world that is "waiting," as Henri Nouwen wrote, "...for new saints, ecstatic men and women who are so deeply rooted in the love of God" that they are free to imagine a radical new political and social reality that reflects compassion and justice. It is this broken world from which Matthew Fox's dream of the Order of Sacred Earth has emerged. And it is this broken world that has called forth the Holy Resistance we witnessed at Standing Rock.

There, the elders of the Lakota Sioux nation showed us what the true meaning of mature spiritual leadership is and how it should be embodied. Upon arrival to the Oceti Sakowin camp, we were told, "This is a place of ceremony. You are here to pray." Indeed, every morning began with a call to prayer and, all day long, elders shared traditional sacred stories via megaphone. Our entire lives—past, present, and future—take place in the context of a larger story, the story of our Mother Earth herself. Not only did every protest action begin with a traditional song or ritual, but every action was itself an act of prayer. The elders listened to and communed with Spirit with the understanding that we were not there to merely protest. We were there to let the Divine act through us. In this way, prayer is not simply a request or demand for what we desire, but a dynamic embodiment, the place from which our whole lives are meant to arise. The new world our hearts know is possible already exists. Not only do our protests need to be demands for a new world, but also the protests themselves need to be examples of this way of life.

Standing Rock attracted people from all over the continent, most of whom were urged by a fierce call to protect the lifeblood of Mother Earth. We saw seasoned activists and faith leaders come together to defend the sacred. However, some people showed up with misguided intentions, looking for a party. Many of them refused to be integrated into the sacred and nonviolent culture of the camp. And yet, the elders never treated these campers, many of them young people, with anger or contempt. Instead the elders treated the misguided young people with a firm, but gentle kindness one would offer a younger sibling who does not yet fully understand the true meaning of living in reciprocity with each other, Mother Earth, and all of Her creatures. Trust was given, not earned, and all who came to Standing Rock were held accountable to principles of cooperation, honesty, and radical nonviolence.

What the world needs now, more than ever, are elders who can help us discover and embody these principles at depths rarely seen. With a glut of self-help books masquerading as "spiritual teachings" and the rising popularity of traditionless meditation, it is clear that many people hunger for a connection to something greater. Yet, there seems to be very little spirituality that can truly offer the depth and rigor that the old monastic orders offered. There is very little spirituality that can prepare people for what is most desperately needed, the kind of action and witness on behalf of those who are hurting, on behalf of the earth and all of Her children.

Matthew Fox is one such elder who has offered decades of prescient and prophetic guidance. He and Skylar Wilson give us a clear-sighted framework that can move us beyond navel gazing and New Age narcissism into a way of life that drinks deeply from the riches of the nonviolent Jesus, Francis and Clare of Assisi, Meister Eckhart, Gandhi, Catherine Doherty, Dorothy Day, Dorothee Solle, Martin Luther King, Jr., Dorothy Stang, and others. This new order can birth leaders who can show up to protests and uprisings with structures of prayer and sacred action, transforming potentially violent struggles into heart-centered spaces of radical mutual care. It is our hope that this order can play a similar role to that of the monastic and friar orders of the Middle Ages—communities of Spirit-oriented people who exist to remind us all why we are here by relocating us in our truth as children of God, as creatures of Mother Earth. It is our hope that this order will empower small groups of friends to move into the margins, to those places the empire has already failed, and reclaim them for the new kingdom/queendom of God. Here, love—not power—is at the center of all.

Perhaps most importantly, these monastics showed us over and over again that saying yes to God requires us to say no to everything that violates God's love, compassion, and justice in the world.

And we pray that this may be so, with Dorothee Solle:
Dream Me God

It's not you who should solve my problems, God,

But I yours, God of the asylum-seekers.

It's not you who should feed the hungry,

But I who should protect your children

From the terror of the banks and armies,

It's not you who should make room for the refugees,

But I who should receive you,

Hardly hidden God of the desolate

You dreamed me, God,

Practicing walking upright

And learning to kneel down

More beautiful than I am now,

Happier than I dare to be

Freer than our country allows.

Don't stop dreaming me, God.

I don't want to stop remembering

That I am your tree,

Planted by the streams

of living water.[1]

---

1   Translated from the German, "Träume Mich, Gott" in *das Brot der Ermutigung* (Stuttgart: Kreuz, 2008)

TO DEFEND MOTHER EARTH
Jeffrey Szilagyi

Our earthly home is the rarest of planets, for it possesses the wondrous yet difficult dream of biological life. Biological life is an extraordinary occurrence in the cosmic sea of infinite night, though to us voyagers, cellular life is most familiar. It is our norm and common enough to seem ordinary.

The destiny of the human condition is shaping the fate of the life on Mother Earth. So it is the human condition that needs not only our love and our kindness but also our understanding. It's not hard to see that humans are at odds with themselves and with nature. With so many crises arising from human life, it is easy to point the finger at human civilizations for the ills that befall us and in our darkest moments say that we are a cancer upon the face of the Earth. It is deeply true that the power and needs of mass, industrial human cultures are changing the course of not just the future human generations, but also the future and the fates of countless life forms and ecological systems. Perhaps the greatest ailment at the root of this unfolding is our unconscious striving against not only nature but human nature.

Mother Earth and her incrementally cultivated biological intelligence, oceans of blood and chlorophyll dispersed into leaf and limb, has her evolutionary hand in our human condition. It's on her loom that rich and ancient drives of biological capacity have been woven. For tens of millions of years and for an unimaginable line of generations, the transfer of biological energy and strategies for acquiring and passing this on have evolved. This is the journey where innumerable changes and adaptations have flowered. This is where the raw elements and the wild forces challenged organisms to survive. This is where dolphins who were once cloven footed wolf-like land mammals found their way to oceans. And this is where our lineage of upright primates emerged and mushroomed into the shocking success of billions.

Because the dream of biological life builds and varies more than it removes, we share common wiring and drives with our ancestral species. As such, each and every human birth is yet another unique living ritual of a cell, reptile, social primate, and homo sapien threaded together. We don't just carry the echoes of the primordial past within; we hear their voices and feel their knowings.

As we reclaim a Sacred Earth, we must also reclaim the sacred journey of biology that has begot our human condition. Not just the parts that feel good and seem safe, but all of it. In particular, it necessitates that we accept the reality that status, threat, power and sex are intrinsic motivators in our human experience. No order will succeed in building momentum without an adequate way to engage the full psycho-social needs which we, the imaginal primates, possess.

Every living organism must find its niche, its way. And while status, threat, power, and sex carry an air of danger, that is only an inflection of our struggle to accept our own human needs for respect, safety, capacity to influence our lives, and ability to participate in the ecstatic regeneration of our own kind. To deny or exaggerate these human experiences is to create internal conflict. If the human family cannot integrate the ancient drives into their culture, then they live themselves out in forms that become problematic.

To make matters worse, cultures, and especially spiritual ones, have shamed the fundamental calculations the animals within care about. At the heart of it, our hardwired orientation to perceive and respond to threats and opportunities is the most primal of biological imperatives. In the modern world, threat consciousness gets slandered as "ego," as if there was something wrong with us for having an instinct to survive. In the ancient world, when we lived in our natural habitat, these drives served more seamlessly. While they may glare in the modern world, it is for the lack of forest than their own nature.

Imagine for a moment a world of adults who grew up with blessings and education for the ancient drives within. The draw toward nobility and influence was recognized in a way that served the greater balance of life. The desire to court, mate, and beget life was celebrated with consciousness. The functionality and limits of threat perceptiveness was fully initiated and expanded to serve not just personal well-being but the well-being of others. But alas, this level of integration is the rare jewel and not the norm. People live, privately containing their own confusion about the complexities of human experience, or worse, act them out in ways that are harmful.

A close relative dies, and the mind flickers toward inheritance and the benefits that would come with that gift. Or one lives in a neighborhood overwhelmed with violence and little resources, and the mind agrees to carry a firearm and sell drugs on the street corner in order to survive. In a moral world at odds with the body, these examples are failures. In a biological world, they are signs of the desire to be adapted and alive. In a sacred world, where the human values and biological motivations are not at odds, the inheritor and drug dealer are seen in the light of compassion for the complexities of the human condition. A human resilience is available because we do not get crossed up with our own conflicts about our human condition.

Humans need resources and the power to secure those resources. Humans gravitate toward efficiency. The lens that there is something wrong with us because of these truths is a deep affront to the old woman in the kitchen who's labored across time to craft the primal intelligences of microbe, lizard, and ape. Evolution does not allow us to disassemble the past, but only to redirect the usefulness of what is there. It is either that or, if we fail to adapt, extinction. The risk for humankind seems less a failure to adapt but to adapt so very well that in the end we harm our own niche. Since, in evolutionarily terms, we can never undo what is, we can only go forward, finding new purposes and expressions for hardwired motivations.

The beauty in the Order of the Sacred Earth is that its vow invites our ancestrally given drives and repurposes them to the reflowering of biological life. We Defend! We Live! We Survive! Not only can my moral compass get behind that, but the accumulated force and wisdom of my body can, too.

The possibility in the Order of the Sacred Earth is to integrate our full humanity in all its layers—to use our drive for power to create sustainable resources, to take our ability for threat calculations and turn them into transforming the dangers in our own human condition, to embrace the procreative urge and celebration that transforms people into joyful beings who care and are invested and engaged in the fate of life, to use our hunger for respect amongst peers to motivate our actions of compassion toward life.

Let this be so, lest we suffer the same problems other orders have found when they stand in opposition to Mother Earth's most precocious molecule, Human DNA.

CALLING US INTO COMMUNION
Susan Coppage Evans

In my kitchen hangs a framed calligraphy of the vows my husband and I exchanged during our wedding. In the most intimate setting, witnessed by our family, we vowed to enter into relationship as an act of compassion and action as well as one of unity and supported autonomy. We committed to support each other even when it wasn't personally beneficial. We committed to the personal work of transformation and to working for the betterment of our community.

Sometimes the framed vows fade into the wall and become something easily forgotten, but then there are times when I stop and read and remember. In these times, I feel my feet squarely on the ground, as an individual with intention and a partner with responsibility. The vows become the compass, reminding me of my intended direction.

The Order of Sacred Earth invites us into a vow that extends our vision from individual and dyadic relationships into a bond with the wider community and Earth itself. The pledge can be said simply, "I Vow to Be the Best Lover and Defender of All of Life." It can become a mantra—said during prayer, in traffic jams, as a response to disheartening evening news, as an awe-filled response to majestic beauty, and when considering an invitation to help any form of life that is suffering.

The Order's invitation into a community bound by a shared vow is one that I find most intriguing. In this time of increasing polarization and the breaking apart of (spiritual) communities into many subsections because participants cannot agree on common values and beliefs, the vow points to something wholly encompassing, which surpasses artificial differences. The vow can be taken by conservatives and liberals, by Christians, Jews, Muslims, Buddhists, Sufis, by the religious and the nonreligious, by scientists and social workers, by workers on Wall Street and Main Street. There need not be distinctions or separations, because we all share in the Life we are pledging to love and protect.

Where distinctions may lie is in how we join together to do the loving and protecting. This is the power and mystery of community. Just as each couple may approach their vows and the way they practice them uniquely, communities may be unique in their expression and implementation of the vow. But there can be no doubt that the vow is emboldened in community.

There is another related mantra that has shaped my life in the last decade. It was seeded in me in Chartres, France, in October 2005. I was there to attend a class that Matthew Fox was teaching entitled "The 12th-Century Renaissance and the 21st-Century Renaissance." I was nearing the end of my Doctorate of Ministry degree and I was wondering how I was going to practically incorporate Creation Spirituality in my life. I had set up a private meeting with Matthew to ask him about a teaching he had shared of "infiltrating and reinventing." I was not inspired to infiltrate the Southern Baptist church of my childhood that had become frozen with patriarchy and with rules that defined a spirituality that no longer called to me. So, I went to this class with a curious mind and heart, wondering how a new renaissance might be emerging. It was during the nights of anticipating our meeting that a new mantra, or guiding directive, came to me.

For three nights, under the shadow of the Chartres Cathedral, I encountered a presence in my small seminary room. It is my only experience of such a presence. I definitely heard it, but not with what I know as sound; I definitely saw it, but not with what I know of as sight. This feminine presence told me that I was to tell Matthew Fox, "*It is time to bring forth a Creation Spirituality Church.*" This seemed unbelievable and improbable to me and I certainly had no intention of acting on something that felt like my mind was falling apart. But after three nights of the same presence with the same message, I called my then fiancé, Leon (now husband), who is a physician/psychiatrist. From the seminary public phone, I whispered to Leon about what was happening to me. I told him my concerns and asked if I was having a psychotic break. Leon listened quietly, asked some questions for clarification, and then said, "No, honey, I think you just need to listen and trust what is happening." He encouraged me to share what I was experiencing with Matt. I learned then that it's a fine line between mental distress and mystical encounter.

Our meeting occurred in the small chapel in the old seminary. We sat knee to knee on facing pews and introduced ourselves. I told him that I came to discuss one topic but it had been rewritten by an unusual experience. But before detailing the presence, I introduced myself—"I am the executive director of a psychiatric treatment facility, I am an administrator, I love budgets!" I described myself as the rational, practical person that I am, someone who likes numbers in columns and my ducks in a row. I tried to explain that presences and voices just don't happen to me. And then I told him about the presence in my room and the message I was to share with him.

Matthew listened quietly to my experience and nodded with interest. I left the meeting feeling listened to and not judged. I had delivered the message and felt complete. I could finally relax. But what I know now is we probably aren't given messages just for other people. Deeply mystical experiences are meant to transform us

The next night at dinner, after Matt finished his meal, he pulled up a chair across from me and said, "So what do we do next?"

As a result of the experience in Chartres and the months of collaboration and discernment that followed, Creation Spirituality Communities formed, and over 10 years later CSC continues to thrive and grow.

The words, "It is time to bring forth Creation Spirituality communities," became a powerful vision for me. It has continued to be the driving force behind supporting the Creation Spirituality movement and the communities that arise from it. The Order of the Sacred Earth continues the Spirit-led calling for sacred community with the message Matt received: "Do It Now."

I imagine that there will be communities within communities; that churches or small groups of all descriptions can welcome the Order of Sacred Earth. Churches affiliated with denominations may choose to also align with the OSE and support one another in practicing the vow. New groups aligned with the Order can be formed and fostered through religious and/or spiritual communities already in existence, such as Creation Spirituality Communities. Small groups of friends and neighbors can transform their hiking or Earth literacy groups and communities into participants of the Order. The best thing about the Order is the accessibility that comes with a shared purpose.

The Order points toward community rather than inviting the life of a hermit. It is in community where we can be supported to be our most compassionate and courageous selves. My entire career in psychiatric healthcare has been in inpatient settings. To help patients to be a part of authentic community, to see them rise to places of leadership, to be vulnerable and practice compassionate communication, is to witness the power of community. Loneliness, isolation, and fear can be confronted and mitigated in community. I have seen people do their deepest and most difficult work in psychiatric settings. Those communities built from the sick getting well are an example of what might happen if we speak up and use our authentic voice, if we share our vulnerabilities and if we communicate a vision and then ask for help to achieve it.

The Order of Sacred Earth and the calling forth of communities invites us to reimagine how we might work and play with others in being the best lovers and defenders of Life. We are invited to let go of preconceived notions of church and community, of the secular and the sacred, and enter into a co-creative process. In Matthew Fox's book *Original Blessing* he confronts our tendency toward dualism and invites the letting go that is necessary to birth new forms of community:

"The Universe was not created by tolerant dualisms but by mutual inter-penetrations. Of course, this implies letting go: hydrogen must let go of it hydrogenness and oxygen of its oxygenness when the two come together and create water. Letting go is demanded as much of religious traditions as it is of individual religious believers."

The courageous work of the Beguines provides an example of com-munity-making that stimulates my own imagination for community. The Beguines were groups of women who came together to live, pray, work, and be of service as early as 1200 CE. At a time in Europe when women barely had the choice to live their lives as committed wives or nuns, these women chose to commit themselves to God and community outside of a known religious structure. They courageously formed new communities that were self-supporting. They let go of cultural norms and were perse-cuted as immoral heretics, but they remained true to their vow of commu-nity and service.

The spiritual vigor and creativity of the Beguines was reflected in every-thing they did. Their communities were diverse in size and location. Their commitment to spiritual study and to loving and defending the weak made them influential enough to challenge and impact unjust political and reli-gious structures. Their movement lasted until 2013 when the last Beguine died in Belgium—the last Beguine of over a million before her. Now, new communities are emerging, using the Beguines as a template.

In 2017, when I hear a sense of hopelessness and despair about anything being better, I am inspired by the Beguines and how courageous they were to imagine a new way of living and then to venture out and practice that new way.

We are having dreams and visions and many of them are communicating the same message. Do it! Participate in communal practices and become awake to the web of life. Bring forth new communities that honor the sacredness of all creation. Call him G-d, call her Mystery, call it the collective unconscious—something is calling us to action on behalf of Life. Something is waking us up at night with a whisper, with a dream, with an invitation.

Growing up in the Protestant church and learning the Bible stories of burning bushes and clairvoyant dreams, I assumed God talking through dreams and messengers was something of the past. But maybe that is because I have learned to like my ducks in a row. Perhaps in a different time and culture I would have gone to sleep and asked for a dream. And then I would have joined a circle and shared the dream, asking leaders for guidance and interpretation.

Maybe in our busy and hectic lives it is only during the night that we can let go enough to be receptive to dreams. I think it would be a mistake to see our dreams and visions as significantly unique and special. Instead, if we understand ourselves as being a part of Cosmic story—connected to every atom of life—we may value our dreams and visions as messages from Life itself, calling us into awareness, into communion. This can happen every day. Life calls to us and we awaken to humbly pledge to use our dreams, visions, intellect, creativity, courage, and compassion to be her Lovers and Defenders.

GOD IN DRAG: DOING ECO-JUSTICE FROM THE EARTH'S POINT OF VIEW
Kristal Parks

A star-studded night sky...
Mountains blanketed in freshly fallen powder...
Meadows splashed with brilliant wildflowers...
The mating call of a bugling elk...
The cacophony of song and sound of birds at dawn...
Baby elephants cavorting with delight...
The intoxicating fragrance of a stargazing lily...
Peacocks with feathers in full fan...

God in drag, all.

I am wildly, madly and passionately in love with all of Creation, from the tiniest ant to the most magnificent whale and am doing everything I can to protect these beings who have no voice but ours. So, when I heard about the vision for a new *Order of the Sacred Earth*, I sprang into a pirouette and have been twirling in joy and gratitude ever since!

Like a candle that can't light the darkness without consenting to its own burning and a mother can't birth a child without excruciating pain[1]; so, the crisis of our time is like a womb about to birth us into our next evolutionary leap.[2] What a glorious time to be alive! As a biologist, conservationist, and activist, I am excited about the possibilities facing us in spite of the fact that we are teetering on the precipice of annihilation.

You see, this is the awakening of humans to the realization that non-human beings are Nations unto themselves with divine and sacred purposes of their own, apart from any association with us. It is the time of the Great Liberation... of the four-legged, finned, feathered, and creepy crawlers. Yes, their time has come. Hurray, hurray, hurrah!

Each thing that exists, marmot, tree, rock or bee, is an expression of the Creator, revealing something about His/Her character. An otter, His playfulness; an elephant, Her gentle power. When any of these beings goes extinct, so does that expression and revelation. *Forever.*

Sentient and sacred, all of them. Here to praise and serve God in their own way. A dandelion as a dandelion; a spider as a spider. Nothing makes me fall on my knees in praise and adoration of the Creator faster than the sight and sound of geese flying overhead or wild bunnies hop, hop, hopping across my yard.

It is time now to abandon our speciesism and remove the chains of terror that most animals feel because of our use, abuse, beating, and eating of them. To harm these, even the least of them, is like doing it to Christ Himself. When sacred rivers are polluted, Amazon Rainforest cathedrals cut down, or the earth heated so that polar bears lose their habitat, it is to me, blasphemy.

If we look closely, we will see a causal connection between the slaughterhouse killing of 56 billion (!) animals[3] per year, and global warming, famine and pollution. As Thich Nhat Hahn poignantly states:

---

1   Rumi, quoted in Andrew Harvey's book: *The Return of the Mother,* pp. 177-178.
2   Andrew Harvey: *The Hope: A Guide to Sacred Activism.*
3   See www.AnimalEquality.net

"Every day forty thousand children die in the world for lack of food. We who overeat in the West, who are feeding grains to animals to make meat, are eating the flesh of these children."[44]

Instead, let us extend the imperative of Love and Nonviolence to embrace all beings. And do eco-justice from the point of view, and in collaboration with, Mother Earth and Her critters. They have knowledge and abilities we can't even begin to imagine and are worthy to be our mentors and elders.

For example, the naturalist Lyle Watson tells this story: He was hired to be the director of a zoo in South Africa. Shortly after he arrived, the staff brought in a wild elephant who they named Delilah. They put her in a small enclosure which she began to investigate with her multipurpose trunk. When she came to a certain corner she froze, as if in fright, backed up and trembled. Then her eyes grew wide as if she got an idea. She went and got some hay and put it in that corner. Dr. Watson, watching all of this, wondered what was going on and asked the zookeeper, who had worked there forever, to explain Delilah's behavior. The zookeeper said: "Twenty years ago, we killed an elephant in that corner." Wow. Somehow Delilah knew what had happened. That's an ability we don't have. And, as you may know, elephants bury their dead by covering them with hay, straw, and leaves.

During the 10 years that my organization, *Pachyderm Power! Love in Action for Elephants*, worked in Kenya to stop the genocide of the Elephant Nation, I had the great fortune of collaborating with local tribes, especially the Maasai and Samburu. They told me that if elephants become extinct, humans will lose their soul and go crazy. These indigenous tribes understand the deep connection and interbeing we have with the natural world. They are the leaders the world needs.

My own intimate embrace with Mother Nature began years ago when I was lured into a forest for a prolonged retreat. I had gone there for a sabbatical of silence, reflection, and inner healing after having been incarcerated

---

4   Thich Nhat Hanh: *Creating True Peace*, p. 77.

in solitary confinement for nonviolent peace actions. I moved into a small, rustic, one room cabin high in the rocky mountains. I spent my days walking in the forest, sitting by streams, watching and listening. Mostly listening. After about two years, nature and silence taught me this:

At the core of all that exists, in every blade of grass, howling coyote and quivering aspen leaf, there exists an energy and vibration of joy, not unlike a giggle.

Take a tree, for example. They do talk but veeeery slowly. Like a good lover, they take their time so you just have to wait patiently. I would sit for hours under an old granddaddy ponderosa pine. He was quite wise. Trees don't talk with words or sounds but they do communicate if you wait and listen long enough. What they herald is a mischievous, wild, and ecstatic joy.

If we wish to take our cues from Nature and work effectively in harmony with and for Her, then we too have to be in the energy of joy.

The *Order of the Sacred Earth* will be like that... full of joy, because it is an invitation to participate in the evolutionary intentions of the Universe. What could be more purposeful and fun than that?! The revolution that Matthew, Skylar, and Jennifer are ushering in and leading is perhaps the most important ever, because we really are on the precipice and everything, *everything* is at stake. So let's take the vow: *I promise to be the best lover and defender of the Earth that I can be*; roll up our sleeves and get to it! Don't forget to bring your banjo and dancing shoes!

IMAGINING THE EARTH'S GUIDANCE FOR BUILDING A SACRED COMMUNITY
Charles Burack, Ph.D.

Shared Identity

My beloved human children, all Earthly beings are equal members of my precious family. It is time to let go of exclusive identification with your human self, family, clan, culture, nation, species. It is time to expand your identity to include larger and larger circles of life. It is time to realize your shared destiny as caring inhabitants of the living Earth, as conscious citizens of the Cosmos, and as cherished offspring of the Sacred Source, however named or conceived.

Community

Our Earth family is a community that is nurtured by communion and communication. Let us co-build an interdependent community that is interhuman, interspecies, interbeing. Let us communicate with words and winds and waters. Let us commune with one another and with the Wellspring of Being. Through holy communion we become interdignified and interdivinized.

Personal Responsibility

The fate of our holy community depends on you. Please take responsibility for your individual and collective actions. Please review your motivations and behaviors, obtain the counsel and support of others, and realign your lives with your highest ideals. Our community will prosper if you stay informed about global initiatives and local projects, test them against your touchstones of care and equality, and form coalitions that promote human and ecological justice.

Spiritual Practice

Ongoing spiritual practices connect you to the Common Ground and its holy powers and possibilities, visions, and values. Through daily practice you expand consciousness, face shadows, cultivate virtues, and contribute to the healing and transformation of self and world. Some vital virtues include: humility, trust, love, empathy, compassion, awareness, openness, understanding, intuition, appreciation, truthfulness, wisdom, joy, gratitude, patience, forgiveness, forbearance, peacefulness, courage, kindness, strength, and overall wellbeing. Every worldly being casts a shadow. Boldly confront, alchemize, and integrate your shadows in service of the Whole.

Inherent Holiness and Limitation

The Holy inheres in every creature. I entreat you to seek out and honor that sacred essence while respectfully acknowledging that all individuals and collectives have limitations. Treat every limitation as a divine invitation to learn and grow from. Respect the sustainable limits of our Earth family.

Diversity-in-Unity

Each creature is a unique and evolving expression of the One. Each one is a wave of the Ocean influencing and being influenced by all other waves. Appreciate the differences among the many modes of existence, the many forms of life, and the many persons and peoples of Earth, while emphasizing the ultimate unity of beings in the Ground of Being.

Joint Activity

How great to engage with diverse others!—not only in dialogue, study, hospitality, justice-building, and peacemaking but also in prayer, meditation, and creative play and ritual. You uplift our Earth community by collaborating on personal and collective change. Please form alliances that cultivate compassion, resist oppression, right inequality, befriend foes, protect the marginalized, and promote the Greater Good. Care for the Whole while attending to the particular needs of each. Let freedom ring. Let love dream. Enjoy the gift of life.

Authentic Encounter

What joy, what sorrow, what passion, what peace, to participate wholeheartedly in the world! Surrender your egos and open your souls to the wonder and awe of existence. Meet the greening, flowering, swimming, flying, squirming, burrowing beings all around. Savor the sacred presence in one another. Protect the rights and existence of all. Celebrate being.

Effort and Grace

Work is good and so is rest. Collaborate with holy intention and effort, remembering that all essential work is ultimately accomplished by grace.

Take time to relax and rejuvenate together. Offer gratitude to the Source for the blessings you receive every moment of every day.

Experiencing and Interpreting the Sacred

Notice how the trees, the breezes, the rains, and the robins proclaim the glory of the Mystery, all in their own elegant song, sonnet, or samba. Explore the sundry ways of experiencing, verbalizing, imaging, symbolizing, and interpreting the sacred, seeking to appreciate both the varieties and the commonalities.

Re-envisioning Conflict

Conflicts can create as well as destroy. I implore you to use nonviolent ways to resolve discords. Reframe tensions as opportunities for creative reconciliation, growth, and connection. Root resolution processes in inclusivity, equity, respect, understanding, compassion, and forgiveness. Seek harmonious solutions that evolve as participants and conditions change. Marry love to justice to birth peace.

Cross-Fertilization

Everyone, everything, is teaching about being. Learn from one another. Share experiences. Investigate the cross-fertilizing flow of insights among religions, arts, philosophies, sciences, and commerce. Become a student of nature's evolving wisdom. Watch a squirrel. Befriend a flower. Apprentice to a cat. Take notes from a newt. Listen to a breeze. Study a stream. Dance with a mountain. Sing with a seagull. All is alive and uttering its truth. All is alight and shining its love.

REBELLION, DIVINE GRACE AND ENDURING LOVE
Zohara M. Hieronimus, D.H.L.

"It's all of us together, or it's all of us, together," I often say with a chuckle. Aren't we all archetypally guided by the same dream of paradise, our soul's native home? Despite our thinking we are separate from each other, aren't we unitary in our origin and purpose, born not for ourselves alone but for the world? The Order of the Sacred Earth celebrates these truths and its formation is literally the fulfillment of an experience I had in 1984. I share in profound gratitude this true story.

In 1957, as a three-year-old toddler, I committed my first of numerous acts of rebellion. I waded with forethought into the deeper waters of our family pool beyond the kiddie step while my parents and other adults were up the hill out of sight. "Come to the light," said the voice I heard, which seemed to mean the shining sunlight on the waters above my head. But I could not right my body from its somersaulting underwater. Realizing I had made a fatal error in thinking I would be able to swim like the older kids around me, I was drowning. Suddenly though, I found myself above the pool in the arms of a beautiful woman as large as the oak trees, as enormous as the clouds, a woman cloaked in a cerulean blue robe and white trim, golden hair, and the pure emanation of love. She cradled me in her arms until I hit the ground on the side of the pool from the force of my mother's saving motions. "Oh, she'll be alright," I heard her say, reassuring everyone now gathered around me. Rebellion has its price and reward.

Seven years later, during my Jewish Sunday school's field trip to a local church to visit children our age, a boy and girl there asked me tauntingly, "Can you show us your horns?" As horrific as that experience was, my focus shifted to a beautiful statue I saw on a pedestal inside the church. This was the lady who had saved me from drowning. Discovering this was a revelation, and in that moment I became a heretic, a Jewish girl who secretly loved the Blessed Mother.

In 1969 I formally became an Earth guardian and social justice advocate when I handed out flyers for a program on acid rain given by Ralph Nader in South East Baltimore. Like so many other elders, I have led or been involved in numerous environmental, social justice, animal rights, and economic change campaigns since then.

In 1984 I founded what is now the oldest and longest freestanding outpatient holistic healing center in America, the Ruscombe Mansion Community Health Center in Baltimore, Maryland. After harvesting what would be the last fruits from a plum tree in the garden there, I had a waking engagement with an apparition that was standing by a century-old pine tree. There she was in stunning light. Dressed in white with a blue trim, her head covered by a flowing white cloth headdress. It was the Blessed Mother who had saved me decades earlier but whom I had not seen since then. Her manifestation in the material realm just 20 feet away from me was incredible. When she spoke her voice was clear, beautiful, precise, compelling, and as spirit behaves when she enters our lives, the Blessed Mother was swift coming and going. Looking directly in my heart, she said, "I want you to start the New Order of the World Mother" and then she was gone. I had no time to ask her, "What do you mean, what should I do, why me?" Adding humorously to the story today, "Besides, I'm Jewish!"

For years I tried to imagine what a New Order of the World Mother would do, who its members might be, how it could carry out activities in the world. I reasoned she meant to care for the Earth, to instill in our lives an "ethos of care," something I learned telepathically from the animals I write about in *White Spirit Animals, Prophets of Change*. A society centered around the welfare of the mother, child, and natural world produces the healthiest and happiest communities. Anyone could join, I thought to myself, and any activity that was life-affirming and elevating could constitute the Order's good works. I have tried to live my life personally fulfilling her request, but I never established the New Order of the World Mother as I was asked to do. It seemed an impossible task for a sensitive woman adversely affected by large crowds and who needs long stretches of solitude for good health.

When I received a print galley of *Order of the Sacred Earth* in preparation for interviewing Mathew Fox about Creation Spirituality on 21stCentury Radio®, I had an immediate recognition and recollection of my own calling. My husband and I have both been grateful to have interviewed Dr. Fox many times over the past 30 years on our new paradigm radio program, but this time was very special. I felt moved to thank Matthew for fulfilling the work the Blessed Mother instructed me to undertake so long ago. The Order of the Sacred Earth offers all of us the opportunity to unite our varied efforts wherever we live and experience the empowering connectedness we truly share.

The universe is reflexive, and like the prophets and prophetesses of prior centuries that I wrote two books about, cultivating courage, imagination and humility activates our soul-given talents. When we accept our roles as visionaries, co-creators, and Earth lovers, we become daring collaborators with each other and all of nature.

I know that divine grace is a power we can invite into our lives, and that we must do all that we can in honorable dedication to prepare the way, as farmers do soil for seed. We are all rooted in paradise, craftsmen of noble souls and mortal bodies whose enabling energy comes from divinity's enduring love. This is what the Order of the Sacred Earth celebrates, to feel deeply interconnected in our planetary and personal destinies of service, galactic citizens in our local habitats, god-like beings destined to evolve together.

MOVING FORWARD

On December 21, 2017 we—Matthew, Skylar, and Jennifer—hosted a Solstice celebration and ritual ceremony launching the Order of the Sacred Earth. About eighty people joined us at the Sacred Stream Center in Berkeley, California, while hundreds of people attended satellite events across the country and countless people live-streamed the event online.

It was a beautiful evening of reflection by our panel with the three of us and essayist Broderick Rodell, followed by contributions from participants. Music and a dance led up to the vow-taking ritual, during which each person held a sacred object, stood around an altar we created for the occasion, and took the vow: "I vow to be the best lover and defender of the Earth I can be."

We received many poignant questions and wise insights and stories from the participants, and we encourage you to visit our website and watch what transpired. (orderofthesacredearth.org)

There are two very important questions that continue to come up about the OSE and we want to answer them, one more time, as succinctly as we can.

(1) Yes, I feel inspired by this vision, but I still don't understand—what *is* the Order of the Sacred Earth? What is its form?

The Order of the Sacred Earth is a self-organizing, emergent movement—a network of individuals and communities who are committing to the pledge "to be the best lover and defender of the Earth I can be." We use the word *self-organizing* very intentionally because we do not want to operate in the old, patriarchal paradigm where we create a rigid structure and set of rules and implement that on anyone who wants to join, and therefore spend inordinate amounts of time, money, and energy on the bureaucratic process of managing the form. Instead, we leave it open. We are encouraging local groups to come up with forms that work for them, and to share them with the three of us so we all might collaborate. We want anyone who feels inspired by our vision to contribute to the form, to share their ideas and visions, and to co-create with others in their area as well as with us.

We have also used the word *order* very intentionally, understanding its double-meaning. The Order of the Sacred Earth is an Order, mirroring revolutionary religious Orders of the past which arose when society's spiritual (and in this case, sociopolitical and environmental) cultural needs were not being met. The word *order* also indicates the natural order of the Earth, and our use of the word mirrors our desire to bring *order* to the many disparate movements and organizations who are already doing the Great Work, as well as to bring *order* to these chaotic, turbulent times.

(2) How do I get involved?

It is of course a little difficult to tell you how to get involved with a movement whose shape is not completely formed. But there is a fundamental way you can join right now, and that is on the individual level. Create for yourself or better, with others living near you, a time and space and a ritual, and take the vow.

What we are now calling OSE Pods are beginning to form in communities all over the country: groups of people who are inspired by this message and are starting their own communities of vow-taking sacred activists to carry on the work and are discussing its fuller implementation in actions they can take. Find one and join it. Or even better, start your own.

The Order of the Sacred Earth is launched! Here are many more ways you can become involved:

1. Take the vow to be the best lover and defender of the Earth that you can be.

2. Start an OSE Pod where you live. Talk about the Order with others where you live and create your own vow-taking ceremony or event.

3. Visit our website to learn more and watch the video of our launch celebration: orderofthesacredearth.org

4. Sign up for our mailing list on the website to stay connected and be informed of all future goings on.

5. Donate to our cause on our Generosity crowdfunding page: http://bit.ly/OSEdonate. If you are moved to donate, we promise a transparent reporting of the use of funds—they are intended to support the building up of the program, including awareness building, correspondence, and future events.

6. Share the book and create study groups to discuss it.

7. Stay tuned for more information about formation classes, including initiation retreats and other classes as well, which we will keep you posted about very soon.

8. Join our blog, and share your story about what you do, and how you are cultivating change in your communities and what visions for the OSE you carry inside. Or, tell us about another community/organization which is participating in change-making and implementing values of the OSE into their work and citizenship.

Let us rise up together as the mystic warriors that we are!

CONTRIBUTOR BIOGRAPHIES
(In Order of Appearance)

Matthew Fox

Matthew Fox has been called a maverick, a rebel, and by some a heretic. In his quest for a viable spirituality, he discovered the ancient (but often suppressed) creation spirituality tradition that honors the sacredness of all creation. He has worked closely with Native spiritual leaders, feminists, scientists, activists, and others, and got himself in trouble with his mother church and the pope. He has written 34 books on spirituality and culture (now translated in 67 languages) and has taught in many schools, including Stanford, the University of Creation Spirituality, which he founded, and the new Fox Institute for Creation Spirituality in Boulder, Colorado. He is also a visiting scholar at the Academy for the Love of Learning. Among his books are *Original Blessing, The Coming of the Cosmic Christ, A Way To God: Thomas Merton's Creation Spirituality Journal, Meister Eckhart: A Mystic Warrior for Our Times.* See matthewfox.org.

Skylar Wilson

Skylar Wilson is the founder and co-director of Wild Awakenings, an adult Rites of Passage organization dedicated to the thriving of Earth, life, and humanity. Over the past 16 years, Skylar has led retreats all over the world focusing on ecological restoration, wilderness knowledge, meditation, and ceremonial practices. Skylar is director of an intercultural ritual called the Cosmic Mass, which brings together the world's spiritual traditions into an embodied, transformational ritual that builds community through music, dancing, and the arts. He works closely with community organizations including the Stepping Stones Project in Berkeley, California, which holds Rites of Passage groups for teenagers, using a community-based curriculum. He enjoys surfing, swimming, climbing, writing, giving and receiving bodywork, as well as facilitating one-on-one integration sessions with people of all ages and backgrounds. He received his master's degree in Philosophy, Cosmology, and Consciousness from the California Institute of Integral Studies in 2012.

Jennifer Berit Listug

Jennifer Berit Listug works in book publishing as a private consultant for authors assisting with manuscript editing and book publicity. She is also the co-director of Wild Awakenings, an adult Rites of Passage organization dedicated to fostering the thriving of Earth, life, and humanity. Jennifer was on the board of trustees at the Unity in Marin Spiritual Community for three years, serving as the board president for 18 months. Also at Unity in Marin, Jennifer was a guest speaker for Sunday mornings, led Rites of Passage groups for teenagers, and founded a young adult interfaith group committed to conscious connection, community service, and social activism. She is a passionate hiker, reader, writer, and public speaker.

Brian Thomas Swimme

Brian Thomas Swimme received his Ph.D. from the Department of Mathematics at the University of Oregon in 1978 for work in gravitational dynamics. He teaches in the Philosophy, Cosmology, and Consciousness program at the California Institute of Integral Studies in San Francisco. Brian brings the context of story to our understanding of the 14-billion-year trajectory of the universe. Such a story, he feels, will assist in the emergence of a flourishing Earth community.

Brian is the author of *The Hidden Heart of the Cosmos* and *The Universe is a Green Dragon*. He is co-author of several books, *Manifesto for a Global Civilization* with Matthew Fox, *The Universe Story* with Thomas Berry, and *The Journey of the Universe*, with Mary Evelyn Tucker. Brian is also the creator of three educational video series: "Canticle to the Cosmos," "Earth's Imagination," and "The Powers of the Universe." Most recently, he hosted the 60 minute film "Journey of the Universe," broadcast on PBS television stations nationwide and winner of the Northern California regional Emmy for Best Documentary in 2011.

Mirabai Starr

Mirabai Starr is author of numerous books, including a memoir, *Caravan of No Despair: A Memoir of Loss and Transformation*; new translations of the Spanish mystics, John of the Cross and Teresa of Avila; *The Showings of Julian of Norwich*, and the award-winning *God of Love: A Guide to the Heart of Judaism, Christianity & Islam*. A leader in the emerging interspiritual movement, Mirabai leads contemplative interspiritual retreats worldwide.

Dr. David Korten

Dr. David Korten is the author of *Change the Story, Change the Future: A Living Economy for a Living Earth*; *Agenda for a New Economy: From Phantom Wealth to Real Wealth*; *The Post-Corporate World: Life after Capitalism*; and the international best-sellers *When Corporations Rule the World*; and *The Great Turning: From Empire to Earth Community*. He is board chair of *YES! Magazine*, president of the Living Economies Forum, a board member of Toward Ecological Civilization, a full member of the Club of Rome,

Contributor Biographies

and an associate fellow of the Institute for Policy Studies. He earned MBA and Ph.D. degrees from the Stanford University Graduate School of Business and served on the faculty of the Harvard Business School.

Geneen Marie Haugen

Geneen Marie Haugen, Ph.D., grew up a little wild, with a run-amok imagination. As a guide to the intertwined mysteries of nature and psyche (animas.org) she delights in multidimensional listening, and in offering perceptive questions, ceremonies, escapades, and reflections that help expand a sense of our own possibilities as individuals (and as a species), and deepen our experience of participation with an intelligent, animate, holy Earth/cosmos. Her writing has appeared in many anthologies and journals, including *Spiritual Ecology: The Cry of the Earth*; *Thomas Berry: Dreamer of the Earth*; *Parabola Journal*; and *High Country News*. She is committed to the world-transforming potential of the human imagination in collaboration with the Earth community.

Joran Oppelt

Joran Slane Oppelt is an international speaker, author, interfaith minister, and award-winning producer and singer/songwriter. He is the owner and founder of the Metta Center of St. Petersburg and Integral Church—an interfaith and interspiritual organization in Tampa Bay, Florida. Joran is the author of *Sentences, The Mountain and the Snow*, and co-author of *Transform Your Life: Expert Advice, Practical Tools, and Personal Stories and Integral Church: An Interfaith Handbook of Ceremonies and Rituals*. He serves as president of Interfaith Tampa Bay, chaplain emeritus at Unity Spiritual Campus, and ambassador of the Council for a Parliament of the World's Religions. He has spoken around the world about spirituality and the innovation of religion.

Carol P. Vaccariello

Rev. Dr. Carol P. Vaccariello, D.Min., MSE, MBA, M.Div., Oblate OSB is an ordained interfaith minister, priest, and bishop. Carol is a recipient of the Siksika/Sac Blackfoot Ancestral Blessing, a spiritual coach, ritual/ retreat leader, captivating speaker and storyteller, an honored Elder in Creation Spirituality Tradition, and is a member of the Braided Way. She participates in Hindu and Buddhist-Christian dialogues and has studied/ taught on six continents.

Carol is the founder of All Peoples Center, Wheel Within the Wheel Ministries, and Ordo Hagia Sophia (Order of Holy Wisdom), an egalitarian spiritual community. She is the author of *The Lion of God: Archangel Ari'El ... Personal Encounters*, published in 2017.

Carol has also produced, directed, and led the Cosmic Mass with Matthew Fox. She facilitates and builds labyrinths, medicine wheels, sacred drums, and sweat lodges. heartspacecommunity.org

Theodore Richards

Theodore Richards is a poet, novelist, director and the founder of the Chicago Wisdom Project, as well as a core faculty member of The Fox Institute. The author of six books, including, most recently, *The Great Re-imagining: Spirituality in an Age of Apocalypse*, Richards is the recipient of numerous literary awards, including two Independent Publisher Awards, the USA Book Award, and the Nautilus Book Award. He lives in Chicago with his wife and daughters. For more information visit his website, theodorerichards.com.

Deidre B. Combs, D.Min.

Dr. Deirdre B. Combs is a cross-cultural leadership and conflict resolution consultant, executive coach, and university professor. She has worked with a myriad of corporate, government, and NGO clients over the past 25 years, including Aveda Corporation; the U.S. Postal Service, Forest Service, and

State Department; IBM; Agenda Ciudadana; and Landmine Survivors Network. Dr. Combs is the author of three books on universal approaches to resolving conflict and overcoming challenges: *The Way of Conflict*; *Worst Enemy, Best Teacher*; and *Thriving Through Tough Times*.

Combs has provided intensive leadership development training to thousands of State Department-sponsored international teachers, students, activists, and business professionals. She has taught in Mexico, the Dominican Republic, India, Turkey, Tunisia, Morocco, and Costa Rica, and served as a professor at the University of Creation Spirituality as well as for Columbia University, Montana State University, and Naropa University.

Broderick Rodell Ph.D., N.D.

Broderick Rodell's role and mission as an educator is to develop learning systems that support humanity's evolution towards the ultimate values of goodness, beauty, and truth. His approach targets the cultivation of multiple intelligences, including cognitive, emotional, moral, social, somatic, creative, and spiritual forms. He takes advantage of classical and contemporary ideas and tools from a broad spectrum of disciplines, including philosophy; psychology; biology; and yoga, a term that connotes the development of the whole being towards its full potential. He also utilizes *capoeira*, a Brazilian dance and martial art that employs the warrior's spirit in developing discipline, creative expression, somatic intelligence, and community. Broderick offers these services to individuals and institutions via workshops, retreats, and ongoing public classes. For more information please visit his website at broderickrodell.com.

Kerri Welch, Ph.D.

Kerri Welch, Ph.D., teaches at California Institute of Integral Studies and Integrity Academy at Casa de Luz Center for Integral Studies and is working on a narrative nonfiction book about the science of temporal perception, *The Texture of Time: A Fractal Topology*. She lives in Austin, Texas.

Mark Youngblood

Mark Youngblood is a lifelong student, teacher, and facilitator of Inner Mastery. His life purpose is to elevate human consciousness and promote spiritual growth, individually and collectively. He founded his company, Inner Mastery, Inc., 20-plus years ago to promote personal and organizational transformation. His outreach presently includes executive coaching with top management, the Inner Mastery Community, Dear Human books, public speaking, and special workshops.

Deborah Santana

Deborah Santana is an author, business manager, and activist for peace and social justice. She founded Do A Little, a nonprofit that serves women and girls in the areas of health, education, and happiness. In 2005, she published a memoir: *Space Between the Stars*. Deborah has produced five short documentary films, four with Emmy award-winning director Barbara Rick: *Road to Ingwavuma*, *Girls of Daraja*, *School of My Dreams*, and *Powerful Beyond Measure*. These films highlight the work of nonprofit partners in South Africa, and Daraja Academy, a free secondary boarding school for girls in Kenya. Deborah holds a Master of Arts in philosophy and religion with a concentration in women's spirituality.

Trevien Stanger

Trevien Stanger is a tree planter, poet, writer, and educator based within the Vermont side of the ancient Champlain Basin. He teaches environmental studies and ecological service learning at Saint Michael's College and the Community College of Vermont, and partners frequently with Burlington's innovative agricultural and conservation hub, the Intervale Center. Trevien lives on a four-acre homestead in the forested foothills of Richmond with his wife, nurse-midwife Whitney Smith; and their cat Birdie, or "Birdhi-sattva." He is currently at work on a coffee table book about creating an eco-centric culture of clean water around Lake Champlain entitled *Our Basin of Relations.*

Claudia Picardi

Claudia Picardi lives and works in Torino, Italy, where she is a researcher and teaching assistant at the local university. She has always been fascinated by the workings of the human mind, which brought her first to a Ph.D. in computer science and artificial intelligence, then to study Buddhist meditation, and finally to a long personal and spiritual journey with transpersonal psychology. In 2012, she earned a Master in Transpersonal Psychology from former ITP, now Sofia University, in California, where she first learned about Creation Spirituality. She has a passion for stories, myths, and fairy tales as mysterious and wondrous sources of revelations on the soul and the Cosmos. Creative expression and being in nature are her favorite meditation practices. Since 2016, she has acted as vice-president of the Italian Association for Creation Spirituality.

Nethaniel Jaye

Nathaniel Jaye (@saintjaye) speaks on human intelligence and meaning design and is creator of 100 House, a coliving community in San Francisco.

Adam Bucko

Adam Bucko is a new monastic, activist, co-founder of the Reciprocity Foundation, and co-author of *Occupy Spirituality: A Radical Vision for the New Generation* and *The New Monasticism: An Interspiritual Manifesto for Contemplative Living.*

Chelsea MacMillan

Chelsea MacMillan is a minister for the spiritual-but-not-religious, writer, activist, and co-founder of Brooklyn Center for Sacred Activism in New York City.

Jeffrey Szilagyi

For more than two decades Jeffrey Szilagyi has crafted his work-life around the healing arts and community initiation practices for adolescents. As a perpetual student of the human body and passionate advocate for ending the unconscious battle culture has with human nature, Jeffrey writes, speaks, and trains on human vitality and stress intelligence. On his off days you can find him trying to be an adequate parent to his two incredible daughters, cultivating his Dao of Soccer, or geeking out on evolutionary biology.

Susan Coppage Evans

Susan Coppage Evans is a nest builder. She has a passion and the skill for creating structures which foster the beauty and sustainability of life-giving organizations. She completed her Doctorate of Ministry from the University of Creation Spirituality while serving as an executive in psychiatric healthcare, and initiated the formation of Creation Spirituality Communities in 2006. She hosts international retreats through her company, WholeHearted, Inc., and in 2017 became founding president of the Fox Institute for Creation Spirituality.

Kristal Parks

For two years, Kristal Parks lived as a hermit in the intimate embrace of a forest and what she learned there guides her vision. Also, she was a human shield for disappearing Mayans during Guatemala's civil war; volunteered in refugee camps in South East Asia; helped end apartheid in South Africa; was imprisoned for nonviolent peace actions; and participated with Ecuadorian tribes to protect the Amazon Rainforest. In 2005, Kristal founded *Pachyderm Power! Love in Action for Elephants* which worked to stop elephant genocide in Kenya for 10 years. Her pivotal efforts there successfully created an army of over 1,000 young people impassioned to save the elephant nation. Additionally, she (with many others) helped end the use of elephants by the Ringling Bros. Circus. Kristal weaves a tapestry of justice woven from various shades, hues, and textures of interconnected liberation movements. She holds a Bachelor's degree in biology and a Master's in justice, peace and social transformation. For more information, visit PachydermPower.org

Charles Burack, Ph.D.

Charles Burack, Ph.D., is an award-winning poet, writer, scholar, and teacher as well as a spiritual counselor and creativity coach. He is the author of three books and numerous essays, poems, and stories. In his latest poetry collection, *Leaves of Light* (Apocryphile, 2016), the sacred Earth comes alive as Burack meets trees, flowers, birds, spiders, cats, seals, and other wondrous and endangered creatures as equals. They share their wisdom and beauty, love and fear, humor and suffering, and inspire in him profound ponderings, playful antics, and startling realizations. Burack is a professor at John F. Kennedy University, where he teaches courses on psychology, spirituality, and literature and has pioneered contemplative and creative approaches to education.

Zohara M. Hieronimus, D.H.L.

J. Zohara Meyerhoff Hieronimus, D.H.L. is an award-winning radio broadcaster (21stcenturyradio.com), author, social justice, environmental and animal activist. She is a pioneer in holistic health care, founding the Ruscombe Mansion Community Health Center in Baltimore, Maryland, in 1984 (Ruscombe.org). A visionary and futurist, Zoh is also a transspecies telepath who communicates with animals both wild and domestic. Dr. Hieronimus is author of *White Spirit Animals: Prophets of Change* (2017), *The Future of Human Experience* (2013), *Sanctuary of the Divine Presence* (2012), and *Kabbalistic Teachings of the Female Prophets* (2008). (zoharaonline.com)